Jacqueline Rose

Sexuality in the Field of Vision

VERSO
The Imprint of New Left Books

British Library
Cataloguing in Publication Data

Rose, Jacqueline
Sexuality in the field of Vision
1. Women in literature and moving pictures
I. Title
791.43'09'09352042   □□   PN1995.W6

First published 1986
©Jacqueline Rose 1986

Verso
6 Meard Street London W1

Filmset in Times by
Morning Litho, London

Printed by The Thetford Press
Thetford, Norfolk

ISBN 0 86091 148 9
ISBN 0 86091 861 0 Pbk

Contents

For my mother

Acknowledgements

We would like to thank the following publishers and journals for permission to reprint these essays: 'Dora — Fragment of an Analysis', *m/f*; 'Femininity and its Discontents', *Feminist Review*; 'Feminine Sexuality — Jacques Lacan and the *école freudienne*', Macmillan Press and W W Norton; 'The Imaginary' and 'The Cinematic Apparatus — Problems in Current Theory', Macmillan Press and St. Martin's Press.

Many people are associated for me with these essays, whether through their encouragement, intellectual advice, or friendship and support. In particular I would like to thank Parveen Adams, Ben Brewster, Constance Penley and Peter Wollen. A number of groups and individual people have at various times been part of a crucial context of discussion and work or have offered detailed advice in relation to separate articles: the Lacan women's study group which met in London between 1975 and 1977; the women at the conference on 'The Cinematic Apparatus' held at the University of Wisconsin-Milwaukee in 1978; the students on the 'Studies in Feminism' course at the University of Sussex, especially in the year 1982-83, and Homi Bhabha, Jonathan Dollimore and Cora Kaplan. I owe a special debt to Juliet Mitchell.

Finally, my thanks, and much more, to Sally Alexander and Robert Young.

Introduction
Feminism and the Psychic

In her *Tribute to Freud,* the American woman poet H.D. writes of the one moment when Freud laid down the law during the brief analysis she conducted with him in 1933. This law ('he does not lay down the law, only this once — only this one law'), coming from someone who still stands in the image of a patriarch with which feminism has not yet settled its accounts, was in fact no law, but a plea — a plea that H.D. should never defend Freud and his work 'at any time, in any circumstance'. Freud goes on to explain this plea with the precision of 'a lesson in geometry' or of a demonstration of the 'inevitable course of a disease once a virus has entered the system'.[1] A law which takes the form of a plea that there should be no defence, or which hovers between geometrical precision and the course of a disease — these are contradictions which we might expect from any discussion which has psychoanalysis as its object or which tries to place itself within its terms.

But there is something outrageous in Freud's demand that psychoanalysis cannot be defended on the grounds that defence will 'drive the hatred or the fear or the prejudice in deeper', since it snatches from the opponent the very rationality by which a critique, no less than a defence, of psychoanalysis should take place.[2] This disarming by Freud of his woman patient draws

---

[1] H.D., *Tribute to Freud, Writing on the Wall* (1944), Boston 1974, p.86.
[2] Ibid.

psychoanalysis back fiercely into its own practice and leaves her with an impasse which H.D. will then resolve — more or less and in her own way — through literary writing, memoirs and, finally, a tribute. A tribute, we could say, is one possible response, and perhaps the only possible response, to the laying down of the law.

On the other hand, Freud's injunction and H.D.'s place within it reveal a dilemma or set of problems in which all the essays that follow are equally caught. First, the problem of writing of psychoanalysis in a context which exceeds its primary institutional and therapeutic domain. Second, the problem of writing in the form of a defence with regard to something — the psychoanalytic concept of the unconscious — which brooks no defence and constantly breaks down the law. Third, the problem of writing as a woman within the terms and discourse largely of two men — Freud, and then the French psychoanalyst Jacques Lacan who also saw his work as a tribute or return to Freud, as nothing less than the preservation of a 'tradition entrusted to our keeping'.[3] Scandalous for many other men of their time, they nonetheless embody the image of the patriarch whose insidious effects at the level of our psychic life they each attempted — with more or less success — to undo or defy.

The question which this introduction will attempt to address, therefore, is what *could* be the purchase of psychoanalysis outside its own specific domain. More specifically, the argument is for psychoanalysis in relation to feminism, and the importance of these together for the larger terms of contemporary political debate. We are in fact witnessing a moment when psychoanalysis is being assimilated into literary method — as it has been before — at the same time as the critique of psychoanalysis outside the academy by feminists and others is being renewed or increased. Feminism inherits and inflects a set of political challenges to psychoanalysis with a long and complex history which this introduction will also attempt to trace. The point being not to serve the essays themselves, but rather to situate them within an ongoing history and set of problems which I see them as part of today.

[3] Jacques Lacan, 'Intervention sur le transfert' (1951), *Ecrits,* Paris 1966, p.216; tr. Jacqueline Rose, 'Intervention on Transference' in *Feminine Sexuality. Jacques Lacan and the école freudienne,* eds. Juliet Mitchell and Jacqueline Rose, London 1982, p.63.

Two letters written by women at the time of Lacan's dissolution of his school in 1980 confront each other on one page of the French radical newspaper *Libération*. Together they can give some sense of the struggles over institutions and power in which Lacanian psychoanalysis has been played out in France, and the place of the woman within it. The first, from Michèle Montrelay, states a refusal: to accept the dissolution of the *école freudienne* declared unilaterally by Lacan, to reaffiliate to his person. This refusal is a matter of love ('what love is being demanded here?') and its fantasies ('in what Christlike position does Lacan thereby find himself placed?'), of the body and its powers ('that massive body which becomes corpus and dogma, blindly putting itself at the service of a power which many would prefer to ignore').[4] The second, from Marie-Christine Hamon, sees, on the other hand, the dissolution of the school not as a 'seizure of power' or as a sign of 'dogmatic intolerance', but rather as the only way of reintroducing the '*dimension of risk* which is proper to discourse'[5] against the transformation of Lacan's theory into style (Lacanianism no less) and that view, which has been so influential outside of France under the brief of 'New French Feminisms', which sees theory itself as a masculine fantasy to which the only response for many women is the dissolution, not just of institutions, but of language itself.

For both writers, however, and despite the different personal decisions to which they individually came, the issue of institutional power is one in which the question of language and its limits is centrally at stake. 'On n'est fou que de sens' ('Only meaning drives you mad' or 'No madness without meaning'), writes Montrelay[6] — the unconscious is the only defence against a language frozen into pure, fixed or institutionalised meaning, and what we call sexuality, in its capacity to unsettle the subject, is a break against the intolerable limits of common sense.

François Roustang has described the way that this problem — how to create an institution in which the effects of the unconscious can be spoken without fossilizing into hereditary transmission and style — has marked the whole history of the psychoanalytic

---

[4] Michèle Montrelay, 'La passion de la perte', *Des femmes analystes parlent, Libération,* 19-20 January 1980, p.9.

[5] Marie-Christine Hamon, 'Les féministes sont misogynes!', *Des femmes analystes parlent, Libération,* 19-20 January 1980, p.9.

[6] Montrelay, p.9.

movement.[7] In this case, however, it is clear that the question of the unconscious brings with it fantasies and images of sexual difference. Above all it leads to a question: how to situate oneself as a woman between the Christlike figure with its powerful and oppressive weight, and the too easy assimilation of the underside of language to an archaic femininity gone wild. That there is another scene to the language through which we most normatively identify and recognise ourselves is the basic tenet of Freudian psychoanalysis. But it is rarely demonstrated with such startling clarity how far the effects of the unconscious are tied into the key fantasies operating at the heart of institutions, and how these in turn are linked into the most fundamental images of sexual difference (adoration to the male, chaos or exclusion to the female) on which the wider culture so centrally turns.

The crisis of the analytic institution therefore leads outside itself and also outside the figure of Lacan. Montrelay herself stresses that her critique is addressed neither to his 'person' nor his 'teaching', although we can notice the strange similarity-cum-difference between Freud's plea to H.D. and Lacan's to his members: the end of all defence and the demise of a school, both of which hold within them the ultimate and most impossible of commands. Yet more importantly, this moment suggests that the question of how an institution defines its limits, or even constitutes itself as an institution, is underpinned by a realm in which sexual fantasy is at play. The interface between these two factors — of institutions and their fantasies — shows the fully social import of the concept of the unconscious, but the disagreement between these two women writers also suggests that the ramifications are not adequately covered, or cannot easily be settled, by recourse to any one-sided concept of power. For if the power clearly goes first to Lacan, and through him to Freud, it is also the case that Lacan's dissolution of his school has led to a proliferation of analytic schools in France, which endlessly divide the name and image of Lacan to which many of them also claim allegiance.

The political import and difficulty of psychoanalysis can, I think, be read out of this moment. In terms of Lacan himself, the history begins with his critique of American ego-psychology, the assimilation, as he saw it, of the concept of the unconscious into a

---

[7] François Roustang, *Un destin si funeste*, Paris 1976; tr. Ned Lukacher, *Dire Mastery*, Baltimore and London 1982.

normative or adaptive psychology which took identity at its word and tried to strengthen it. But behind that lies the divisions of the analytic community in France and Lacan's dissociation in 1953 from the *Société psychanalytique de Paris* because (amongst other reasons) of the autocratic way it was being governed. The critique of autocracy and the critique of the ego should be taken together, since an ego in place which has held off the challenge from the unconscious, or transformed it into something which can simply be known and controlled, will be autocratic above all else. For women especially, the supremest of autocrats is a father whose status goes without question and beyond which there is no appeal. Feminism describes this structure as patriarchal. It is no coincidence therefore that Lacan's attempts to undo the effects of autocracy inside the analytic institution, and their hideous return, should have brought into such sharp relief his own symbolic status and the crisis for women of their relationship to it.

For someone like Montrelay, however, the only way to deal with that crisis is to continue to *be* an analyst, that is, to continue to create a space in which the problem of identification and its laws, in all their force and impossibility, can repeatedly be experienced.

The question of identity — how it is constituted and maintained — is, therefore, the central issue through which psychoanalysis enters the political field. This is one reason why Lacanian psychoanalysis came into English intellectual life, via Althusser's concept of ideology, through the two paths of feminism and the analysis of film (a fact often used to discredit all three). Feminism because the issue of how individuals recognise themselves as male or female, the demand that they do so, seems to stand in such fundamental relation to the forms of inequality and subordination which it is feminism's objective to change. Film because its power as an ideological apparatus rests on the mechanisms of identification and sexual fantasy which we all seem to participate in, but which — outside the cinema — are, for the most part, only ever admitted on the couch. If ideology is effective, it is because it works at the most rudimentary levels of psychic identity and the drives. As early as 1935, Otto Fenichel saw this as the chief contribution which psychoanalysis had to make to political analysis:

> The study of the modifications of instinct is in no way an unessential bagatelle, but is of the greatest importance theoretically

as well as practically. The statement that the production and dissemination of the ideology of a society must be understood from the actual economic conditions of this society, the 'superstructure' of which is the ideology; that further they are to be understood from the fact that this 'superstructure' by means of the actions of human beings, reacts back again upon the 'foundation', the economic conditions modifying them — these statements are correct but general. They become more specific when we succeed in comprehending scientifically the details of the mechanisms of these transformations, and only psychoanalysis is able to help us in that.[8]

Fenichel's objective was a form of analysis which would understand the psychic force of ideological process while avoiding the twin pitfalls of sociological and psychological reductionism — the sociologists dismissing the psychic investments of social life as 'mere bagatelle', the psychoanalysts, as he saw it, falling into an equivalent trap which makes the realm of the psychic the primary determining factor in the social mechanisms which it serves to drive (Fenichel on Glover: 'all psychological factors which partake of war he treats as the cause of war'; and on money: 'nothing justifies the assertion that its symbolic significance is the cause of the origin of money'[9]).

But this objective of Fenichel's, to use psychoanalysis in order to understand the internalisation, effectivity and persistence of some of the most oppressive social norms is striking for the way that it anticipates, in the similarity of terms, the argument with which Juliet Mitchell introduced the case for psychoanalysis and feminism in 1974:

> The way we live as 'ideas' the necessary laws of human society is not so much conscious as *unconscious* — the particular task of psychoanalysis is to decipher how we acquire our heritage of the ideas and laws of human society within the unconscious mind, or, to put it another way, the unconscious mind *is* the way we acquire these laws ... where Marxist theory explains the historical and economic situation, psychoanalysis, in conjunction with the

[8] Otto Fenichel, 'The Drive to Amass Wealth' (1934), *Collected Papers,* second series, London 1955, p.107.

[9] Fenichel, 'Über Psychoanalyse, Krieg und Frieden', *Internationales Ärztliches Bulletin,* 2, 1935, p.39 (cit. Russell Jacoby, *The Repression of Psychoanalysis: Otto Fenichel and the Political Freudians,* New York 1983, p.114); 'The Drive to Amass Wealth', p.100.

notions of ideology already gained by dialectical materialism, is the way into understanding ideology and sexuality.[10]

The feminist move was, accordingly, to add sexuality to the historically established links between psychoanalysis and the understanding of how ideology works. It was in this context that sexual difference was analysed as one of the most fundamental, if not *the* most fundamental, of human laws. This was therefore a theoretical case for a political necessity: that sexual difference should be acknowledged in the fullest range of its effects and then privileged in political understanding and debate. By presenting this case through psychoanalysis, Juliet Mitchell was not, however, only arguing for the importance of psychoanalysis for feminism. She was equally inserting the question of femininity back into a project which, as long ago as the 1930s, had seen psychoanalysis as the only means of explaining the exact mechanisms whereby ideological processes are transformed, via individual subjects, into human actions and beliefs.

Like Marxism, psychoanalysis sees the mechanisms which produce those transformations as determinant, but also as leaving something in excess. If psychoanalysis can give an account of how women experience the path to femininity, it also insists, through the concept of the unconscious, that femininity is neither simply achieved nor is it ever complete. The political case for psychoanalysis rests on these two insights together — otherwise it would be indistinguishable from a functionalist account of the internalisation of norms. In fact the argument from a biological pre-given and the argument from sociological role have in common the image of utter passivity they produce: the woman receives her natural destiny or else is marked over by an equally ineluctable social world.

The difficulty is to pull psychoanalysis in the direction of both of these insights — towards a recognition of the fully social constitution of identity and norms, and then back again to that point of tension between ego and unconscious where they are endlessly remodelled and endlessly break. In the 1930s, neither the celebration of the unconscious as pure force (Wilhelm Reich), nor the accusation of the restrictiveness of culture which forgets or

[10] Juliet Mitchell, *Psychoanalysis and Feminism,* London 1974, Introduction, pp.xvi, xxii.

would ideally abandon the unconscious altogether (culturalists such as Karen Horney) were adequate to that dynamic. The problem at that time was as it still is: how to articulate the unconscious as a point of resistance or defence without filling it out with visions of psychic and/or social utopia, whether one calls this unbound genital energy as Reich did then, or another femininity — site of an absolute or uncontaminated truth — as we are sometimes tempted to do now. The alternate discarding and reification of the unconscious has been the constant refrain (curse almost) of the Freudian left.

The feminist debate about psychoanalysis is therefore a repetition with a significant difference. We know now that the radical feminist critique of Freud's phallocentrism was anticipated by the quarrels of the 1920s and 30s when analysts such as Jones, Horney and Klein objected to Freud's account of sexual difference because of a fundamental asymmetry which was seen to work to the actual, as well as theoretical, disadvantage of the female. Turning that objection around, Juliet Mitchell could argue that asymmetry at the level of psychic life was precisely what psychoanalysis could be used to explain. But this quarrel should also be referred outside itself to the discussion of the political import of the Freudian concept of the unconscious and the sexual drive simultaneously conducted by analysts like Otto Fenichel and his group. Looking back at this moment, it is rather as if the theoretical/clinical debate about female sexuality and the more explictly Marxist debate about ideology and its forms were historically severed from each other — at least until feminism itself forged, or rather demonstrated, the links.

Thus in the 1930s, the controversy over Freud's account of femininity (roughly the division between the London and Vienna schools) was paralleled by the simultaneous controversy over the political import of psychoanalysis (again roughly the division between Vienna and Berlin).[11] The objective of Fenichel and the Berlin group was a political psychoanalysis which would use Freudian insights into psychic processes as the basis for a radical social critique — an issue never broached in the debate over femininity which was then simultaneously taking place. The Berlin group was in no sense simply opposed to Vienna, which had been the site of Reich's own seminars in the thirties, but their Marxism

[11] A detailed account of the Berlin group is given in Russell Jacoby.

distinguished them as a group. At the same time their commitment to the basic psychoanalytic concepts of the unconscious and the sexual drive was constant, and this cut them off from the psychic utopianism of the better known Freudian left, whose simplistic notion of libidinal repression collapsed the concept of unconscious psychic conflict into that of cultural malaise.

In this debate we can see the deployment of all the terms within which the political controversy about psychoanalysis continues to be played out to this day. Fenichel himself was clearly caught between the theorisation of the unconscious and sexuality in all their complex difficulty on the one hand, and the need to give an account of the repressiveness of social norms on the other. The uniqueness of his position (one which is wholly travestied by the idea that he was simply put down or repressed)[12] is the fact that he refused to go over to either side. Which meant that the account of social constraint was always matched by a recognition of the perverse and aberrant nature of the sexual forces bound over into the oppressive and unjust services of social forms.

For historically, whenever the political argument is made for psychoanalysis, this dynamic is polarised into a crude opposition between inside and outside — a radical Freudianism always having to argue that the social produces the misery of the psychic in a one-way process, which utterly divests the psychic of its own mechanisms and drives. Each time the psychoanalytic description of internal conflict and psychic division is referred to its social conditions, the latter absorb the former, and the unconscious shifts — in that same moment — from the site of a division into the vision of an ideal unity to come. As if the tension between the unconscious and the image to which we cling of ourselves as unified subjects were split off from each other, and the second were idealised and then projected forward into historical time. Thus sexual radicalism seems to construct its image of a free sexuality in the image of the ego, without flaw or error, as the pre-condition, or ultimate object, of revolutionary change. Idealisation of the unconscous and externalisation of the event have gone together in the attempt to construct a political Freud. That this is a dualism — psychic or philosophical or indeed both — in the classic sense is

---

[12] This is the polemic of Jacoby's book, but the material he presents demonstrates that the situation was more complicated; on p.14 of the introduction, Jacoby himself acknowledges that the term 'repression' is misleading.

clear from the way that the argument constantly crystallises into the inside/outside distinction.

It seems that from the outset, this issue has been at the heart of the earlier political, but also the feminist, critique of Freud. Reich's rejection of the death drive, for instance, is expressed in exactly these terms: "He [Freud] sensed something in the human organism which was deadly. But he thought in terms of instinct. So he hit upon the term 'death instinct'. That was wrong. 'Death' was right. 'Instinct' was wrong. Because it's not something that the organism wants. *It's something that happens to the organism.*"[13]

And when, later, Habermas describes the unconscious as an interrupted communication between subject and self, he too makes of it the mere repository of 'socially unsanctioned needs', a type of interference with what would otherwise be the perfect self-communication and self-knowledge of subjects.[14] The unconscious as the distorted effect of an oppressive social world — this was also the basis of the radical feminist critique of Freud which unilaterally shifted the emphasis from the subjectivity of the infant in the throes of unmanageable queries, envies and demands, onto the social institution of the family within which they are played out. Which is not to argue for a reversal of this dogma and grant primacy to the psychic, which would leave social misery or inequality as its simple effect, but to notice the strain *on* and *of* psychoanalytic theory in its attempt to describe in a non-reductive way the vicissitudes of psychic and sexual life.

In relation to psychoanalysis, feminism therefore finds itself with a dual inheritance: the quarrel over femininity in the thirties, but equally important, the terms of what was already then the more explicitly political debate. Read 'ideology' as 'femininity', 'cultural norms' as 'the family' and you produce the position of Shulamith Firestone, for whom psychic conflict — the problem of female identity — is the direct reflection of institutionally regulated forms of control (the link runs historically as well as theoretically from both the culturalists and the radical Freud).[15] Add the question of femininity to Fenichel's concern to insist,

[13] Wilhelm Reich, *Reich Speaks of Freud, Conversations with Kurt Eissler,* ed. Mary Higgins and C.M. Raphael, New York 1967, p.89n (my italics).

[14] Jürgen Habermas, *Knowledge and Human Interests,* London 1972, p.271.

[15] Shulamith Firestone, *The Dialectic of Sex* (1970), London 1979, especially chapter 3, 'Freudianism: The Misguided Feminism'.

against this reduction, on the importance of the unconscious and sexuality to any political psychoanalysis, and you have the precise intervention for feminism made by Juliet Mitchell in 1974. The dialogue between psychoanalysis and feminism is prefigured in this earlier, and still unresolved, debate. When someone like Elizabeth Wilson objects to any consideration of sexuality which cannot be mapped directly onto the immediately observable forms of gender inequality and oppression, her argument merely unwittingly repeats a historical and theoretical tension one half of which it blithely presents as a contemporary political fact.[16]

The same tension might explain the constant side-stepping of psychoanalysis and feminism in their mutual relation within recent Marxist debate. Thus Perry Anderson dismisses the feminist turn to Freud as a 'precarious resort to less scientific bodies of thought [than socialism]'; Fredric Jameson overlooks the links between psychoanalysis and feminism in a book devoted to the place of the unconscious in cultural form (although radical feminism is recognised, it is later re-absorbed into a priority of class division and the category of the subject is dismissed as 'anarchic'); Terry Eagleton about turns at the end of *Literary Theory,* and posits socialism and feminism over and above the forms of analysis, including psychoanalysis, he has covered in the book.[17] In Jameson's case, psychoanalysis returns in a footnote via Reich as a possible path to the analysis of the collective fantasies of religion, nationalism and fascism. In Anderson's case, the moral-aesthetic utopias of the Frankfurt school, and in particular Habermas, appear — once psychoanalysis has been divested of its feminist interest — as the political end-point of the book. As indeed they do for Eagleton at the close of his chapter on psychoanalysis and the literary text.[18] What is at issue here is not the political impetus of these books, but something which looks like a conspicuous omission or marginalisation of a crucial political link. And it seems to come in direct response to that

[16] Angela Weir and Elizabeth Wilson, 'The British Women's Movement', *New Left Review* 148, November-December 1984, pp.95-98; also Elizabeth Wilson, 'Psychoanalysis: Psychic Law and Order', *Feminist Review* 8, Summer 1981.

[17] Perry Anderson, *In the Tracks of Historical Materialism,* London 1983, p.88; Fredric Jameson, *The Political Unconscious: Narrative as a Socially Symbolic Act,* New York and London 1981, pp.100, 286; Terry Eagleton, *Literary Theory: An Introduction,* Oxford 1983, p.204.

[18] Jameson, p.291n; Anderson, p.98; Eagleton, p.193.

moment when feminism brings the most fundamental problems of the psychic back onto the political agenda. It is as if feminism can be acknowledged as part of a critique of Marxism, and psychoanalysis can be incorporated into an account of collective fantasy, but they cannot be taken together. For then the concept of psychic life which accompanies the feminist challenge to sexual division presents itself too starkly against the terms of a traditional political critique. The unconscious as ideology (its present oppressiveness), or as pleasure (its future emancipation), but not something which hovers uncomfortably in between. This was the problem in the thirties as it re-presents itself to Marxism, and also feminism, today.

The most recent form taken by the polarity between inside and outside is the dispute which has broken out over Jeffrey Masson's assault on Freud for relinquishing the seduction theory of neurosis in favour of the analysis of fantasy life.[19] Seen in these terms, it might lose something of the originality and drama which it claims for itself. A radical feminist issue (not just because Masson now chooses to describe himself as such), this polemic states more clearly than any other that the concept of an internal psychic dynamic is detrimental to politics — in this case explicitly feminism — since it denies to women an unequivocal accusation of the real. There must be no internal conflict, no desire and no dialogue; conflict must be external, the event must be wholly outside, if women are to have a legitimate voice. The psychoanalytic concept of the unconscious becomes a male conspiracy which takes from women the truth value of their speech. Kate Millett puts the argument better than Masson in the Barnard anthology on sexual politics:

> Reich was the first to address the sexuality of the young in an age when Freud was analysing and curing young persons with sexual disorders on order and payment from their parents. Freud often dealt with children, especially females, who had been sexually abused; he resolved the entire problem by deciding that it was an Oedipal fantasy on their part. So female children were not only sexually abused, they had to assent that they imagined it. This process undermines sanity, since if what takes place isn't real but

[19] Jeffrey Masson, *Freud: The Assault on Truth. Freud's Suppression of the Seduction Theory,* Boston and London 1984; for a critique of Masson, see A. Davidson, 'Assault on Freud', *London Review of Books,* 5 July 1984.

imaginary, then you are at fault: you are illogical, as well as naughty, to have imagined an unimaginable act: incest. You ascribed guilt to your father, and you are also a very guilty, sexy little creature yourself. So much for you.[20]

Freud in fact never treated children, and the only child he had access to analytically — even indirectly — was male. But more important is the way that the idea of a conflictual, divided subjectivity, caught up in the register of fantasy, is directly opposed to the idea of legitimate protest as it is politically understood. The debate about political causality and the real event resolves itself into the issue of language. Political truth relies, therefore, on the concept of full speech. This throws slips and symptoms alike back into the outer darkness of aberration from which the Freudian attention to fantasy and the unconscious had originally served to rescue them.

The psychoanalytic attention to fantasy does not, however, discredit the utterance of the patient. To argue that Freud dismissed the traumas of his patients as 'the fantasies of hysterical women who invented stories and told lies' is a total misconstrual of the status psychoanalysis accords to fantasy, which was never assigned by Freud to the category of wilful untruth.[21] In fact Freud's move was the reverse — towards a dimension of reality all the more important for the subject because it goes way beyond anything that can, or needs to be, attested as fact. By seeing fantasy as a degradation of speech, by turning reality into nothing more than what can be empirically established as the case, it is Masson himself who places human subjects in the dock.

What can this discarding of the concept of fantasy make, for instance, of one of Masson's own examples — the case of a twenty-nine-year-old woman who has sexual fantasies to the point of hallucination about her three-year-old nephew and who compulsively seeks reassurance from those around her that the event has *not* taken place? This example — in which desire belongs

---

[20] Kate Millett, 'Beyond Politics? Children and Sexuality', in *Pleasure and Danger: Exploring Female Sexuality,* ed. Carole S. Vance, Boston and London 1984, p.222; see also Chris Reed, 'How Freud Changed His Mind And Became A Chauvinist', 'Guardian Women' *Guardian,* 20 February 1985; a lengthy article by Masson has also appeared in the American radical feminist journal *Mother Jones.*

[21] Masson, p.11; yet on p.112, Masson acknowledges that Freud did *not* say that the hysterical fantasy was a lie.

to the woman in relation to a male child and where what does not happen is hallucinated as if it had — is offered by Masson, without a trace of irony, as evidence that sexual impulses 'which often lead to sexual acts' on the part of adults towards children were *'real'*.[22] Doesn't this very example illustrate the vexed relation between actuality, memory, and fantasy which is the domain of the Freudian unconscious? And if we use this example to insist on the reality of seduction, where does that leave the woman if not simply accused, when her far more painful reality leaves her suspended between fantasy and the reality of the event? And again what should we make of the tension between Masson's unequivocal appeal to 'an actual world of sadness, misery and cruelty' and his own recognition of a 'need to repeat early sorrows' which he recognises in his conclusion as one of the most genuine discoveries of Freud?[23]

Fantasy and the compulsion to repeat — these appear as the concepts against which the idea of a more fully political objection to injustice constantly stalls. It seems to me that this is the ground on to which the feminist debate about psychoanalysis has now moved; but in doing so it has merely underlined a more general problem for political analysis which has always been present in the radical readings of Freud. Which is how to reconcile the problem of subjectivity which assigns activity (but not guilt), fantasy (but not error), conflict (but not stupidity) to individual subjects — in this case women — with a form of analysis which can also recognise the force of structures in urgent need of social change?

I would argue that the importance of psychoanalysis is precisely the way that it throws into crisis the dichotomy on which the appeal to the reality of the event (amongst others) clearly rests. Perhaps for women it is of particular importance that we find a language which allows us to recognise our part in intolerable structures — but in a way which renders us neither the pure victims nor the sole agents of our distress. In its strange attention to an involvement in a structure (say, sexual difference) no more reducible to false consciousness or complicity than to adaptation or ease, psychoanalysis might in fact allow us to rethink this vexed political question.

Let's turn the critique of psychoanalysis around for a moment

[22] Masson, pp.28-29.
[23] Ibid., pp.144, 188.

and say, not that the concept of a divided subjectivity is incompatible with political analysis and demand, but that feminism, through its foregrounding of sexuality (site of fantasies, impasses, conflict and desire) and of sexual difference (the structure towards which all of this constantly tends but against which it just as constantly breaks) is in a privileged position to challenge the dualities (inside/outside, victim/ aggressor, real event/fantasy, and even good/evil) upon which so much traditional political analysis has so often relied. For it remains the case that — without reifying the idea of a pure fragmentation which would be as futile as it would be psychically unmanageable for the subject — only the concept of a subjectivity at odds with itself gives back to women the right to an impasse at the point of sexual identity, with no nostalgia whatsoever for its possible or future integration into a norm. Which is why someone like Habermas, coming from a very different position, who looks to psychoanalysis to solve the problem of how a class comes to knowledge of itself, and hence as a means to the pure rationality of the integrated political subject, so utterly misses the point.

It does seem to me, however, that it is precisely because of what psychoanalysis throws into question at just this level that feminism too, which has centred sexuality on the political stage, often about turns on psychoanalysis when faced with the twists and vicissitudes which psychoanalysis exposes at the heart of sexuality itself. Today the terms of the objections have shifted from the critique of phallocentrism to the argument that feminism needs access to an integrated subjectivity more than its demise.[24] Or else it takes the form of a new asserted politics of sexuality in all its multiplicity, but one from which any idea of the psychic as an area of difficulty has been dropped.[25]

In all of this, what is worth noting is the strange relationship of psychoanalysis to the changing terms of feminist analysis and debate. Thus feminism asks psychoanalysis for an account of how ideologies are imposed upon subjects and how female identity is acquired, only to find that the concepts of fantasy and the

---

[24] Nancy Miller, 'A Conversation Between Adrienne Rich and Roland Barthes', *Feminism/Theory/Politics,* Conference held at the Pembroke Center for Teaching and Research on Women, March 1985 (to be published 1987).

[25] Gayle Rubin, 'Thinking Sex: Notes for a Radical Theory of the Politics of Sexuality', in *Pleasure and Danger.*

unconscious rule any notion of pure imposition or full acquisition out of bounds. Or more recently, as feminism turns to the practices and limits of sexuality, calling for a pluralism which the analytic concept of a multifarious sexual disposition might appear to legitimate or support, it finds itself up against the problem of *any* sexual identity for the subject and the lie of any simple assertion of self. Perhaps even more difficult, as feminism turns to questions of censorship, violence and sado-masochism, psychoanalysis hands back to it a fundamental violence of the psychic realm — hands back to it, therefore, nothing less than the difficulty of sexuality itself.

For if psychic life has its own violence; if there is an aggression in the very movement of the drives; if sexual difference, because of the forcing it requires, leaves the subject divided against the sexual other as well as herself or himself; if the earliest instances of female sexuality contain a difficulty not solely explicable in terms of the violent repudiation with which the little girl leaves them behind — if any of these statements have any force (they can be attributed respectively, if loosely, to Melanie Klein, Jacques Lacan and Julia Kristeva), then there can be no analysis for women which sees violence solely as accident, imposition or external event. Only a rigid dualism pits fantasy against the real; only an attempt to reduce the difference between them by making one a pure reflection of the other has, finally, to set them so totally apart.

Thus feminism inherits the debates of the 1920s and 30s, not even in two, but in three stages. First the quarrel over sexual difference (the dispute over the phallocentrism of Freud); then the concept of ideology (femininity as a norm); and now the concept of the death drive which was no less controversial than the other two. For the debates over the real event and the limits of what is tolerable in sexual life, clearly contain within them this question of how, or where, violence should be placed. 'Where does the misery come from?' — this was the question put by Reich to Freud when he rejected the concept of the death drive, which has been the point at which more than one radical Freudian has broken with psychoanalysis.[26] Fenichel also criticised the concept precisely for

---

[26] Reich, pp.42-43; the same cut-off point, specifically around the concept of the death drive and the 'inevitability of conflict', appears in *Free Associations,* the journal of the Radical Science collective on psychoanalysis; see David Ingleby, 'The Ambivalence of Psychoanalysis', *Radical Science* 15, 1984.

the way it could be misused to 'eliminate the social factor from the etiology of the neuroses', but in the rest of this same paper, although these points are rarely quoted, he argues for the destructive character of the earliest psychic impulses and, against the dualism inherent in Freud's own conception, posits Nirvana as a *general* principle of instinctual life.[27] If this is important today, it is only because we seem to be gravitating to a point where that same break with psychoanalysis is taking place. Thus sexual violence enters the political scene for reasons which go way beyond psychoanalysis (sexual politics in the immediate sense), only to find itself drawn once again into the confrontation with Freud. In response to which, violence is relegated wholly to the outside. But at that same moment — and with an almost moral distaste — it is the psychic dynamic of sexuality *per se* which is discarded.

At the same time, in this overall clash between psychoanalysis and a politics of sexuality based on assertion and will, the historical and national differences between the different emphases is important. The different feminist responses to, and uses of, Freud can only be properly understood in terms of the context in which they emerged. Thus the radical feminist rejection of Freud is in part a response to the analytic institution in America where, once the case for lay analysis was lost, then the 'defeminisation' no less than the depoliticisation of the analytic community was assured.[28] In France, on the other hand, the first links of Lacanian psychoanalysis were with avant-garde artistic practice and surrealism which guaranteed it a position of contestation in relation to bourgeois culture and norms, as well as at least partly explaining its attention to the slippages of language. Further-more, its specific object of criticism was the very form of psychoanalysis which writers like Millett and Firestone were later to attack. In England, the feminist case comes through Marxism and the theory of ideology which connects with that much earlier radical Freudian project. If we take Montrelay, Mitchell and Millett, they can obviously be set against each other in the uses they make (or do not make) of Freud, but the attention to the play

---

[27] Fenichel, 'A Critique of the Death Instinct' (1935), *Collected Papers,* first series, London 1954, p.370; Jacoby gives the quotation, but does not mention the rest of the argument.

[28] See Jacoby, pp.12-14, 18-19.

of language in all its dislocating effects, to the constraints of ideology, and to the politics of self-expression, identity and power, also point to crucial historical differences which should perhaps not be theoretically reduced to each other, and then resolved.

One strand of that institutional history and of the cross-currents between different cultures and politics should finally, if briefly, be mentioned. This is the recent assimilation of a literary Freud into the academic establishment. For while the feminist critique of psychoanalysis repeats itself outside, or even against, institution and academy, albeit in new terms, psychoanalysis is being incorporated into literary method, a strange relic of the link in France at least — for this is a French Freud — between psychoanalysis and the avant-garde text. Decisively informing a whole strand of artistic production in the visual image, photography and film, psychoanalysis simultaneously moves into literary analysis in conjunction with what is in fact a sustained and influential critique by Derrida of Lacan and, through him, of Freud.[29] Lacan himself always argued that only those who were alert to the processes of literary writing would understand his linguistic reading of Freud. But we need to ask what price this absorption of psychoanalysis — as practice and institution — into writing and reading has for the understanding of subjectivity and for feminism alike.

On the far side of the earlier critiques, this engagement with psychoanalysis aims for all those points in psychoanalytic discourse which reinforce the category of the subject, which Derrida sees as a vestige of the logocentrism of the West. Here the phallocentrism of Freud is objected to, not as a manifestation of

[29] The move into literature is most strongly represented by Shoshana Felman ed., *Literature and Psychoanalysis — The Question of Reading: Otherwise, Yale French Studies* 55/56, 1977; also Felman, *La folie et la chose littéraire*, Paris 1978 (trs. N.M. Evans and Shoshana Felman, *Writing and Madness*, Ithaca 1986);for the Derridean reading of Freud, see Samuel Weber, *The Legend of Freud*, Minneapolis 1982. For a key moment of reversal between psychoanalysis and deconstruction, see also Paul de Man, *Allegories of Reading*, New Haven and London 1979: 'Far from seeing language as an instrument in the service of a psychic energy, the possibility now arises that the entire construction of the drive, substitutions, repressions, and representations is the aberrant, metaphorical correlative of the absolute randomness of language, prior to any figuration or meaning.' (p.299.) For a discussion of these developments between literary theory and psychoanalysis see Robert Young, 'Psychoanalytic Criticism: Has It Got Beyond a Joke?', *Paragraph* 4, October 1984.

male institutional power nor in the name of an identity of women, but in terms of the whole order of representation which supports it. One in which the phallic term receives its inscription at the level of a wholly general metaphysical law. Against that order of representation, Derrida posits *différance,* the sliding of language which only arbitrarily and repressively fixes into identity and reference alike. *Différance* is explicitly opposed to sexual difference in which Derrida identifies a classic binarism that closes off the potentially freer play of its terms.[30]

This is a criticism which accordingly places itself at the opposite pole to the other political critiques, since where they see in psychoanalysis too little of a subject, Derrida sees if anything too much. But the two positions can be politically related — for while the first claims an identity rendered corrupt only through its exclusive possession by the male, the second goes for the same object by displacing or undercutting the form of identity itself. This is a traditional opposition between equality and difference as historical alternatives for feminism. Feminists have been attracted to Derrida's reading precisely because of the possibility it seems to engender for a wholly other discursive and, by implication, political space.

But in so far as Derrida's critique of psychoanalysis is part of a challenge to 'the history of symbolic possibility *in general'*, and through that to cultural form,[31] it comes remarkably close at times to earlier radical repudiations of Freud. For Reich also criticised Freud for his commitment to the necessity of culture (*'Die Kultur*

---

[30] Derrida's writing on psychoanalysis is extensive. The key texts, whose detail is in no sense covered here, are 'Freud et la scène de l'écriture', *L'écriture et la différence,* Paris 1967 (tr. Alan Bass, 'Freud and the Scene of Writing', *Writing and Difference,* Chicago and London 1978); 'La double séance', *La dissémination,* Paris 1972 (tr. Barbara Johnson, 'The Double Session' *Dissemination,* Chicago and London 1981); 'La Facteur de la Verité', *Poétique* 21, 1975 (trs. Willis Domingo *et al.,* 'The Purveyor of Truth', *Yale French Studies* 52, 1976); 'Fors', preface to Nicolas Abraham and Maria Torok, *Cryptomanie, le verbier de l'homme aux loups,* Paris 1976 (tr. 'Fors: the Anglish Words of Nicolas Abraham and Maria Torok', *The Georgia Review* 31:1, 1977); *La carte postale, de Socrate à Freud et au delà,* Paris 1980. On Derrida's critique of Lacan, see Barbara Johnson, 'The Frame of Reference: Poe, Lacan, Derrida' in *Literature and Psychoanalysis,* and in Robert Young ed., *Untying the Text,* London 1981.

[31] 'Freud and the Scene of Writing', p.197 (emphasis in the original); see also 'Cogito et histoire de la folie', *L'écriture et la différence;* 'Cogito and the History of Madness', *Writing and Difference,* especially p.54.

geht vor'),[32] and although *différance* is in no sense unbound genital energy, a reference to energy runs through Derrida's writing.[33] For Derrida, that movement (that energy) is held down by a drive to mastery ('*la pulsion du propre*') which links the narcissistic and self-identified subject to the forms of propriety and propriation which characterise the logocentrism of the West. Likewise psychoanalysis is criticised as ethics and institution. In its strongest moments this is a criticism which points to the boundaries the analytic community sets for itself in relation to the political realities of the societies of which it forms a part.[34] But behind these more local designations, it is the concept of identity and subjectivity which is at stake. The analytic community draws in its boundaries protectively (remember Freud's injunction to H.D.), and constitutes itself as an identity in that moment for which its ultimate reinforcement of the category of the subject is merely the logical sequel.

In Derrida there is therefore an endless dispersal of subjectivity. If it seems to go so much further than earlier criticisms in its disruption of categories and the transcending of norms, that is only because the scope of its critique is so much vaster (the phallogocentrism of the West). The dispersal of the subject across the space of representation then allows for the assimilation of this psychoanalysis into the literary/academic institution as a reading and writing effect (the bypassing of one institution leads straight into another).

For feminism, the critique of identity and difference has its obvious force — the production of what might be another representational space, and the resulting idea that sexual difference is not just internally unstable but can be moved off centre-stage, away from the privileged position which the psychoanalytic attention to the Oedipal moment undoubtedly

---

[32] Freud cit. in Reich, p.45. The points of connection are most striking in a long and crucial footnote to 'The Purveyor of Truth' (p.97 n.34) on the phallocentrism of psychoanalysis, in which Derrida finally bases his critique on the 'ethico-institutional' status of psychoanalysis which he locates in Lacan's statement: 'All human formations have as their essence, and not by accident, the restraint of *jouissance*'.

[33] See, for example, 'Freud and the Scene of Writing', p.212.

[34] Derrida, 'Géopsychanalyse "and the rest of the world" ', *Géopsychanalyse, les souterrains de l'institution,* 'Rencontre franco-latine-américaine', ed. René Major, Paris 1981.

accords it. Yet identity returns in Derrida through the category of mastery as the metaconceptual and transcendent drive, so that something in the order of a psychic exigency seems to underpin the logos itself. Behind the Western logos of presence, Derrida locates an archi-trace or *différance* which that logos would ideally forget, but this then requires a psychic account of how/why that forgetting takes place.[35] And sexual difference also returns with all the trappings of the binary polarisation which Derrida seeks to displace. For the effect of this general dispersal of subjectivity into a writing process where narrative, naming and propriation are undone, is the constant identification of the woman with the underside of truth. Precisely as a logical consequence of the 'critique of humanism as phallogocentrism', the woman comes to occupy the place 'of a general critique of Western thought'[36] — at once the fantasy on which male propriation relies as well as the excluded fact of that propriation which gives back to it the lie. But the effect is a massive sexualisation of Derrida's own discourse as the concepts of 'hymen' and 'double chiasmatic invagination of the borders' appear as the terms through which the failure of Western representation is most aptly embodied or thought.[37] The critique of the psychoanalytic focus on the Oedipal triangle and of the phallogocentrism of language can only be pursued, therefore, in terms of the very sexual antagonism which it was intended to displace. That the woman then comes to be set up in a classic position of otherness is only the most striking effect of this move.[38]

---

[35] *La carte postale,* p.419; hence, I would argue, the whole return of Derrida to the question of the psychic apparatus in *La carte postale.* For a very similar reading to Derrida's, see Samuel Weber.

[36] Gayatri Spivak, 'Love Me, Love My Ombre, Elle', *Diacritics,* Winter 1984, pp.24, 22.

[37] See in particular, 'The Double Session' and *La carte postale,* p.417.

[38] Gayatri Spivak writes: 'To see indeterminacy in the figure of the woman might be the effect of an ethicolegal narrative whose oppressive hegemony remains largely unquestioned' — the 'reversal' of a classic dualism 'rather than its accomplished displacement, whatever that might be'. ('Love Me, Love My Ombre, Elle', pp.22, 29.) On Derrida's use of the terms 'reproduction' and 'hymen', Spivak also comments: 'one might have expected a deconstitution of the sedimentation of these metaphors'. (p.28.) I suspect, however, that our criticisms meet from a position of difference. For Spivak, this repetition follows from Derrida not following through his own deconstructive project to its own (non) end (for example, failing to undo the structure/empiricism binary opposition). For me it follows from the very drive of the project and what it attempts to by-pass or circumvent. Hence the problem starts here: 'If a good definition of the "I" (ego) is

An exposure of fantasy at the basis of language — or its mere repetition? (The question can also be asked of Lacan.) But thrown onto the underside of language, this fantasy cannot be *analysed* at the point of its psychic effectivity for subjects. It can only be played out, or discarded along with western discourse, perhaps.

Finally, if the challenge to subject, ethics and institution (psychoanalysis no less) leads to such a repetition, then we might also ask whether all or any of these can in fact be wholly displaced. Whether in fact only an institution that knows the necessity and impossibility of its own limits and, like the subject, can only operate on that edge, might be — instead of the antithesis of all politics — the pre-condition or site where any politics must take place. Suspended between the too little and too much of a subject, psychoanalysis can only be grasped — as practice and in its wider effects — from some such position as this.

For Derrida the critique of logocentrism leads to the end of the institution in which he rightly locates the oppressions of our world. But in going over to the other side he merely starts to repeat the sexual fantasmagoria which was there in the collapse of the *école freudienne*. And if we go back again to that moment, which is where I started, we find another woman analyst — Jeanne Favret Saada — who had resigned in 1977 over a colleague (also a woman) who had committed suicide after trying to make her way into full theoretical membership of the school through a procedure called '*la passe*'[39]. Saada analyses the impossible transference which such a passage entails and resigns from the school, but she considers herself no less (rather more) of an analyst for that. The problem of the transmission of psychoanalysis and its 'knowledge' of the unconscious, she recognises, is not resolved by her gesture, any more than the '*passe*' could be said in some simple way to have caused the death of her friend. Rather, as she sees it, it became the impossible repository of whatever was 'unanalysed' in her (Derrida's ultimate question to the analytic institution is also that of its founding relation to the 'unanalysed' of Freud[40]).

a staggered contingent set of postal relays arriving at multiple points at the same time'. (p.28.) I don't think it is a good definition and suspect that it might also lead straight to the return of 'uniqueness' and 'properness' that Spivak remarks on in Derrida's discourse on love.

[39] Jeanne Favret Saada, 'Excusez-moi, je ne faisais que passer', *Les Temps Modernes* 371, June 1977.

[40] *La carte postale*, pp.547-549.

No recourse to a place simply outside the process of analysis, and no simple dichotomy between inside and outside. From Masson to Saada the question of how to locate the violence of institutions and of subjects returns as the issue of psychoanalysis in relation to the social today. In relation to Derrida, and for feminism, I would merely suggest that it is only the dispatching of the subject and its dissolution into a writing strategy which leads to the political demands for its return.[41] For the political necessity of the subject is met in part by the psychic necessity of the subject, but in a way which finds itself suspended between each of these demands, for this subject is neither pure assertion nor play. More than writing, but less than the event, psychoanalysis continues to point to an instance which cannot be caught by the infinite play of language any more than it can be answered by class, economy or power. That has always been its political importance and its difficulty, although it is through feminism that this has been articulated more clearly than anywhere else. To understand subjectivity, sexual difference and fantasy in a way which neither entrenches the terms nor denies them still seems to me to be a crucial task for today. Not a luxury, but rather the key processes through which — as women and as men — we experience, and then question, our fully political fates.

---

[41] Angela McRobbie, 'Strategies of Vigilance — An Interview with Gayatri Chakravorty Spivak', *Block* 10, 1985, p. 9.

Part One
Femininity and Representation

Part One
Formality and Representation

1
Dora-Fragment of an Analysis

The word is understood only as an extension of the body which is
there in the process of speaking.... To the extent that it does not
know repression, femininity is the downfall of interpretation.
> Michèle Montrelay, 'Inquiry Into Femininity,' *m/f* 1,
> 1978, p.89.

Filmed sequence — it is the body of Dora which speaks pain,
desire, speaks a force divided and contained.
> Hélène Cixous, *Portrait de Dora* (Paris 1976), p.36.

What would it mean to reopen the case of Dora now?[1] The
quotations above point to an urgency that is nothing less than that
of the present dialogue between psychoanalysis and feminism, a
dialogue that seems crucial and yet constantly slides away from
the point of a possible encounter, psychoanalysis attempting to
delimit an area that might be called femininity within the confines
of the drive, within a theory of sexuality that constantly places and
displaces the concept of sexual difference, feminism starting
precisely from that difference which it then addresses to
psychoanalysis as a demand, the demand for the theory of its
construction. Feminism, therefore, first turns to psychoanalysis
because it is seen as the best place to describe the coming into

---

[1] This essay was first published in *m/f* 2, 1978, pp.5-21; it was reprinted in *In
Dora's Case, Freud, Hysteria, Feminism*, eds. Charles Bernheimer and Claire
Kahane, New York and London 1985.

being of femininity, which, in a next stage, it can be accused of producing or at least reproducing, sanctioning somehow within its own discourse. And then, where it fails, as it did with Dora, this can be taken as the sign of the impossibility of its own project, the impossibility then becoming the feminine, which, by a twist that turns the language of psychoanalysis against itself, it *represses*. Quite simply, the case of Dora is seen to fail because Dora is repressed as a woman by psychoanalysis and what is left of Dora as somehow retrievable is the insistence of the body as feminine, and since it is a case of hysteria, in which the symptom speaks across the body itself, the feminine is placed not only as source (origin and exclusion) but also as manifestation (the symptom). Within this definition, hysteria is assimilated to a body as site of the feminine, outside discourse, silent finally, or, at best, 'dancing'.

What I want to do in this essay is look at some of these difficulties through the case of Dora — not simply to accuse the case of its failure, which failure must, however, be described and interrogated; not to produce an alternative reading whose content would be the feminine; but nonetheless to bring out some of the problems of the case precisely as the problem of the feminine within psychoanalysis in its urgency for us now. To do this will involve a discussion of the case itself, how its failure relates to changes in the concept of sexuality, and how these changes, which come at least partly in response to that failure, make certain conceptions of the feminine problematic.

The essay falls into three parts: (1) the failure of the case, its relation to Freud's concept of femininity; (2) the relation of changes in the concept of femininity to changes in that of analytic practice (transference), and then to the concept of the unconscious in its relation to representation (hysterical and schizophrenic language); and (3) how these changes make impossible any notion of the feminine that would be outside representation,[2] the failure of the case of Dora being precisely the failure to articulate the relation between these two terms.

The case of Dora

The case of Dora was first drafted under the title 'Dreams and

[2] See Parveen Adams, 'Representation and Sexuality', *m/f* 1, 1978.

Hysteria' in 1901, the year after the publication of *The Interpretation of Dreams*. Yet it did not appear until 1905, in the same year as the *Three Essays on the Theory of Sexuality*. The space between the two dates is punctuated by Freud's own comments on his hesitancy regarding a case that had promised so much, that he had in fact promised as nothing less than the sequel to *The Interpretation of Dreams*, as the link between clinical practice and dream analysis, between the etiology of the symptom and the primary process. The history of the case, its hesitancy, in this sense speaks for itself, for it is caught quite literally between those two aspects of Freud's work, the theory of the unconscious and the theory of sexuality, whose relation or distance is what still concerns us today, as if the case of Dora could only appear finally at the point where the implications of its failure had already been displaced onto a theory of sexuality, by no means complete and still highly problematic, but at least acknowledged as such. Dora then falls, or fails, in the space between these two texts, and Freud himself writes: "While the case history before us seems particularly favoured as regards the utilization of dreams, in other respects it has turned out poorer than I could have wished".[3]

What then was wrong with Dora? First, in the simple sense of diagnosis and/or symptom, leaving aside at this stage the question of the status of the diagnostic category itself, not forgetting however that it was from this very question that psychoanalysis set out (rejection of hysteria as an independent clinical entity[4]). Dora, then, as first presented or brought to Freud, was suffering from *tussis nervosa* and periodic attacks of aphonia (nervous cough and loss of voice), 'possibly migraines, together with depression, hysterical unsociability, and a *taedium vitae* which was probably not entirely genuine'.[5] Her entering into the treatment had been precipitated by the discovery of a suicide note by her parents and a momentary loss of consciousness after a row with her father, subsequently covered by amnesia. The symptoms are so slight, in a sense, that Freud feels it necessary to

---

[3] Sigmund Freud, 'Fragment of an Analysis of a Case of Hysteria (*Dora*)' (1905), *The Standard Edition of the Complete Psychological Works* (SE), London 1955-74, SE 7, p.11; *The Pelican Freud Library* (PF), Harmondsworth 1976-85, PF 8, p.40.

[4] Josef Breuer and Sigmund Freud, *Studies on Hysteria* (1893-95), SE 2, p.259; PF 3, p.342.

[5] *Dora*, p.24; p.54.

excuse to the reader the attention he is to give to the case, the status he is granting it as exemplary of a neurotic disorder whose etiology he sets himself to describe.

The situation is all the more complex in that the case is offered as a 'fragment', and this in a number of different senses: first, the case was broken off by the patient; second, it was not committed to writing until after the completion of the treatment (only the words of the dreams were recorded immediately after the session); and third, as a corollary to the second factor, only the results of the analysis and not its process were transcribed. Finally, Freud explicitly states that, where the etiology of the case stalled, he appeals to other cases to fill in the gaps, always indicating the point at which 'the authentic part ends and my construction begins'.[6]

Each of these notions of fragment are crucial for the case, and each is double-edged. If the case is broken off after three months, this only 'fragments' it insofar as the whole practice of psychoanalysis had changed from the immediate analysis of the symptom to an engagement with whatever presented itself to the mind of the patient in any one session, so that the inadequacy of the time span is the consequence of a new privileging of the discourse of the patient herself. Thus the distinction between the results and the process of analysis, which is the basis of the second and third notions of fragment, in one sense collapses on the first (this incidentally should be remembered in any simple dismissal of the case as the suppression of the patient's 'own' language). On the other hand, the process *is* missing from the case in another and more crucial sense, that of the relation between the analyst and the patient, which Freud calls the transference, and to whose neglect he partly ascribes its failure. All these points should be borne in mind as the signs of this failure, and yet each is a paradox: the process is there, but it is somehow elided; a meaning or interpretation of Dora's 'complaint' is produced, but it is clearly inadequate.

To give a history of the case is therefore impossible, but a number of central points can be disengaged that I hope will be of help in the discussion to follow:[7]

[6] Ibid, p.12; p.41.
[7] For a fuller discussion of the sequence of this case see Jacques Lacan, 'Intervention on Transference'.

1. The parameters of the case are defined by the sexual circuit that runs between Dora's parents and their 'intimate' friends, Herr and Frau K., in which Dora herself is caught.

2. Thus, Dora is courted by Herr K., and the crisis that leads to the treatment is partly precipitated by an attempted seduction on his part, which she repudiates.

3. Behind this is the affair between Dora's father and Frau K.; behind this, crucially, the absence of Dora's mother in her relationship both to Dora ('unfriendly')[8] and to Dora's father (hence his relationship with Frau K.).

4. Behind this again, there is an intimacy which is first that between the two families but which also completes the sexual circuit between them — the intimacy of Dora and Frau K., whose precise content is never given and that functions exactly as the 'secret' of the case, the source of the sexual knowledge that Dora undoubtedly has, and that thus cuts straight across from the 'manifest' behaviour of the participants to the 'latent' etiology of the symptoms (Freud's theory of hysteria).

Put at its most crude, Freud's interpretation of the case is based on a simple identification of the Oedipal triangle, and starts with Dora's protest at her place in the relationship between Frau K. and her father, that is, with Dora as a pawn who is proferred to Herr K. Thus her repudiation of the latter is the inevitable consequence of an outrage that takes Herr K. as its immediate object, and yet behind which is the figure of the father, who is the object of real reproach. In this way Dora's rejection of Herr K., 'still quite young and of prepossessing appearance' (sic)[9] can be seen as simultaneously Oedipal *and* hysterical (repudiation of her own desire). Dora's own desire is defined here as unproblematic — heterosexual and genital. At this stage Freud was still bound to the traumatic theory of neurosis, and he thus traces the repudiation on the part of Dora to an attempted embrace by Herr K. when she was fourteen, which was also repulsed — 'the behaviour of this child of fourteen was already entirely and completely hysterical'.[10] To be more precise, therefore, we would have to say that the Oedipal triangle is there in the case history but that it is held off by this

[8] *Dora*, p.20; p.50.
[9] Ibid., p.29n; p.60n.
[10] Ibid., p.28; p.59.

notion of trauma, which makes of Herr K. the first repudiated object (the seducer). In his analysis of Dora's first dream, there is no doubt that Freud interprets it as a summoning up of an infantile affection for the father *secondarily*, as a defense against Dora's persistent and unquestioned desire for Herr K. (The second dream is then interpreted as revealing the vengeance/hostility against her father that could not achieve expression in the first.)

Now the way in which the case history is laid out immediately spoils the picture, or the 'fine poetic conflict'[11] as Freud himself puts it, since Dora has been totally complicit in the affair between her father and Frau K., and it had in fact been entirely through her complicity that the situation had been able to continue. Furthermore, Dora's symptom, her cough, reveals an unmistakable identification with her father, a masculine identification confirmed by the appearance of her brother at three points in the case history — each time as the object of identification, whether as recollection, screen memory, or manifest content of the dream. The revealing of this masculine identification leads directly to the uncovering of the 'true' object of Dora's jealousy (made clear if for no other reason by the overinsistence of her reproaches against her father), that is, Frau K. herself, with whom Dora had shared such intimacy, secrecy, and confessions, even about Frau K.'s unsatisfactory relationship with her husband — in which case, Freud asks, how on earth could Dora in fact be in love with Herr K.? We may well ask.

What we therefore have in the case is a series of contradictions, which Freud then attempts to resolve by a mandatory appeal to the properties of the unconscious itself ('thoughts in the unconscious live very comfortably side by side, and even contraries get on together without disputes'),[12] revealing a theory of interpretation actually functioning as 'resistance' to the pressing need to develop a theory of sexuality, whose complexity or difficulty manifests itself time and again in the case. Thus in his analysis of the hysterical symptom — aphonia, or loss of voice — Freud is forced toward the beginnings of a concept of component sexuality (a sexuality multiple and fragmented and not bound to the genital function), since the symptom is clearly not only the response to the absence of Herr K. (impossibility of the

[11] Ibid., p.59; p.94.
[12] Ibid., p.61; p.96.

communication desired) but also a fantasied identification with a scene of imagined sexual satisfaction between Dora's father and Frau K. This is the fullest discussion of sexuality in the book, which anticipates many of the theses of the *Three Essays*, but it is conducted by Freud as an apology for Dora (and himself) — a justification of the discussion of sexual matters with a young girl (the question therefore being that of censorship, Freud's discovery reduced to the articulation of sexuality *to* a woman) and then as insistence on the perverse and undifferentiated nature of infantile sexuality so that Dora's envisaging of a scene of oral gratification — for that is what it is — might be less of a scandal.

The difficulties therefore clearly relate to the whole concept of sexuality, and not just to the nature of the object (for the importance of this, see later in this essay on the concept of the sexual aim), but Freud's own resistance appears most strongly in relation to Frau K.'s status as an object of desire for Dora. Thus this aspect of the case surfaces only symptomatically in the text, at the end of the clinical picture that it closes, and in a series of footnotes and additions to the interpretation of the second dream and in the postscript.

It is in her second dream that the identification of Dora with a man (her own suitor) is unquestionable, and since the analysis reveals a latent obsession with the body of the woman, the Madonna, defloration, and finally childbirth, the recuperation of a primary autoeroticism (the masturbation discerned behind the first dream) by a masculine fantasy of self-possession now charted across the question of sexual difference is clear.[13] Yet Freud makes of the dream an act of vengeance, as he does the breaking off of the case, which perhaps not suprisingly is its immediate sequel. The way this dream raises the question of sexual difference will be discussed below. It should already serve as a caution against any assimilation of Dora's homosexual desire for Frau K. to a simple preoedipal instance. Note for the moment that Freud is so keen to hang onto a notion of genital heterosexuality that it leads him, first, to identify the fantasy of childbirth that analysis revealed behind the

---

[13] Note Freud's discussion of this dream: 'What was most evident was that in the first part of the dream she was identifying herself with a young man — it would have been appropriate for the goal to have been the possession of a woman, of herself'. (Ibid., pp.96-97; pp.116-117.)

second dream as an obscure 'maternal longing'[14] outdoing in advance Karen Horney's appeals to such a longing as natural, biological and pregiven in her attacks on Freud's later work on femininity; and second, to classify Dora's masculine identification and desire for Frau K. as 'gynaecophilic' and to make it 'typical of the unconscious erotic life of hysterical girls'[15], that is, to use as an explanation of hysteria the very factor that needs to be explained.

Finally, it should be pointed out that the insistence on a normal genital sexuality is obviously related to the question of transference. Freud himself attributes the failure of the case to his failure in 'mastering the transference in good time',[16] while his constant footnoting of this discussion with references to his overlooking the homosexual desire of this patient indicates that the relation between these two aspects of the case remains unformulated. At one level it is easy that Freud's failure to understand his own implication in the case (countertransference) produced a certain definition of sexuality as a *demand* on Dora, which, it should be noted, she rejects (walks out). On the other hand, and more crucially, Freud's own definition of transference in its relation to the cure can be seen as caught in the same trap as that of his theory of sexuality, since he sees the former as the obstacle to the uncovering of 'new memories, dealing, probably, with actual events'[17] (relics of the seduction theory), just as he defines neurosis as the 'incapacity for meeting a *real* erotic demand',[18] and even allows (thereby undermining the whole discovery of psychoanalysis) that neurosis might ultimately be vanquished by 'reality'.[19] The concept of a possible recovery from neurosis through reality and that of an unproblematic feminine sexuality are coincident in the case.

'In fact she was a feminist'

The reference comes from Freud's case on the 'Psychogenesis of

14 Ibid., p.104n; p.145n.
15 Ibid., p.63; p.98.
16 Ibid., p.118; p.160.
17 Ibid., p.119; p.160.
18 Ibid., p.110; p.151.
19 Ibid., p.110; p.152.

Homosexuality in a Woman',[20] and in one sense the step from the failure of the case of Dora to this case, which appeared in 1920, is irresistible — not, however, in order to classify Dora as homosexual in any simple sense, but precisely because in this case Freud was led to an acknowledgement of the homosexual factor in all feminine sexuality, an acknowledgement which was to lead to his revision of his theories of the Oedipus complex for the girl. For in this article he is in a way at his most radical, rejecting the concept of cure, insisting that the most psychoanalysis can do is restore the original bisexual disposition of the patient, defining homosexuality as nonneurotic. Yet, at the same time, his explanation of this last factor — the lack of neurosis ascribed to the fact that the object-choice was established not in infancy but after puberty — is then undermined by his being obliged to trace back the homosexual attraction to a moment prior to the oedipal instance, the early attachment to the mother, in which case either the girl is neurotic (which she clearly is not) or all women are neurotic (which indeed they might be).

The temptation is therefore to see the case of Dora as anticipating, through the insistence of Dora's desire for Frau K. as substitute for the absent mother in the case ('the mystery turns upon your mother'[21], Freud says in relation to the first dream), the nature of the preoedipal attachment between mother and girl child, an attachment Freud finally makes specific to feminine sexuality in its persistence and difficulty. All recent work on the concept of a feminine sexuality that resists or exceeds the reproductive or genital function stems from this, and since the Oedipus complex is properly the insertion of the woman into the circuit of symbolic exchange (nothing could be clearer in the case of Dora), then her resistance to this positioning is assigned a radical status. The woman, therefore, is outside exchange, an exchange put into play or sanctioned by nothing other than language itself, which thus produces the question of her place and *her* language simultaneously. The transition to a concept of hysterical discourse as some privileged relation to the maternal body is then easy; it is partly supported by Freud's own 'suspicion' that 'this phase of attachment to the mother is especially

[20] Freud, 'The Psychogenesis of a Case of Homosexuality in a Woman' (1920), SE 18; PF 9.

[21] *Dora*, p.70; p.105.

intimately related to the aetiology of hysteria, which is not surprising when we reflect that both the phase and the neurosis are characteristically feminine'.[22]

What seems to happen is that the desire to validate the preoedipal instance as resistance to the oedipal structure itself leads to a 'materialization' of the *bodily* relation that underpins it, so that the body of the mother, or more properly the girl's relation to it, is then placed as being somehow outside repression. What we then have is a constant assimilation in feminist texts of the maternal body and the unrepressed (see Montrelay, quoted at the beginning of this article), or of the maternal body and the dream (Kristeva: 'different, close to the dream or the maternal body'), or of the maternal body and a primary autoeroticism (Irigaray) whose return would apparently mean the return of the (feminine) exile.[23] In the case of Kristeva, the relation to differing modes of language is made explicit to the point of identifying a preoedipal lingustic register (rhythms, intonations) and a postoedipal linguistic register (the phonologico-syntactic structure of the sentence). Hysteria, therefore, and the poetic language of the woman (which becomes the language of women poets, — Woolf, Plath, etc.) are properly then the return of this primary and bodily mode of expressivity.[24] It is no coincidence that at this stage it is schizophrenia that is invoked as frequently as hysteria, since the relation between schizophrenia and poetic discourse is a recognized and accredited one within psychoanalysis itself. It is in a sense a feminist version of Laing, but having to include the transference neurosis (hysteria) since the relation of the latter to the feminine is too heavily attested to be ignored. More often than not, the two forms are assimilated the one to the other, so that what happens is that the specificity of the two types of disorder is

[22] Freud, 'Female Sexuality' (1931), SE 21, p.227; PF 7, p.373.

[23] Julia Kristeva, *Des Chinoises,* Paris 1974, p.34 (tr. Anita Barrows, *About Chinese Women,* London and New York 1977, p.29); Luce Irigaray, *Speculum de l'autre femme,* Paris 1974 (tr. Gillian Gill, *Speculum of the Other Woman,* Ithaca 1985). For a fuller discussion of the work of Julia Kristeva, see 'Julia Kristeva — Take Two' in this collection.

[24] It can also be objected to these arguments that they reproduce the classical definition of woman/the feminine as irrational, outside discourse, language, etc., with clearly reactionary implications for women. For discussion of this, see Monique Plaza, 'Pouvoir "phallomorphique" et psychologie de "la Femme" ', *Questions féministes* 1, 1977 (tr. ' "Phallomorphic" Power and the Psychology of "Women" — A Patriarchal Chain', *Ideology and Consciousness* 4, 1978).

lost. It is worth, therefore, looking again at Dora's symptoms, and then (in the next section) at what Freud said about schizophrenia in its relation to language, in order to see whether such a position can be theoretically sustained.

A number of points about Dora first. First, as we saw above, Dora's bodily symptoms (the aphonia, the cough) are the expression of a masculine identification, through which identification alone access to the maternal and feminine body is possible. This access then threatens Dora with a physical or bodily fragmentation, which constitutes the symptoms of conversion. Thus access to the (maternal) body is only possible now through a masculine identification, which access then threatens the very category of identification itself, that is, Dora as subject. Thus at neither point of her desire for Frau K. can Dora be placed as a 'true' feminine, since either she is identified with a man or else the movement is toward an instance in which the category of sexual difference is not established and that of the subject, on which such difference depends, is threatened.

Second, in the second dream, in which Dora's desire could be defined as the desire for self-possession, her position as subject is at its most precarious. The dream most clearly articulates the split between the subject and object of enunciation at the root of any linguistic utterance (the speaking subject and the subject of the statement),[25] here seen in its relation to the question of sexual difference. Thus, if Dora is there to be possessed, then she is not there as a woman (she is a man), and if she is not there to be possessed, her place as a woman is assured (she remains feminine) but she is not there (Lacan's lethal *vel*).[26]

Third, and as a corollary to this, what is revealed behind this dream is nothing other than this question of woman *as* representation: 'Here for the third time we come upon "picture"

---

[25] This is the linguistic distinction between the subject of the enunciation or statement and the subject of the enunciated or utterance. See Emile Benveniste, 'De la subjectivité dans le langage', *Problèmes de linguistique générale,* Paris 1966 (tr. 'Subjectivity in Language', *Problems in General Linguistics,* Miami 1971). It is a distinction I deliberately reformulate here. For a discussion of the concept for psychoanalysis, see Lacan, 'Analyse et vérité ou la fermeture de l'inconscient', *Le séminaire XI: Les quatre concepts fondamentaux de la psychanalyse,* (1964), Paris 1973 (tr. Alan Sheridan, 'Analysis and Truth or Closure of the Unconscious', *The Four Fundamental Concepts of Psychoanalysis,* London 1977, New York, 1978).

[26] See Adams, p.72.

(views of towns, the Dresden gallery), but in a much more significant connection. Because of what appears in the picture (the wood, the nymphs), the "Bild" (picture) is turned into a "Weibsbild" (literally "picture of a woman")',[27] and then of woman *as* query, posed by Dora herself, of her relationship to a knowledge designated as present and not present — the sexual knowledge that is the *secret* behind her relation with Frau K.: 'Her *knowing* all about such things and, at the same time, her always *pretending not to know where her knowledge came from* was really too remarkable. I ought to have attacked this *riddle* and looked for the motive of such an extraordinary piece of repression'.[28] Thus nothing in Dora's position can be assimilated to an unproblematic concept of the feminine or to any simple notion of the body, since where desire is genital it is charted across a masculine identification, and where it is oral it reveals itself as a query addressed to the category of sexuality itself (Frau K. as the unmistakable *'oral* source of information').[29]

Perhaps we should remember here that Freud's work on hysteria started precisely with a rejection of any simple mapping of the symptom onto the body (Charcot's hysterogenic zones). By so doing he made of hysteria a language (made it speak) but one whose relation to the body was decentered, since if the body spoke it was precisely because there was something called the unconscious that could not. At this point the relation of dreams and hysteria, from which we started out, can be reasserted as nothing other than the inflection of the body *through* language in its relation to the unconscious (indirect representation). When Lacan writes that 'there is nothing in the unconscious which accords with the body', he means this, and he continues: 'The unconscious is discordant. The unconscious is that which, by speaking, determines the subject as being, but as a being to be struck through with that metonymy by which I support desire, insofar as it is endlessly impossible to speak as such.'[30] We saw this above in the split between subject and object of enunciation, Dora as subject literally fading before her presence in the dream.

---

[27] *Dora,* p.99n; p.139n.

[28] Ibid, p.120n; p.162n (my italics).

[29] Ibid., p.105n; p.145n. See Freud's whole footnote here, pp.104-105n, also p.110-111n and p.120n; p.145n, p.152n, p.162n.

[30] Lacan, 'Séminaire du 21 janvier, 1975', *Ornicar? (Bulletin périodique du champ freudien),* 3 May 1975, p.105 (tr. in *Feminine Sexuality,* p.165).

Word-presentations and thing-presentations

Freud's discussion of schizophrenic and hysterical language is at its most explicit in chapter 7 of his metapsychological paper on the unconscious.[31] That this discussion should take up the chapter entitled 'Assessment of the Unconscious' indicates its importance, and it is in fact the distinction between these two types of disorder that produces Freud's definition of the concept **ucs** (the unconscious in his system: unconscious, preconscious, and conscious). Freud starts with schizophrenia in its inaccessibility to analysis, involving as it does a complete withdrawal of object-cathexes in their reversion to the ego. Note that what this produces is unmitigated narcissism, so that while the definition indicates Freud still basing his diagnostic categories on a differential relation to reality, what emerges at another level is a concept of schizophrenia as the 'embodiment' of the category of the ego and hence of identification (as opposed to the embodiment of the body). What then appears as symptom is what Freud calls organ-speech, in which 'the patient's relation to a bodily organ [arrogates] to itself the representation of the whole content [of her thoughts]'.[32] Thus the precondition of organ-speech is a reversion to narcissism, and the function of the body is the representation of a thought-content, which, in both of the examples given, reveals the patient's identification with her lover; this as distinct from the hysterical symptom, where there is not the verbal articulation of a certain relation to the body but the bodily symptom itself, i.e. conversion.

Hence there can be no equating of schizophrenia and hysteria and no assimilation of either to the body in an unmediated form. On the other hand, if the attempt to construct a theory of feminine discourse tends to produce such an identification, it is because of the attraction for such a theory of what Freud says about the schizophrenic's privileged relation to words (subject to the primary processes and obeying the laws of the unconscious) and the definition that this then leads to of unconscious representation itself: 'We now seem to know all at once what the difference is between conscious and an unconscious presentation ... the conscious presentation comprises the presentation of the thing

---

[31] Freud 'The Unconscious', *Papers in Metapsychology* (1914), SE 14; PF 11.
[32] Ibid., p.198; p.203.

and the presentation of the word belonging to it, while the unconscious presentation is the presentation of the thing alone'.[33] The distinction does in fact appear to be predicated on the notion of some direct ('truer' even) relation to the object itself: 'The system **ucs** contains the thing-cathexes of the objects, the first and true object-cathexes'.[34]

It is on the collapse of this concept, in Freud's text itself, that the assimilation schizophrenia/body/unconscious can again be seen to fail. First, Freud does in fact state even within this definition that what is involved in the first (primary) cathexis of the object is the memory-*trace* of the object, and in the appendix on aphasia he states the relation between object and thing-presentation to be a mediate one. Second, in the choice that his distinction leaves him — for if the unconscious comprises the thing-presentation alone, repression involving a withdrawal of the word, then for the schizophrenic either there is no repression or else the schizophrenic's use of language indicates the first stage of a *recovery*, the recovery of the object-cathexes themselves. The schizophrenic's relation to the word would therefore reveal at its most transparent the loss of the object that is at the root of linguistic representation ('These endeavours are directed towards *regaining the lost object*').[35] This is the concept at the basis of the concept of the unconscious as the *effect* of the subject's insertion into language: the loss of the object and production of the subject in that moment (the moment of its fading).

A number of conceptions about language that underpin discussion about the feminine and discourse, the feminine *as* discourse can now be disengaged. First, the idea of an unmediated relation between the body and language is contrary to the linguistic definition of the sign, implying as it does a type of anatomical mimesis of language on the body (for example, Irigaray's 'two lips' as indicating the place of woman outside (phallo-)monistic discourse). Second, the concept of the feminine as outside discourse involves a theory of language in which a nonexcentric relation to language would be possible, the subject as control and origin of meaning, which is to render meaningless both the concept of the unconscious and that of the subject.

[33] Ibid., p.201; p.207.
[34] Ibid.
[35] Ibid., p.204; p.209 (my italics).

It is on this latter factor that the relation of psychoanalysis to language exceeds that of linguistics, precisely insofar as it poses this problem of the subject's relation to discourse. Freud did not formulate this as such, but it is there in the contradictions of his text, in this further sense, too, and most clearly, I would suggest, in what he has to say about feminine sexuality and transference — which brings us back to the case of Dora.

The question of femininity

In this final section I want to look at the two 'vanishing points' of the case of Dora — the theory of feminine sexuality and the concept of transference. For if the case failed it was because Freud failed to recognize the specificity of either of these two factors, and where he saw their pertinence (addenda, postscript, footnote) they were left in a type of offstage of the case, as the thing that was missing (the 'secret') or the element that he had failed to 'master', as if both were a content, an object to be identified, placed, and resolved (transference as the recovery of an actual event). What I want to do here, therefore, is to show how in both of these concepts something of the subject's relation to discourse as we saw it emerging above — in Dora's second dream, and then in the schizophrenic relation to the word — can be discerned and to suggest the pertinence of that theory for discussion of the feminine not *as* discourse but, within discourse, as a relationship to it.

First, the transference, as it was elaborated by Freud in his papers on technique ('The Dynamics of Transference', 'Remembering, Repeating, and Working-Through', 'Observations on Transference-Love'),[36] where he starts again with a definition of neurosis as a libidinal turning away from reality, is first seen as a resistance in the chain of associations that would lead logically to the repairing or completing of the patient's memory. Dora's case also started, in Freud's discussion of the fragment, with this insistence that cure of the symptom and completion of memory were synonymous — psychoanalysis being defined here as the creation of a full history to which the subject would be restored. It is a concept also present at the beginning of Lacan's work on the

---

[36] All in Freud, *Papers on Technique* (1911-15), SE 12.

idea of full speech,[37] retranscription of the history of the patient *through* language, before the development of the concept of the unconscious precisely as the effect *of* language, and hence behind it a moment of failing that can never be restored, that is nothing other than that of the subject itself (primary repression). Thus Freud starts by stressing transference as the obstacle to the reality of the patient's history, in a simple sense corresponding to the notion that behind neurosis is an event (seduction theory) and in front of it, if all goes well, another event (neurosis vanquished by reality), transference appearing here as something that 'flings' the patient 'out of his real relation to the doctor'.[38]

Yet, taken together, these three texts inscribe an opposite movement. In the discussion of recollection ('Remembering, Repeating, and Working-Through'), Freud interpolates a discussion of amnesia that starts with the concept of total recall as the objective of analysis but ends up with a discussion of primary or primal fantasy, indicating that concept of Freud's which was most completely to undermine the concept of the cure as the retrieval of a real occurrence. In fact, in his article on the two principles of mental functioning,[39] Freud assigned to fantasy the whole domain of sexuality, whereby it escapes the reality principle altogether (pleasure in sexuality revealing itself as pleasure in the act of representation itself).[40]

Through this a different concept of the transference emerges, one seen most clearly in 'Observations on Transference-Love', where what is objected to in transference is its status as a demand (the demand for love) and, more important, one that insists on being recognized as *real* (which it is, Freud has to concede), so that what now 'irrupts' into the analytic situation is reality itself, a reality that is totally out of place: 'There is a complete change of scene; it is as though some piece of make-believe had been stopped

[37] Lacan, 'Fonction et champ de la parole et du langage en psychanalyse' (1953), *Ecrits,* Paris 1966 (tr. Alan Sheridan, 'The Function and Field of Speech and Language in Psychoanalysis', *Ecrits: A Selection,* London and New York 1977).

[38] 'The Dynamics of Transference', *Papers on Technique,* p.107.

[39] Freud, 'Formulations on the Two Principles of Mental Functioning' (1911), SE 12; PF 11.

[40] See Moustapha Safouan, *L'échec du principe du plaisir,* Paris 1979 (tr. Ben Brewster, *Pleasure and Being, Hedonism from a Psychoanalytic Point of View,* London 1983).

by the sudden irruption of reality'.[41] The patient insists therefore on repeating 'in real life' what should only have been reproduced as 'psychical material' — thus the relationship to the real has been reversed. What this indicates for this discussion is that Freud himself was forced to correct or to revise the concept of transference to which he ascribed the failure of the case of Dora, and this in a way that is not satisfactorily or exhaustively defined by reference to the countertransference (Freud's implication in the case). For what is at stake is transference as an impossible demand for recognition (a return of love in 'Observations on the Transference-Love'), a demand that has to be displaced onto another register, indicated here by the corresponding emphasis on the concepts of fantasy ('make-believe'), representation, psychical material (the only meaning of material that has any value here). Note the proximity of these terms to the query, image, *Bild,* of Dora's second dream, sexuality precisely not as demand (the demand for love) but as question.

In the discussion of the case itself, I suggested that Freud's concept of the transference as the retrieval of an event corresponded to the concept of a pregiven normal feminine sexuality, neurosis being defined as the failure to meet a 'real erotic demand'. Thus if the concept of reality has to go in relation to the notion of transference, we can reasonably assume that it also goes in relation to that of sexuality itself. I have already suggested briefly that it does, in what Freud says about the pleasure principle. What is important to grasp is that, while it is undoubtedly correct to state that Freud's analysis of Dora failed because of the theory of feminine sexuality to which he then held, this concept cannot be corrected by a simple reference to his later theses on feminine sexuality (preoedipality, etc.), crucial as these may be, since that is simply to replace one content with another, whereas what must be seen in Freud's work on femininity is exactly the same movement we have just seen in the concept of transference, which is nothing less than the collapse of the category of sexuality as *content* altogether.

Freud starts both his papers on femininity ('Female Sexuality' and 'Femininity') with recognition of the girl's preoedipal attachment to the mother, its strength and duration, as it had been overlooked within psychoanalytic theory, thus feminine sexuality

---

[41] 'Observations on Transference Love', p.162.

as an earlier stage, a more repressed content, something archaic. Yet although the two papers in one sense say the same thing, their logic or sequence is different, and the difference has important effects on the level of theory.

'Female Sexuality' (1931) starts with the preoedipal factor and its necessary relinquishment, which is then discussed in terms of the castration complex and penis envy. But this does not exhaust the question of the girl's renunciation of her mother, a question that then persists in a series of references to 'premature' weaning, the advent of a rival, the necessary frustration and final ambivalence of the child's demand for love. None of these factors, however, constitute a sufficient explanation: 'All these motives seem nevertheless insufficient to justify the girl's final hostility',[42] which cannot be attributed to the ambivalence of the infantile relation to the object, since this would be true of the boy child too. Thus a question persists that reveals itself as *the* question, hanging over from that of a demand that has been frustrated and a renunciation that still has not been explained: 'A further question arises: "What does the little girl require of her mother?" '.[43]

Freud can only answer this question by reference to the nature of the infantile sexual aim — its activity (rejection of a male/female biological chemistry, a single libido with both active and passive aims), an activity that is not only a corrective to the idea of a naturally passive femininity but functions as *repetition* (the child repeats a distressing experience through play). Correlating this with the definition of infantile sexuality given earlier in the paper ('It has, in point of fact, no aim, and is incapable of obtaining complete satifaction; and principally for that reason is doomed to end in disappointment'.[44]) it emerges that what specifies the little girl's aim, and her demand, is that she does not have one. The question persists, or is repeated, therefore, as the impossibility of satisfaction.

In 'Femininity' (1933), the sequence is in a sense reversed. The paper starts with the caution against the biological definition of sexual difference and then reposes the question of the girl's relinquishment of the preoedipal attachment to the mother. The motives for renunciation are listed again — oral frustration,

---

[42] 'Female Sexuality', p.234; p.382.
[43] Ibid., p.235; p.383.
[44] Ibid., p.231; p.378.

jealousy, prohibition, ambivalence — but in this case the question of how these can explain such renunciation when they apply equally to the boy is answered with the concept of penis envy, with which the question is in a sense closed (the discussion moves on to a consideration of adult modes of feminine sexuality). Thus the question is answered here, and it is as answer that the concept of penis envy has produced, rightly, the anger against Freud. For looking at the paper again, it is clear that nothing has been answered at all, since Freud characterizes each of the earlier motives specifically in terms of its impossibility (see above): oral demand as 'insatiable', 'a child's demands for love are immoderate' (rivalry), 'multifarious sexual wishes ... which cannot for the most part be satisfied', 'the immoderate charater of the demand for love and the impossibility of fulfilling their sexual wishes'.[45] Now, if what characterizes all these demands is the impossibility of their satisfaction, then the fact that there is another impossible demand ('the wish to get the longed-for penis')[46] cannot strictly explain anything at all, other than the persistence of the demand itself — the question, therefore, of the earlier paper, 'What does the little girl require of her mother?'[47]

The question persists, therefore, only insofar as it cannot be answered, and what I want to suggest here is that what we see opening up in the gap between the demand and its impossibility is desire itself, what Lacan calls the effect of the articulation of need as demand, 'desire endlessly impossible to speak as such'. This is why the demand for love in the transference blocks the passage of the treatment insofar as it insists precisely on its own reality (the possibility of satisfaction). What Freud's papers on femininity reveal, therefore, is nothing less than the emergence of this concept of desire as the *question* of sexual difference: how does the little girl become a woman, or does she?

To return to dreams and hysteria, isn't this exactly the question that reveals itself in the dream of the hysteric analyzed in *The*

---

[45] Freud, 'Femininity' (1933), *New Introductory Lectures,* SE 22, pp.122-124; PF 2, pp.156-157.

[46] Ibid., p.125; p.159.

[47] See 'La sexualité féminine dans la doctrine psychanalytique', *Scilicet, Revue du champ freudien* 5, 1975, reprinted as chapter 1 of Moustapha Safouan, *La sexualité féminine dans la doctrine freudienne,* Paris 1976 (tr. 'Feminine Sexuality in Psychoanalytic Doctrine' in *Feminine Sexuality*).

Interpretation of Dreams[48] who dreamt that her own wish was *not* fulfilled, through an identification with the woman she posited as her sexual rival? Her desire, therefore, is the desire for an unsatisfied desire: 'She likes caviar,' writes Lacan, 'but she doesn't want any. It is in that that she desires it.'[49] And behind that wish (and that identification) can be seen the question of the woman as object of desire, of how her husband could desire a woman who was incapable of giving him satisfaction (she knows he does not want her), the identification being, therefore, with the question itself: 'This being the question put forward, which is very generally that of hysterical identification ... whereby the woman identifies herself with the man.'[50] This can be referred directly back to the case of Dora, woman as object and subject of desire — the impossibility of either position, for if object of desire then whose desire, and if subject of desire then its own impossibility, the impossibility of subject *and* desire (the one implying the fading of the other). Thus Dora rejects Herr K. at the exact moment when he states that he does not desire his own wife, the very woman through whom the whole question for Dora was posed (the scene at the lake).

Thus what feminine sexuality reveals in these examples is the persistence of the question of desire *as* a question (exactly the opposite of the feminine as sexual content, substance, or whatever). Finally, to return to the hysterical symptom itself:

> It is to the extent that a need gets caught up in the function of desire that the psychosomatic can be conceived of as something more than the idle commonplace which consists in saying that there is a psychic backing to everything somatic. That much we have known for a long time. If we speak of the psychosomatic it is insofar as what must intervene is desire.[51]

I want to conclude with this, not because I think it answers anything but because I believe it to be a necessary caution to

[48] Freud, *The Interpretation of Dreams* (1900), SE 4-5, pp.147-151, 228; PF 4, pp.229-233, 260-261.

[49] For a full discussion of this dream, see Lacan, 'La direction de la cure et les principes de son pouvoir' (1958), *Ecrits* (tr. 'The Direction of the Treatment and the Principles of its Power' in *Ecrits: A Selection,* pp.256-265).

[50] Ibid., p.262 (translation modified).

[51] *The Four Fundamental Concepts,* p.228 (tr. modified).

certain current developments within feminist theory. What seems to me to need attention is precisely this movement of psychoanalysis away from sexuality as content (preoedipal or otherwise) to a concept of sexuality as caught up in the register of demand and desire. What does emerge from the above is that it was on the failings in the concept of the feminine (the case of Dora) that this problem emerged in Freud's own work. To relinquish the idea of a specific feminine discourse may be less discouraging if what it leads to is work on the place of the feminine as somehow revealing more urgently the impossibility of the position of the woman within a discourse that would prefer to suppress the question of desire as such (the question of its splitting). I would suggest that the case of Dora reveals no more, and no less, than this.

Bernini: 'The Ecstasy of Saint Teresa' with Cardinal Cornero, one of the cardinals and doges of the city in accompanying gallery, Santa Maria della Vittoria, Rome.

2
Feminine Sexuality: Jacques Lacan and the *école freudienne*

Freud argues that the only libido is masculine. Meaning what? other than that a whole field, which is hardly negligible, is thereby ignored. This is the field of all those beings who take on the status of the woman — if, indeed, this being takes on anything whatsoever of her fate.

Lacan, *Le séminaire XX: Encore* (1972-3), Paris 1975, p. 75; (tr. *Feminine Sexuality*, p. 151.)

The works of Jacques Lacan and the *école freudienne* on female sexuality return to and extend the psychoanalytic debate of the 1920s and 30s over femininity and sexual difference in Freud.[1] They return to it by insisting that its implications for

[1] This essay was originally published as the second part of the Introduction to *Feminine Sexuality – Jacques Lacan and the école freudienne*, edited by Juliet Mitchell and Jacqueline Rose, London 1982, New York 1983, a collection of articles relating to the question of feminine sexuality by the French psychoanalyst Jacques Lacan and members of his school of psychoanalysis, the *école freudienne*, founded in 1964 and dissolved by Lacan in 1980. The articles were put together and edited by Juliet Mitchell and myself with separate, but complementary, introductions tracing the terms of the psychoanalytic debate about femininity instigated in the 1920s and continued in the work of Lacan and in the responses to his writing. In the first part, Juliet Mitchell gave an extensive account of the dispute which took place in the 1920s and 30s over Freud's theories of femininity and the castration complex. For details of this dispute, readers are referred to Juliet Mitchell's Introduction, *Feminine Sexuality,* reprinted in Juliet Mitchell, *Women: The Longest Revolution,* London and New York 1984, as well as to the articles by Melanie Klein, Ernest Jones and Karen Horney in the bibliography included here.

psychoanalysis have still not been understood; they extend it in so far as the issue itself — the question of feminine sexuality — goes beyond psychoanalysis to feminism, as part of its questioning of how that sexuality comes to be defined.

In this sense, the writing examined in this essay bears all the signs of a repetition, a resurfacing of an area of disagreement or disturbance, but one in which the issue at stake has been thrown into starker relief. It is as if the more or less peaceful co-existence which closed the debate of the 1920s and 1930s ('left, in a tacit understanding, to the goodwill of individual interpretation'),[2] and the lull which it produced ('the lull experienced after the breakdown of the debate'),[3] concealed a trouble which was bound to emerge again with renewed urgency. Today, that urgency can be seen explicitly as political, so much so that in the controversy over Lacan's dissolution of his school in 1980, the French newspaper *Le Monde* could point to the debate about femininity as the clearest statement of the political repercussions of psychoanalysis itself (*Le Monde*, 1 June 1980, p.xvi). Psychoanalysis is now recognised as crucial in the discussion of femininity — how it comes into being and what it might mean. Lacan addressed this issue increasingly during the course of his work, and has been at the centre of the controversies produced by that recognition.

In this context, the idea of a 'return to Freud' most commonly associated with Lacan has a very specific meaning. It is not so much a return to the letter of Freud's text as the re-opening of a case, a case which has already been fought and one which, if anything, in relation to feminism, Freud could be said to have lost. In fact the relationship between psychoanalysis and feminism might seem to start at the point where Freud's account of sexual difference was rejected by analysts specifically arguing *for* women ('men analysts have been led to adopt an unduly phallocentric view').[4] Most analysts have since agreed on the limitations and difficulties of Freud's account. Those difficulties were fully recognised by Lacan, but he considered that attempts to resolve

---

[2] Lacan, 'Propos directifs pour un congrès sur la sexualité féminine' (1958), *Ecrits* (tr. 'Guiding Remarks for a Congress on Feminine Sexuality', *Feminine Sexuality*, pp. 88-89).

[3] Ibid., p. 89.

[4] Ernest Jones, 'The Early Development of Female Sexuality', *International Journal of Psychoanalysis* 8, 1927, p. 459.

them within psychoanalysis had systematically fallen into a trap. For they failed to see that the concept of the phallus in Freud's account of human sexuality was part of his awareness of the problematic, if not impossible, nature of sexual identity itself. They answered it, therefore, by reference to a pre-given sexual difference aimed at securing that identity for both sexes. In doing so, they lost sight of Freud's sense that sexual difference is constructed at a price and that it involves subjection to a law which exceeds any natural or biological division. The concept of the phallus stands for that subjection, and for the way in which women are very precisely implicated in its process.

The history of psychoanalysis can in many ways be seen entirely in terms of its engagement with this question of feminine sexuality. Freud himself started with the analysis of the hysterical patient[5] (whom, it should be noted, he insisted could also be male[6]). It was then his failure to analyse one such patient — 'Dora' — in terms of a normative concept of what a woman should be, or want, that led him to recognise the fragmented and aberrant nature of sexuality itself. Normal sexuality is, therefore, strictly an *ordering*, one which the hysteric refuses (falls ill). The rest of Freud's work can then be read as a description of how that ordering takes place, which led him back, necessarily, to the question of femininity, because its persistence as a difficulty revealed the cost of that order.

Moreover, Freud returned to this question at the moment when he was reformulating his theory of human subjectivity. Lacan took Freud's concept of the unconscious, as extended and developed by the later texts[7] as the basis of his own account of femininity (the frequent criticism of Lacan that he disregarded the later works is totally unfounded here). He argued that failure to recognise the interdependency of these two concerns in Freud's work — the theory of subjectivity and femininity together — has led psychoanalysts into an ideologically loaded mistake, that is, an attempt to resolve the difficulties of Freud's account of femininity by aiming to resolve the difficulty of femininity itself. For by

[5] Breuer and Freud, *Studies on Hysteria.*
[6] Freud, 'Observation of a Severe Case of Hemi-Anaesthesia in a Hysterical Male' (1886), SE 1.
[7] Freud, *Beyond the Pleasure Principle* (1920), SE 18, PF 11; 'Splitting of the Ego in the Process of Defence' (1938), SE 23, PF 11.

restoring the woman to her place and identity (which, they argue, Freud out of 'prejudice' failed to see), they have missed Freud's corresponding stress on the division and precariousness of human subjectivity itself, which was, for Lacan, central to psychoanalysis' most radical insights. Attempts by and for women to answer Freud have tended to relinquish those insights, discarding either the concept of the unconscious (the sign of that division) or that of bisexuality (the sign of that precariousness). And this has been true of positions as diverse as that of Jones (and Horney) in the 1920s and 1930s and that of Nancy Chodorow[8] speaking from psychoanalysis for feminism today.

Re-opening the debate on feminine sexuality must start, therefore, with the link between sexuality and the unconscious. No account of Lacan's work which attempts to separate the two can make sense. For Lacan, the unconscious undermines the subject from any position of certainty, from any relation of knowledge to his or her psychic processes and history, and *simultaneously* reveals the fictional nature of the sexual category to which every human subject is none the less assigned. In Lacan's account, sexual identity operates as a law — it is something enjoined on the subject. For him, the fact that individuals must line up according to an opposition (having or not having the phallus) makes that clear. But it is the constant difficulty, or even impossibility, of that process which Lacan emphasised. Exposure of that difficulty within psychoanalysis and for feminism is, therefore, part of one and the same project.

I

The link between sexuality and the unconscious is one that was constantly stressed by Lacan: 'we should not overlook the fact that sexuality is crucially underlined by Freud as being strictly consubstantial to the dimension of the unconscious'.[9] Other accounts, such as that of Ernest Jones, described the acquisition of sexual identity in terms of ego development and/or the

---

[8] Nancy Chodorow, *The Reproduction of Mothering, Psychoanalysis and the Sociology of Gender*, Berkeley and Los Angeles 1978, London 1979; see note 28 below.

[9] Lacan, *The Four Fundamental Concepts*, p. 146.

maturation of the drives. Lacan considered that each of these concepts rests on the myth of a subjective cohesion which the concept of the unconscious properly subverts. For Lacan, the description of sexuality in developmental terms invariably loses sight of Freud's most fundamental discovery — that the unconscious never ceases to challenge our apparent identity as subjects.

Lacan's account of subjectivity was always developed with reference to the idea of a fiction. Thus, in the 1930s he introduced the concept of the 'mirror stage',[10] which took the child's mirror image as the model and basis for its future identifications. This image is a fiction because it conceals, or freezes, the infant's lack of motor co-ordination and the fragmentation of its drives, But it is salutary for the child, since it gives it the first sense of a coherent identity in which it can recognise itself. For Lacan, however, this is already a fantasy — the very image which places the child divides its identity into two. Furthermore, that moment only has meaning in relation to the presence and the look of the mother who guarantees its reality for the child. The mother does not (as in D.W. Winnicott's account)[11] mirror the child to itself; she grants an image *to* the child, which her presence instantly deflects. Holding the child is, therefore, to be understood not only as a containing, but as process of referring, which fractures the unity it seems to offer. The mirror image is central to Lacan's account of subjectivity, because its apparent smoothness and totality is a myth. The image in which we first recognise ourselves is a *misrecognition*. Lacan is careful to stress, however, that his point is not restricted to the field of the visible alone: 'the idea of the mirror should be understood as an object which reflects — not just the visible, but also what is heard, touched and willed by the child'.[12]

Lacan then takes the mirror image as the model of the ego function itself, the category which enables the subject to operate as 'I'. He supports his argument from linguistics, which designates

[10] Lacan, 'Le stade du miroir comme formateur de la fonction du Je' (1936), *Ecrits* (tr. 'The mirror stage as formative of the function of the I', *Ecrits: A Selection).*

[11] D.W. Winnicott, 'Mirror-Role of Mother and Family in Child Development' (1967), *Playing and Reality,* London 1971.

[12] Lacan, 'Cure psychanalytique à l'aide de la poupée fleur', *Revue française de la psychanalyse* 4, October-December 1949, p. 567.

the pronoun as a 'shifter'.[13] The 'I' with which we speak stands for our identity as subjects in language, but it is the least stable entity in language, since its meaning is purely a function of the moment of utterance. The 'I' can shift, and change places, because it only ever refers to whoever happens to be using it at the time.

For Lacan the subject is constituted through language — the mirror image represents the moment when the subject is located in an order outside itself to which it will henceforth refer. The subject is the subject *of* speech (Lacan's *'parle-être'*), and subject *to* that order. But if there is division in the image, and instability in the pronoun, there is equally loss, and difficulty, in the word. Language can only operate by designating an object in its absence. Lacan takes this further, and states that symbolisation turns on the object *as* absence. He gives as his reference Freud's early account of the child's hallucinatory cathexis of the object for which it cries, and his later description in *Beyond the Pleasure principle* of the child's symbolisation of the absent mother in play.[14] In the first example, the child hallucinates the object it desires; in the second, it throws a cotton reel out of its cot in order to symbolise the absence and the presence of the mother. Symbolisation starts, therefore, when the child gets its first sense that something could be missing; words stand for objects, because they only have to be spoken at the moment when the first object is lost. For Lacan, the subject can only operate within language by constantly repeating that moment of fundamental and irreducible division. The subject is therefore constituted in language *as* this division or splitting (Freud's *Ichspaltung,* or splitting of the ego).

Lacan termed the order of language the symbolic, that of the ego and its identifications the imaginary (the stress, therefore, is quite deliberately on symbol and image, the idea of something which 'stands in'). The real was then his term for the moment of impossibility onto which both are grafted, the point of that moment's endless return.[15]

---

[13] Emile Benveniste, 'La nature des pronoms', *Problèmes de linguistique générale* (tr. 'The Nature of Pronouns', *Problems in General Linguistics).*

[14] Freud, *Project for a Scientific Psychology* (1895), SE 1, p. 319; *Beyond the Pleasure Principle,* pp. 14-17; pp. 283-287.

[15] This can be compared with, for example, Melanie Klein's account of symbol-formation (Melanie Klein, 'The Importance of Symbol Formation in the Development of the Ego', *IJPA* 11, 1930) and also with Hannah Segal's ('Notes on Symbol formation', *IJPA* 38, 1957), where symbolisation is an effect of anxiety and

Lacan's account of childhood then follows his basic premise that identity is constructed in language, but only at a cost. Identity shifts, and language speaks the loss which lay behind that first moment of symbolisation. When the child asks something of its mother, that loss will persist over and above anything which she can possibly give, or say, in reply. Demand always 'bears on something other than the satisfaction which it calls for'[16], and each time the demand of the child is answered by the satisfaction of its needs, so this 'something other' is relegated to the place of its original impossibility. Lacan terms this 'desire'. It can be defined as the 'remainder' of the subject, something which is always left over, but which has no content as such. Desire functions much as the zero unit in the numerical chain - its place is both constitutive *and* empty.

The concept of desire is crucial to Lacan's account of sexuality. He considered that the failure to grasp its implications leads inevitably to a reduction of sexuality back into the order of a need (something, therefore, which could be satisfied). Against this, he quoted Freud's statement: 'we must reckon with the possibility that something in the nature of the sexual instinct itself is unfavourable to the realisation of complete satisfaction'.[17]

At the same time 'identity' and 'wholeness' remain precisely at the level of fantasy. Subjects in language persist in their belief that somewhere there is a point of certainty, of knowledge and of truth. When the subject addresses its demand outside itself to another,

---

a means of transcending it on the path to reality, a path which is increasingly assured by the strengthening of the ego itself. Cf. also Lacan's specific critique of Ernest Jones's famous article on symbolism (Ernest Jones, 'The Theory of Symbolism', *British Journal of Psychoanalysis* 11:2, 1916 and Jacques Lacan, 'A la mémoire d'Ernest Jones: sur sa théorie de symbolisme' (1959), *Ecrits*) which he criticised for its definition of language in terms of an increasing mastery or appropriation of reality, and for failing to see, therefore, the structure of metaphor (or substitution) which lies at the root of, and is endlessly repeated within, subjectivity in its relation to the unconscious. It is in this sense also that Lacan's emphasis on language should be differentiated from what he defined as 'culturalism', that is, from any conception of language as a social phenomenon which does not take into account its fundamental instability (language as constantly placing, and *displacing,* the subject).

[16] Lacan, 'La signification du phallus' (1958), *Ecrits* (tr. 'The Meaning of the Phallus', *Feminine Sexuality,* p. 80).

[17] Freud, 'On the Universal Tendency to Debasement in the Sphere of Love' (1912), SE 11, pp. 188-189; PF 7, p. 258.

this other becomes the fantasied place of just such a knowledge or certainty. Lacan calls this the Other — the site of language to which the speaking subject necessarily refers. The Other appears to hold the 'truth' of the subject and the power to make good its loss. But this is the ultimate fantasy. Language is the place where meaning circulates — the meaning of each linguistic unit can only be established by reference to another, and it is arbitrarily fixed. Lacan, therefore, draws from Saussure's concept of the arbitrary nature of the linguistic sign — introduced in his *Course in General Linguistics* — the implication that there can be no final guarantee or securing of language. There is, Lacan writes, 'no Other of the Other', and anyone who claims to take up this place is an imposter (the Master and/or psychotic).

Sexuality belongs in this area of instability played out in the register of demand and desire, each sex coming to stand, mythically and exclusively, for that which could satisfy and complete the other. It is when the categories 'male' and 'female' are seen to represent an absolute and complementary division that they fall prey to a mystification in which the difficulty of sexuality instantly disappears: 'to disguise this gap by relying on the virtue of the "genital" to resolve it through the maturation of tenderness..., however piously intended, is nonetheless a fraud'.[18] Lacan therefore argued that psychoanalysis should not try to produce 'male' and 'female' as complementary entities, sure of each other and of their own identity, but should expose the fantasy on which this notion rests.

There is a tendency, when arguing for the pre-given nature of sexual difference, for the specificity of male and female drives, to lose sight of the more radical aspects of Freud's work on sexuality — his insistence on the disjunction between the sexual object and the sexual aim, his difficult challenge to the concept of perversion, and his demand that heterosexual object-choice be explained and not assumed.[19] For Lacan, the 'vicissitudes' of the instinct ('instinct' was the original English translation for the German word *trieb*) cannot be understood as a deviation, accident or defence on the path to a normal heterosexuality which would ideally be secured. Rather the term 'vicissitude' indicates a

---

[18] 'The Meaning of the Phallus', p. 81.
[19] Freud, *Three Essays on the Theory of Sexuality* (1905), SE 7, pp. 144-146n; PF 7, p. 57n.

fundamental difficulty inherent in human sexuality, which can be seen in the very concept of the drive.

The concept of the drive is crucial to the discussion of sexuality because of the relative ease with which it can be used to collapse psychoanalysis into biology, the dimension from which, for Lacan, it most urgently needed to be retrieved. He rejected the idea of a gradual 'maturation' of the drive, with its associated emphasis on genital identity (the 'virtue' of the genital) because of the way it implies a quasi-biological sequence of sexual life. Instead he stressed the resistance of the drive to any biological definition.

The drive is not the instinct precisely because it cannot be reduced to the order of need (Freud defined it as an internal stimulus only to distinguish it immediately from hunger and thirst). The drive is divisible into pressure, source, object and aim; and it challenges any straightforward concept of satisfaction — the drive can be sublimated and Freud described its object as 'indifferent'. What matters, therefore, is not what the drive *achieves,* but its *process.* For Lacan, that process reveals all the difficulty which characterises the subject's relationship to the Other. In his account, the drive is something in the nature of an appeal, or searching out, which always goes beyond the actual relationships on which it turns. Although Freud did at times describe the drive in terms of an economy of pleasure (the idea that tension is resolved when the drive achieves its aim), Lacan points to an opposite stress in Freud's work. In *Beyond the Pleasure Principle,* when Freud described the child's game with the cotton reel, what he identified in that game was a process of pure repetition which revolved around the object as lost. Freud termed this the death drive. Analysts since Freud (specifically Melanie Klein) have taken this to refer to a primordial instinct of aggression. For Freud there could be no such instinct, in that all instincts are characterised by their aggression, their tenacity or insistence (exactly their *drive*). It is this very insistence which places the drive outside any register of need, and beyond an economy of pleasure. The drive touches on an area of excess (it is 'too much'). Lacan calls this *jouissance* (literally 'orgasm', but used by Lacan to refer to something more than pleasure which can easily tip into its opposite).

In Lacan's description of the transformation of the drive (its stages), the emphasis is always on the loss of the object around which it revolves, and hence on the drive itself as a representation.

Lacan therefore took one step further Freud's own assertion that the drive can only be understood in terms of the representation to which it is attached, by arguing that the structure of representation is present in the very process of the drive. For Lacan, there is always distance in the drive and always a reference to the Other (he added to the oral and anal drives the scopic and invocatory drives whose objects are the look and the voice). But because of its relation to the question of sexual difference, he made a special case for the genital drive in order to retrieve it from the residual biologism to which it is so easily assimilated: 'There is no genital drive. It can go and get f...[...] on the side of the Other'.[20] In one of his final statements, Lacan again insisted that Freud had seen this, despite his equation of the genital and the reproductive at certain moments of his work.[21]

When Lacan himself did refer to biology, it was in order to remind us of the paradox inherent in reproduction itself, which, as Freud pointed out, represents a victory of the species over the indivual. The 'fact' of sexed reproduction marks the subject as *'subject to'* death.[22] There is a parallel here with the subject's submission to language, just as there is an analogy between the endless circulation of the drive and the structure of meaning itself ('a topological unity of the gaps in play').[23] At moments, therefore, it looks as if Lacan too is grounding his theory of representation in the biological facts of life. But the significant stress was away from this, to an understanding of how representation determines the limits within which we experience our sexual life. If there is no straightforward biological sequence, and no satisfaction of the drive, then the idea of a complete and assured sexual identity belongs in the realm of fantasy.

The structure of the drive and what Lacan calls the 'nodal point' of desire are the two concepts in his work as a whole which undermine a normative account of human sexuality, and they have repercussions right across the analytic setting. Lacan considered that an emphasis on genital maturation tends to produce a

---

[20] *The Four Fundamental Concepts*, p.189.
[21] *Ornicar?* 20-21, Summer 1980, p. 16. *Ornicar?* is the periodical of the department of psychoanalysis, under Lacan's direction up to 1981, at the University of Paris VIII (Vincennes).
[22] *The Four Fundamental Concepts*, p.205.
[23] Ibid., p. 181.

dualism of the analytic relationship which can only reinforce the imaginary identifications of the subject. The case of Dora illustrates only too well that the question of feminine sexuality brings with it that of psychoanalytic technique.[24] Thus by insisting to Dora that she was in love with Herr K., Freud was not only defining her in terms of a normative concept of genital heterosexuality, he also failed to see his own place within the analytic relationship, and reduced it to a dual dimension operating on the axes of identification and demand. By asking Dora to realise her 'identity' through Herr K., Freud was simultaneously asking her to meet, or reflect, his own demand. On both counts, he was binding her to a dual relationship in which the problem of desire has no place. For Lacan, there was always this risk that psychoanalysis will strengthen for the patient the idea of self-completion through another, which was the fantasy behind the earliest mother-child relationship. If the analyst indicates to the patient that she or he 'desires this or that object',[25] this can only block the emergence of desire itself.

Lacan therefore defined the objective of analysis as the breaking of any imaginary relationship between patient and analyst through the intervention of a third term which throws them both onto the axis of the symbolic. The intervention of a third term is the precondition of language (the use of the three basic pronouns 'I'/'you'/'he-she-it'), and it can be seen in the structure of the Oedipus complex itself. What matters here, however, is that the symbolic sets a limit to the 'imaginary' of the analytic situation. Both analyst and patient must come to see how they are constituted by an order which goes beyond their interaction as such: 'The imaginary economy only has a meaning and we only have a relation to it in so far as it is inscribed in a symbolic order which imposes a ternary relation'.[26]

By focusing on what he calls the symbolic order, Lacan was doing no more than taking to its logical conclusion Freud's preoccupation with an 'historic event' in the determination of

[24] See Lacan, 'Intervention on Transference'; also 'Dora — Fragment of an Analysis' in this collection.

[25] Lacan, *Le séminaire II: Le moi dans la théorie de Freud et dans la technique de la psychanalyse* (1954-55), Paris 1978, p. 267 (tr. Sylvana Tomaselli, *The Ego in Freud's Theory and in the Technique of Psychoanalysis,* forthcoming, Cambridge 1987).

[26] Ibid., p. 296.

human subjectivity (the myth of the primal horde). But for Lacan this is not some mythical moment of our past; it is the present order in which every individual subject must take up her or his place. His concern to break the duality of the analytic situation was part of his desire to bring this dimension back into the centre of our understanding of psychic life. The subject and the analytic process must break out of the imaginary dyad which blinds them to what is happening outside. As was the case with Freud, the concept of castration came into Lacan's account of sexuality as the direct effect of this emphasis. For Lacan, the increasing stress on the mother-child relationship in analytic theory, and the rejection of the concept of castration had to be seen as related developments, because the latter only makes sense with reference to the wider symbolic order in which that relationship is played out:

> Taking the experience of psychoanalysis in its development over sixty years, it comes as no surprise to note that whereas the first outcome of its origins was a conception of the castration complex based on paternal repression, it has progressively directed its interests towards the frustrations coming from the mother, not that such a distortion has shed any light on the complex.[27]

This was at the heart of Lacan's polemic. He considered that it was the failure to grasp the concept of the symbolic which has led psychoanalysis to concentrate increasingly on the adequacies and inadequacies of the mother-child relationship, an emphasis which tends to be complicit with the idea of a maternal role (the concept of mothering).[28] The concept of castration was central to Lacan because of the reference which it always contains to paternal law.

[27] 'Guiding Remarks', p. 87

[28] Nancy Chodorow's reading of psychoanalysis for feminism *(The Reproduction of Mothering)* paradoxically also belongs here, and it touches on all the problems raised so far. The book attempts to use psychoanalysis to account for the acquisition and reproduction of mothering, but it can only do so by displacing the concepts of the unconscious and bisexuality in favour of a notion of gender imprinting ('the establishment of an unambiguous and unquestioned gender identity', p. 158 — the concept comes from Robert Stoller, 'A Contribution to the Study of Gender Identity', *IJPA* 45, 1965) which is compatible with a sociological conception of role. Thus the problem needing to be addressed — the acquisition of sexual identity and its difficulty — is sidestepped in the account. The book sets itself to question sexual *roles*, but only within the limits of an assumed sexual *identity*.

Addressing Melanie Klein, Lacan makes it clear that the argument for a reintroduction of the concept of desire into the definition of human sexuality is a return to, and a reformulation of, the law and the place of the father as it was originally defined by Freud (' a dimension...increasingly evaded since Freud'[29]):

> Melanie Klein describes the relationship to the mother as a mirrored relationship: the maternal body becomes the receptacle of the drives which the child projects onto it, drives motivated by aggression born of a fundamental disappointment. This is to neglect the fact that the outside is given for the subject as the place where the desire of the Other is situated, and where he or she will encounter the third term, the father.[30]

Lacan argued, therefore, for a return to the concept of the father, but this concept is now defined in relation to that of desire. What matters is that the relationship of the child to the mother is not simply based on 'frustration and satisfaction' ('the notion of frustration (which was never employed by Freud)'),[31] but on the recognition of her desire. The mother is refused to the child in so far as a prohibition falls on the child's desire to be what the mother desires (not the same, note, as a desire to possess or enjoy the mother in the sense normally understood):

> What we meet as an accident in the child's development is linked to the fact that the child does not find himself or herself alone in front of the mother, and that the phallus forbids the child the satisfaction of his or her own desire, which is the desire to be the exclusive desire of the mother.[32]

The duality of the relation between mother and child must be broken, just as the analytic relation must be thrown onto the axis of desire. In Lacan's account, the phallus stands for that moment

---

[29] 'La phase phallique et la portée subjective du complexe de castration, *Scilicet* 1, 1968; tr. 'The Phallic Phase and the Subjective Import of the Castration Complex, *Feminine Sexuality*, p.117. *Scilicet* was the review published in Lacan's series, *Le champ freudien*, at Editions du Seuil in Paris; apart from those by Lacan, the articles in the first issues were unsigned.

[30] Lacan, 'Les formations de l'inconscient', *Bulletin de Psychologie* 2, 1957-58, p. 13.

[31] 'The Meaning of the Phallus', p. 80.

[32] 'Les formations de l'inconscient', p. 14.

of rupture. It refers mother and child to the dimension of the symbolic which is figured by the father's place. The mother is taken to desire the phallus not because she contains it (Klein), but precisely because she does not. The phallus therefore belongs somewhere else; it breaks the two-term relation and initiates the order of exchange. For Lacan, it takes on this value as a function of the androcentric nature of the symbolic order itself (cf. pp.69-70 below). But its status is in itself false, and must be recognised by the child as such. Castration means first of all this — that the child's desire for the mother does not refer *to* her but *beyond* her, to an object, the phallus, whose status is first imaginary (the object presumed to satisfy her desire) and then symbolic (recognition that desire cannot be satisfied).

The place of the phallus in the account, therefore, follows from Lacan's return to the position and law of the father, but this concept has been reformulated in relation to that of desire. Lacan uses the term 'paternal metaphor', metaphor having a very specific meaning here. First, as a reference to the act of substitution (substitution is the very law of metaphoric operation), whereby the prohibition of the father takes up the place originally figured by the absence of the mother. Secondly, as a reference to the status of paternity itself which can only ever logically be *inferred*. And thirdly, as part of an insistence that the father stands for a place and a function which is not reducible to the presence or absence of the real father as such:

> To speak of the Name of the Father is by no means the same thing as invoking paternal deficiency (which is often done). We know today that an Oedipus complex can be constituted perfectly well even if the father is not there, while originally it was the excessive presence of the father which was held responsible for all dramas. But it is not in an environmental perspective that the answer to these questions can be found. So as to make the link between the Name of the Father, in so far as he can at times be missing, and the father whose effective presence is not always necessary for him not to be missing, I will introduce the expression *paternal metaphor*.[33]

Finally, the concept is used to separate the father's function from the idealised or imaginary father with which it is so easily confused and which is exactly the figure to be got round, or past: 'Any

[33] Ibid., p. 8.

discourse on the Oedipus complex which fails to bring out this figure will be inscribed within the very effects of the complex'.[34]

Thus when Lacan calls for a return to the place of the father he is crucially distinguishing himself from any sociological conception of role. The father is a function and refers to a law, the place outside the imaginary dyad and against which it breaks. To make of him a referent is to fall into an ideological trap: the 'prejudice which falsifies the conception of the Oedipus complex from the start, by making it define as natural, rather than normative, the predominance of the paternal figure'.[35]

There is, therefore, no assumption about the ways in which the places come to be fulfilled (it is this very assumption which is questioned). This is why, in talking of the genetic link between the mother and child, Lacan could refer to the 'vast social connivance' which *makes* of her the 'privileged site of prohibitions'.[36] And why Safouan, in an article on the function of the real father, recognises that it is the intervention of the third term which counts, and that nothing of itself requires that this should be embodied by the father as such.[37] Lacan's position should be read against two alternative emphases — on the actual behaviour of the mother alone (adequacy and inadequacy), and on a literally present or absent father (his idealisation and/or deficiency).

The concept of the phallus and the castration complex can only be understood in terms of this reference to prohibition and the law, just as rejection of these concepts tends to lose sight of this reference. The phallus needs to be placed on the axis of desire before it can be understood, or questioned, as the differential mark of sexual identification (boy or girl, having or not having the phallus). By breaking the imaginary dyad, the phallus represents a moment of division (Lacan calls this the subject's 'lack-in-being') which re-enacts the fundamental splitting of subjectivity itself. And by jarring against any naturalist account of sexuality ('phallocentrism ... strictly impossible to deduce from any pre-established harmony of the said psyche to the nature it

[34] Moustapha Safouan, 'Is the Oedipus Complex Universal?' (tr. Ben Brewster from chapter 7 of *Etudes sur l'oedipe,* Paris 1974), *m/f* 5-6, 1981, p. 9.

[35] 'Intervention on Transference', p. 69.

[36] Lacan, *Le séminaire XVII: L'envers de la psychanalyse* (1969-70), 6, p. 10 (unpublished seminar, references to week and page of the typescript).

[37] Safouan, p. 127.

expresses'),[38] the phallus relegates sexuality to a strictly other dimension — the order of the symbolic outside of which, for Lacan, sexuality cannot be understood. The importance of the phallus is that its status in the development of human sexuality is something which nature *cannot* account for.

When Lacan is reproached with phallocentrism at the level of his theory, what is most often missed is that the subject's entry into the symbolic order is equally an exposure of the value of the phallus itself. The subject has to recognise that there is desire, or lack in the place of the Other, that there is no ultimate certainty or truth, and that the status of the phallus is a fraud (this is, for Lacan, the meaning of castration). The phallus can only take up its place by indicating the precariousness of any identity assumed by the subject on the basis of its token. Thus the phallus stands for that moment when prohibition must function, in the sense of whom may be assigned to whom in the triangle made up of mother, father and child, but at that same moment it signals to the subject that 'having' only functions at the price of a loss and 'being' as an effect of division. Only if this is dropped from the account can the phallus be taken to represent an unproblematic assertion of male privilege, or else lead to reformulations intended to guarantee the continuity of sexual development for both sexes (Jones).

It is that very continuity which is challenged in Lacan's account. The concept of the phallus and the castration complex testify above all to the problematic nature of the subject's insertion into his or her sexual identity, to an impossibility writ large over that insertion at the point where it might be taken to coincide with the genital drive. Looking back at Jones's answer to Freud, it is clear that his opposition to Freud's concept of the phallic phase involves a rejection of the dimension of desire, of the loss of the object, of the difficulty inherent in subjectivity itself. Just as it was Freud's failure to apply the concept of castration literally to the girl child which brought him up against the concept of desire.[39]

The subject then takes up his or her identity with reference to

---

[38] Lacan, 'D'une question préliminaire à tout traitement possible de la psychose' (1955-56), *Ecrits* (tr. 'On a question preliminary to any possible treatment of psychosis', *Ecrits: A Selection*, p. 198).

[39] For a fuller discussion of both of these points see 'The Phallic Phase', and 'Feminine Sexuality in Psychoanalytic Doctrine', in *Feminine Sexuality*.

the phallus, but that identity is thereby designated symbolic (it is something enjoined on the subject). Lacan inverts Saussure's formula for the linguistic sign (the opposition between signifier and signified), giving primacy to the signifier over that which it signifies (or rather creates in that act of signification). For it is essential to his argument that sexual difference is a legislative divide which creates and reproduces its categories. Thus Lacan replaces Saussure's model for the arbitrary nature of the linguistic sign:

TREE

(which is indeed open to the objection that it seems to reflect a theory of language based on a correspondence between words and things), with this model:[40]

LADIES   **GENTS**

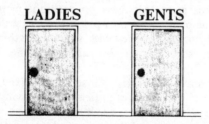

'Any speaking being whatever' must line up on one or other side of the divide.[41]

[40] Lacan, 'L'instance de la lettre dans l'inconscient ou la raison depuis Freud' (1957), *Ecrits* (tr. 'The agency of the letter in the unconscious or reason since Freud', *Ecrits: A Selection*, p. 151).

[41] Lacan, 'Une lettre d'âmour', *Le séminaire XX: Encore* (1972-73), Paris 1975 (tr. 'A Love Letter', *Feminine Sexuality*, p. 150).

Sexual difference is then assigned according to whether individual subjects do or do not possess the phallus, which means not that anatomical difference *is* sexual difference (the one as strictly deducible from the other), but that anatomical difference comes to *figure* sexual difference, that is, it becomes the sole representative of what that difference is allowed to be. It thus covers over the complexity of the child's early sexual life with a crude opposition in which that very complexity is refused or repressed. The phallus thus indicates the reduction of difference to an instance of visible perception, a *seeming* value.

Freud gave the moment when the boy and girl child saw that they were different the status of a trauma in which the girl is seen to be lacking (the objections often start here). But something can only be *seen* to be missing according to a pre-existing hierarchy of values ('there is nothing missing in the real').[42] What counts is not the perception but its already assigned meaning — the moment therefore belongs in the symbolic. And if Lacan states that the symbolic usage of the phallus stems from its visibility (something for which he was often criticised), it is only in so far as the order of the visible, the apparent, the seeming is the object of his attack. In fact he constantly refused any crude identification of the phallus with the order of the visible or real ('one might say that this signifier is chosen as what stands out as most easily seized upon in the real of sexual copulation'),[43] and he referred it instead to that function of 'veiling' in which he locates the fundamental duplicity of the linguistic sign: 'All these propositions merely veil over the fact that the phallus can only play its role as veiled, that is, as in itself the sign of the latency with which everything signifiable is struck as soon as it is raised to the function of signifier'.[44]

Meaning is only ever erected, it is set up and fixed. The phallus symbolises the effects of the signifier in that having no value in itself, it can represent that to which value *accrues*.

Lacan's statements on language need to be taken in two directions — towards the fixing of meaning itself (that which is

---

[42] 'The Phallic Phase', p. 113.
[43] 'The Meaning of the Phallus', p. 82.
[44] Ibid., p. 82.

enjoined on the subject), and away from that very fixing to the point of its constant slippage, the risk or vanishing-point which it always contains (the unconscious). Sexuality is placed on both these dimensions at once. The difficulty is to hold these two emphases together — sexuality in the symbolic (an ordering), sexuality as that which constantly fails. Once the relationship between these two aspects of psychoanalysis can be seen, then the terms in which feminine sexuality can be described undergo a radical shift. The concept of the symbolic states that the woman's sexuality is inseparable from the representations through which it is produced ('images and symbols *for* the woman cannot be isolated from images and symbols *of* the woman ... it is the representation of sexuality which conditions how it comes into play'),[45] but those very representations will reveal the splitting through which they are constituted as such. The question of what a woman is in this account always stalls on the crucial acknowledgement that there is absolutely no guarantee that she *is* at all (cf. below pp.72-74). But if she takes up her place according to the process described, then her sexuality will betray, necessarily, the impasses of its history.

Sexuality belongs for Lacan in the realm of masquerade. The term comes from Joan Rivière for whom it indicated a failed femininity.[46] For Lacan, masquerade is the very definition of 'femininity' precisely because it is constructed with reference to a male sign. The question of frigidity (on which, Lacan recognised, psychoanalysis 'gave up')[47] also belongs here, and it is described in 'The Meaning of the Phallus' as the effect of the status of the phallic term. But this does not imply that there is a physiology to which women could somehow be returned, or into which they could be freed. Rather the term 'frigidity' stands, on the side of the woman, for the difficulty inherent in sexuality itself, the disjunction laid over the body by desire, at the point where it is inscribed into the genital relation. Psychoanalysis now recognises that any simple criterion of femininity in terms of a shift of pleasure from clitoris to vagina is a travesty, but what matters is the fantasies implicated in either (or both). For both sexes,

---

[45] 'Guiding Remarks', p. 90.

[46] Joan Rivière, 'Womanliness as Masquerade', *IJPA* 10, 1929; reprinted in *Formations of Fantasy*, London 1986.

[47] 'Guiding Remarks', p. 89.

sexuality will necessarily touch on the duplicity which underpins its fundamental divide. As for 'normal' vaginal femininity, which might be taken as the recognition of the value of the male sign (a 'coming to' that recognition), it will always evoke the splitting on which its value is erected ('why not acknowledge that if there is no virility which castration does not consecrate, then for the woman it is a castrated lover or a dead man ... who hides behind the veil where he calls on her adoration').[48]

The description of feminine sexuality is, therefore, an exposure of the terms of its definition, the very opposite of a demand as to what that sexuality should be. Where such a definition is given — 'identification with her mother as desiring and a recognition of the phallus in the real father',[49] it involves precisely a collapse of the phallus into the real and of desire into recognition — giving the lie, we could say, to the whole problem outlined.[50]

II

Three points emerge from what has been described so far:

1. anatomy is what figures in the account: 'for me "anatomy is not destiny", but that does not mean that anatomy does not figure',[51] but it *only figures* (it is a sham);

---

[48] Ibid., p. 95.

[49] Safouan, *La sexualité féminine dans la doctrine freudienne*, p. 110.

[50] The difficulty of these terms is recognised by Safouan, but the problem remains; cf. also Eugénie Lemoine-Luccioni, *Partage des femmes* (Paris 1976) where there is the same collapse between the Other to be recognised by the woman in her advent to desire, and the real man whom, ideally, she comes to accept ('the Other, the man', p. 83; 'the Other, the man as subject', p. 87). There seems to be a constant tendency to literalise the terms of Lacan's account and it is when this happens that the definitions most easily recognised as reactionary tend to appear. We can see this in such apparently different areas as Maud Mannoni's translation of the name of the father into a therapeutic practice which seeks to establish the paternal genealogy of the psychotic child (Maud Mannoni, *L'enfant, sa 'maladie' et les autres*, Paris 1967; tr. *The Child, its 'Illness' and the Others*, London 1970) and in Lemoine-Luccioni's account of the real Other who ensures castration to the woman otherwise condemned to pure narcissism. Lemoine-Luccioni's account is in many ways reminiscent of that of Helene Deutsch ('The Significance of Masochism in the Mental Life of Women', *IJPA* 11, 1930) who described the transition to femininity in terms of a desire for castration which is produced across the woman's body by the man.

[51] Safouan, *La sexualité féminine*, p. 131.

2. the phallus stands at its own expense and any male privilege erected upon it is an imposture: 'what might be called a man, the male speaking being, strictly disappears as an effect of discourse,... by being inscribed within it solely as castration';[52]

3. woman is not inferior, she is *subjected:*

> That the woman should be inscribed in an order of exchange of which she is the object, is what makes for the fundamentally conflictual, and, I would say, insoluble, character of her position: the symbolic order literally submits her, it transcends her ... There is for her something insurmountable, something unacceptable, in the fact of being placed as an object in a symbolic order to which, at the same time, she is subjected just as much as the man.[53]

It is the strength of the concept of the symbolic that it systematically repudiates any account of sexuality which assumes the pre-given nature of sexual difference — the polemic within psychoanalysis and the challenge to any such 'nature' by feminism appear at their closest here. But a problem remains. Lacan's use of the symbolic at this stage relied heavily on Lévi-Strauss's notion of kinship in which women are defined as objects of exchange. As such it is open to the same objections as Lévi-Strauss's account in that it presupposes the subordination which it is intended to explain.[54] Thus while at first glance these remarks by Lacan seem most critical of the order described, they are in another sense complicit with that order and any argument constructed on their basis is likely to be circular.[55]

I think it is crucial that at the point where Lacan made these remarks he had a concept of full speech, of access to the symbolic order whose subjective equivalent is a successful linguistic exchange.[56] But his work underwent a shift, which totally undercut any such conception of language as mediation, in favour of an increasing stress on its fundamental division, and the effects

---

[52] *L'envers de la psychanalyse,* 12, p. 4.

[53] *Le moi dans la théorie de Freud,* pp. 304-305.

[54] See Elizabeth Cowie, 'Woman as Sign', *m/f* 1, 1978.

[55] Cf., for example, Gayle Rubin, 'The Traffic in Women', in Rayna M. Reiter, *Towards an Anthropology of Women* (New York 1975), which describes psychoanalysis as a 'theory about the reproduction of Kinship', losing sight, again, of the concept of the unconscious and the whole problem of sexual identity, reducing the relations described to a quite literal set of acts of exchange.

[56] 'The Function and Field of Speech and Language'.

of that division on the level of sexuality itself.

'There is no sexual relation' — this became the emphasis of his account. 'There is no sexual relation' because the unconscious divides subjects to and from each other, and because it is the myth of that relation which acts as a barrier against the division, setting up a unity through which this division is persistently disavowed. Hence the related and opposite formula 'There is something of One' (the two formulas should be taken together) which refers to that fantasied unity of relation *('We are as one.* Of course everyone knows that it has never happened for two to make one, but still *we are as one.* That's what the idea of love starts out from ... the problem then being how on earth there could be love for another'),[57] refers also to its suppression of division and difference ('Love your neighbour as yourself ... the commandment lays down the abolition of sexual difference'),[58] to the very ideology of oneness and completion which, for Lacan, closes off the gap of human desire.

In the earlier texts, the unity was assigned to the imaginary, the symbolic was at least potentially its break. In the later texts, Lacan located the fantasy of 'sameness' within language and the sexual relation at one and the same time. 'There is no sexual relation' because subjects relate through what makes sense in *lalangue.*[59] This 'making sense' is a supplement, a making good of the lack of subjectivity and language, of the subject *in* language, against which lack it is set. Psychoanalysis states meaning to be sexual but it has left behind any notion of a repressed sexuality which it would somehow allow to speak. Meaning can only be described as sexual by taking the limits of meaning into account, for meaning in itself operates *at* the limit, the limits of its own failing: 'Meaning indicates the direction in which it fails'.[60] The stress, therefore, is

[57] *Encore*, p. 46.

[58] Lacan, *Le séminaire XXI: Les non-dupes errent* (1973-74), unpublished typescript, 4, p. 3.

[59] Lacan's term for Saussure's *langue* (language) from the latter's distinction between *langue* (the formal organisation of language) and *parole* (speech), the individual utterance. Lacan's term displaces this opposition in so far as, for him, the organisation of language can only be understood in terms of the subject's relationship to it. *Lalangue* indicates that part of language which reflects the laws of unconscious processess, but whose effects go beyond that reflection, and escape the grasp of the subject. (See *Encore*, pp. 126-127.)

[60] 'A Love Letter', p. 150.

on the constant failing within language and sexuality, which meaning attempts to supplement or conceal: 'Everything implied by the analytic engagement with human behaviour indicates not that meaning reflects the sexual but that it makes up for it'.[61] Sexuality is the vanishing-point of meaning. Love, on the other hand, belongs to the *Lust-Ich* or pleasure-ego which disguises that failing in the reflection of like to like (love as the ultimate form of self-recognition).

We could say that Lacan has taken the relationship between the unconscious and sexuality and has pushed it to its furthest extreme, producing an account of sexuality solely in terms of its divisions — the division *of* the subject, division *between* subjects (as opposed to relation). Hence the increasing focus on enunciation,[62] on language's internal division, and also the deliberate formalisation of the account — sexual difference as a divide, something to be laid out (exactly a formality, a question of form (the graph of *Encore*).[63] The challenge to the unity of the subject, its seeming coherence, is then addressed to the discourse of sexuality itself: 'instead of one signifier we need to interrogate, we should interrogate the signifier One'.[64] Thus there is no longer imaginary 'unity' and then symbolic difference or exchange, but rather an indictment of the symbolic for the imaginary unity which its most persistent myths continue to promote.

Within this process, woman is constructed as an absolute category (excluded and elevated at one and the same time), a category which serves to guarantee that unity on the side of the man. The man places the woman at the basis of his fantasy, or constitutes fantasy through the woman. Lacan moved away, therefore, from the idea of a problematic but socially assured process of exchange (women as objects) to the construction of woman as a category within language (woman as *the* object, the fantasy of her definition). What is now exposed in the account is 'a

---

[61] *Les non-dupes errent,* 15, p. 9.

[62] The term comes from Benveniste, his distinction between *énoncé* and *énonciation*, between the subject of the statement and the subject of the utterance itself. (See note 25 to 'Dora: Fragment of an Analysis' above.) Lacan sites the unconscious at the radical division of these instances, seen at its most transparent in the statement 'I am lying' where there are clearly two subjects, the one who is lying and the one who is not.

[63] 'A Love Letter', p. 149.

[64] *Encore,* p. 23.

carrying over onto the woman of the difficulty inherent in sexuality' itself.[65]

Lacan's later work on femininity, especially the seminar *Encore*, belong to this development. It goes further than, and can be seen as an attempt to take up the problems raised by, the work that precedes it. For whereas in the earlier texts the emphasis was on the circulation of the phallus in the process of sexual exchange, it is now effectively stated that if it is the phallus that circulates then there is no exchange (or relation). The question then becomes not so much the 'difficulty' of feminine sexuality consequent on phallic division, as what it means, given that division, to speak of the 'woman' at all. It is in many ways a more fundamental or 'radical' enquiry:

> whatever can be stated about the constitution of the feminine position in the Oedipus complex or in the sexual 'relation' concerns only a second stage, one in which the rules governing a certain type of exchange based on a common value have already been established. It is at a more radical stage, constitutive of those very rules themselves, that Freud points to one last question by indicating that it is the woman who comes to act as their support.[66]

In the later texts, the central term is the *object small a [objet a]*, Lacan's formula for the lost object which underpins symbolisation, cause of and 'stand in' for desire. What the man relates to is this object and the 'whole of his realisation in the sexual relation comes down to fantasy'.[67] As the place onto which lack is projected, and through which it is simultaneously disavowed, woman is a 'symptom' for the man.

Defined as such, reduced to being nothing other than this fantasmatic place, the woman does not exist. Lacan's statement 'The woman does not exist' is, therefore, the corollary of his accusation, or charge, against sexual fantasy. It means, not that women do not exist, but that her status as an absolute category and guarantor of fantasy (exactly *The* woman) is false (The). Lacan sees courtly love as the elevation of the woman into the place where her absence or inaccessibility stands in for male lack ('For the man, whose lady was entirely, in the most servile sense of the

[65] 'The Phallic Phase', p. 118.
[66] Ibid., pp. 118-119.
[67] 'A Love Letter, p. 157.

term, his female subject, courtly love is the only way of coming off elegantly from the absence of sexual relation),[68] just as he sees her denigration as the precondition for man's belief in his own soul ('For the soul to come into being, she, the woman, is differentiated from it ... called woman and defamed').[69] In relation to the man, woman comes to stand for both difference and loss: 'On the one hand, the woman becomes, or is produced, precisely as what he is not, that is, sexual difference, and on the other, as what he has to renounce, that is, *jouissance*'.[70]

Within the phallic definition, the woman is constituted as 'not all', in so far as the phallic function rests on an exception (the 'not') which is assigned to her. Woman is excluded *by* the nature of words, meaning that the definition poses her as exclusion. Note that this is not the same thing as saying that woman is excluded *from* the nature of words, a misreading which leads to the recasting of the whole problem in terms of woman's place outside language, the idea that women might have of themselves an entirely different speech.

For Lacan, men and women are only ever in language ('Men and women are signifiers bound to the common usage of language').[71] All speaking beings must line themselves up on one side or the other of this division, but anyone can cross over and inscribe themselves on the opposite side from that to which they are anatomically destined.[72] It is, we could say, an either/or situation, but one whose fantasmatic nature was endlessly reiterated by Lacan: 'these are not positions able to satisfy us, so much so that we can state the unconscious to be defined by the fact

---

[68] Lacan, 'Dieu et la jouissance de ~~La~~ femme', *Encore* (tr. 'God and the Jouissance of ~~The~~ Woman', *Feminine Sexuality,* p. 141).

[69] 'A Love Letter', p. 156.

[70] Lacan, *Le séminaire XVIII: D'un discours qui ne sera pas semblant* (1970-71), 6, pp.9-10; see also Otto Fenichel, in a paper to which Lacan often referred, on the refusal of difference which underpins the girl = phallus equation frequently located as a male fantasy: 'the differentness of woman is denied in both cases; in the one case, in the attempt to repress women altogether, in the other, in denying their individuality'. (Otto Fenichel, 'The Symbolic Equation: Girl = Phallus', *Psychoanalytic Quarterly* 18:3, 1949, p. 13.)

[71] *Encore,* p. 36.

[72] Note how this simultaneously shifts the concept of bisexuality — not an undifferentiated sexual nature prior to symbolic difference (Freud's earlier sense), but the availability to all subjects of both positions in relation to that difference itself.

that it has a much clearer idea of what is going on than the truth that man is not woman'.[73]

The woman, therefore, is *not*, because she is defined purely against the man (she is the negative of that definition — 'man is *not* woman'), and because this very definition is designated fantasy, a set which may well be empty. If woman is 'not all', writes Lacan, then 'she' can hardly refer to all women.

As negative to the man, woman becomes a total object of fantasy (or an object of total fantasy), elevated into the place of the Other and made to stand for its truth. Since the place of the Other is also the place of God, this is the ultimate form of mystification ('the more man may ascribe to the woman in confusion with God...the less he is'). In so far as God 'has not made his exit',[74] so the woman becomes the support of his symbolic place. In his later work Lacan defined the objective of psychoanalysis as breaking the confusion behind this mystification, a rupture between the *object a* and the Other, whose conflation he saw as the elevation of fantasy into the order of truth. The *object a,* cause of desire and support of male fantasy, gets transposed onto the image of the woman as Other who then acts as its guarantee. The absolute 'Otherness' of the woman, therefore, serves to secure for the man his own self-knowledge and truth. Remember that for Lacan there can be no such guarantee — there is no 'Other of the Other'. His rejection of the category 'Woman', therefore, belonged to his assault on any unqualified belief in the Other as such: 'This The [of the woman] crossed through ... relates to the signifier O when it is crossed through (Ø)'.[75]

Increasingly this led Lacan to challenge the notions of 'knowledge' and 'belief', and the myths on which they necessarily rely. All Lacan's statements against belief in the woman, against her status as knowing, problematic as they are, can only be understood as part of this constant undercutting of the terms on which they rest. In the later writing, Lacan continually returns to the 'subject supposed to know', the claim of a subject to know (the claim to know oneself as subject), and the different forms of discourse which can be organised around this position.[76]

[73] *Les non-dupes errent,* 6, p. 9.
[74] 'A Love Letter', pp. 160, 154.
[75] Ibid., p. 151.
[76] Much of the difficulty of Lacan's work stemmed from his attempt to subvert

'Knowing' is only ever such a claim, just as 'belief' rests entirely on the supposition of what is false. To believe in The Woman is simply a way of closing off the division or uncertainty which also underpins conviction as such. And when Lacan says that women do not know, while at one level he relegates women outside, and against, the very mastery of his own statement, he was also recognising the binding, or restricting, of the parameters of knowledge itself ('masculine knowledge irredeemably an erring').[77]

The Other crossed through (Ø) stands against this knowledge as the place of division where meaning falters, where it slips and shifts. It is the place of *signifiance,* Lacan's term for this very movement in language against, or away from, the positions of coherence which language simultaneously constructs. The Other threfore stands against the phallus — its pretence to meaning and false consistency. It is from the Other that the phallus seeks authority and is refused.

The woman belongs on the side of the Other in this second sense, for in so far as *jouissance* is defined as phallic so she might be said to belong somewhere else. The woman is implicated, of necessity, in phallic sexuality, but at the same time it is 'elsewhere that she upholds the question of her own *jouissance*',[78] that is, the question of her status as desiring subject. Lacan designates this *jouissance* supplementary so as to avoid any notion of complement, of woman as a complement to man's phallic nature (which is precisely the fantasy). But it is also a recognition of the 'something more', the 'more than *jouissance*',[79] which Lacan locates in the Freudian concept of repetition — what escapes or is left over from the phallic function, and exceeds it. Woman is,

that position from within his own utterance, to rejoin the place of 'non-knowledge' which he designated the unconscious, by the constant slippage or escape of his speech, and thereby to undercut the very mastery which his own position as speaker (master and analyst) necessarily constructs. In fact one can carry out the same operation on the statment 'I do not know' as Lacan performed on the utterance 'I am lying' (cf. note 62 above) — for, if I do not know, then how come I know enough to know that I do not know and if I do know that I do not know, then it is not true that I do not know. Lacan was undoubtedly trapped in this paradox of his own utterance.

[77] *Les non-dupes errent,* 6, p. 11.

[78] 'The Phallic Phase', p. 121.

[79] At times *jouissance* is opposed to the idea of pleasure as the site of this excess, but where *jouissance* is defined as phallic, Lacan introduces the concept of the supplement ('more than') with which to oppose it.

therefore, placed *beyond* (beyond the phallus). That 'beyond' refers at once to her total mystification as absolute Other (and hence nothing other than other), and to a *question,* the question of her own *jouissance,* of her greater or lesser access to the residue of the dialectic to which she is constantly subjected. The problem is that once the notion of 'woman' has been so relentlessly exposed as a fantasy, then any such question becomes an almost impossible one to pose.

Lacan's reference to woman as Other needs, therefore, to be seen as an attempt to hold apart two moments which are in constant danger of collapsing into each other — that which assigns woman to the negative place of its own (phallic) system, and that which asks the question as to whether women might, as a very effect of that assignation, break against and beyond that system itself. For Lacan, that break is always within language, it is the break of the subject *in* language. The concept of *jouissance* (what escapes in sexuality) and the concept of *signifiance* (what shifts within language) are inseparable.

Only when this is seen can we properly locate the tension which runs right through *Encore* between his critique of the forms of mystification latent to the category Woman, and the repeated question as to what her 'otherness' might be. A tension which can be recognised in the very query 'What does a woman want?' on which Freud stalled and to which Lacan returned. That tension is clearest in Lacan's appeal to St Theresa, whose statue by Bernini in Rome[80] he took as the model for an-other *jouissance* — the woman therefore as 'mystical' but, he insisted, this is not 'not political',[81] in so far as mysticism is one of the available forms of expression where such 'otherness' in sexuality utters its most forceful complaint. And if we cut across for a moment from Lacan's appeal to her image as executed by the man, to St Theresa's own writings, to her commentary on 'The Song of Songs', we find its sexuality in the form of a disturbance which, crucially, she locates not on the

---

[80] 'What is her *jouissance,* her *coming* from?' ('God and the Jouissance of The Woman', p.147) — a question made apparently redundant by the angel with arrow poised above her (the 'piercing' of Saint Theresa), and one whose problematic nature is best illustrated by the cardinals and doges in the gallery on either side of the 'proscenium' — *witnesses* to the staging of an act which, because of the perspective lines, they cannot actually *see* (Bernini, 'The Ecstasy of Saint Theresa', Santa Maria della Vittoria, Rome).

[81] 'God and the Jouissance of The Woman', p.146.

level of the sexual content of the song, but on the level of its enunciation, in the instability of its pronouns — a precariousness in language which reveals that neither the subject nor God can be placed ('speaking with one person, asking for peace from another, and then speaking to the person in whose presence she is').[82] Sexuality belongs, therefore, on the level of its, and the subject's, *shifting*.

Towards the end of his work, Lacan talked of woman's 'anti-phallic' nature as leaving her open to that 'which of the unconscious cannot be spoken' (a reference to women analysts in which we can recognise, ironically, the echo of Freud's conviction that they would have access to a different strata of psychic life).[83] In relation to the earlier texts we could say that woman no longer masquerades, she *defaults:* 'the *jouissance* of the woman does not go without saying, that is, without the saying of truth', whereas for the man 'his *jouissance* suffices which is precisely why he understands nothing'.[84] There is a risk, here, of giving back to the woman a status as truth (the very mythology denounced). But for Lacan, this 'truth' of the unconscious is only ever that moment of fundamental division through which the subject entered into language and sexuality, and the constant failing of position within both.

This is the force of Lacan's account — his insistence that

[82] Saint Theresa, *The Complete Works,* ed. Silverio de Santa Teresa P., English edition, Peers, London 1946, p. 359. Commentary on the line from the 'Song of Songs' — 'Let the Lord kiss me with the kiss of his mouth, for thy breasts are sweeter than wine'.

[83] *Ornicar?,* 20-21, Summer 1980, p. 12. At the time of writing Lacan had just dissolved his school in Paris, rejoining in the utterance through which he represented that act — 'Je père-sévère' ('I persevere' — the pun is on 'per' and 'père' (father)) — the whole problem of mastery and paternity which has cut across the institutional history of his work. From the early stand against a context which he (and others) considered authoritarian, and the cancellation, as its effect, of his seminar on the Name of the Father in 1953, to the question of mastery and transference which lay behind the further break in 1964, and which so clearly surfaces in the dissolution here. It has been the endless paradox of Lacan's position that he has provided the most systematic critique of forms of identification and transference which, by dint of this very fact, he has come most totally to represent. That a number of women analysts (cf. note 85, and Introduction pp.3-5) have found their position in relation to this to be an impossible one, only confirms the close relation between the question of feminine sexuality and the institutional divisions and difficulties of psychoanalysis itself.

[84] *Les non-dupes errent,* 7, p. 16.

femininity can only be understood in terms of its construction, an insistence which produced in reply the same reinstatment of women, the same argument for *her* sexual nature as was seen in the 1920s and 1930s in response to Freud. This time the question of symbolisation, which was latent in the earlier debate, has been at the centre of that response. This is all the more clear in that the specificity of feminine sexuality in the more recent discussion[85] has explicitly become the issue of women's relationship to language. In so far as it is the order of language which structures sexuality around the male term, or the privileging of that term which shows sexuality to be constructed within language, so this raises the issue of women's relationship to that language and that sexuality simultaneously. The question of the body of the girl child (what she may or may not know of that body) as posed in the earlier debate, becomes the question of the woman's body as language (what, of that body, can achieve symbolisation). The objective is to retrieve the woman from the dominance of the phallic term and from language at one and the same time. What this means is that femininity is assigned to a point of origin prior to the mark of symbolic difference and the law. The privileged relationship of women to that origin gives them access to an archaic form of expressivity outside the circuit of linguistic exchange.

This point of origin is the maternal body, an undifferentiated space, and yet one in which the girl child recognises herself. The girl then has to suppress or devalue that fullness of recognition in order to line up within the order of the phallic term. In the argument for a primordial femininity, it is clear that the relation between the mother and child is conceived of as dyadic and simply reflective (one to one — the girl child fully *knows* herself in the

[85] In this last section I will be referring predominantly to the work of Michèle Montrelay and Luce Irigaray, the former a member of Lacan's school prior to its dissolution in January 1980 when she dissociated herself from him, the latter working within his school up to 1974 when she was dismissed from the newly reorganised department of psychoanalysis at the University of Paris VIII (Vincennes) on publication of her book, *Speculum de l'autre femme*. Both are practising psychoanalysts. Montrelay takes up the Freud-Jones controversy specifically in terms of women's access to language in her article 'Recherches sur la féminité' (*Critique* 26, 1970; tr. Parveen Adams, 'Inquiry into Femininity'). Irigaray's book *Speculum* contained a critique of Freud's papers on femininity; her later *Ce sexe qui n'en est pas un* (Paris 1977; tr. Catherine Porter, *This Sex Which Is Not One,* Ithaca 1985) contains a chapter ('Cosi fan tutti') directly addressed to Lacan's *Encore.*

mother) which once again precludes the concept of desire. Feminine specificity is, therefore, predicated directly onto the concept of an unmediated and unproblematic relation to origin.

The positions taken up have not been identical, but they have a shared stress on the specificity of the feminine drives, a stress which was at the basis of the earlier response to Freud. They take a number of their concepts directly from that debate (the concept of concentric feminine drives in Montrelay comes directly from Jones and Klein). But the effects of the position are different. Thus whereas for Jones, for example, those drives ideally anticipated and ensured the heterosexual identity of the girl child, now those same drives put at risk her access to any object at all (Montrelay)[86] or else they secure the woman to herself and, through that, to other women (Irigaray). Women are *returned*, therefore, in the account and to each other — against the phallic term but also against the loss of origin which Lacan's account is seen to imply. It is therefore a refusal of division which gives the woman access to a different strata of language, where words and things are not differentiated, and the real of the maternal body threatens or holds off woman's access to prohibition and the law.

There is a strength in this account, which has been recognised by feminism. At its most forceful it expresses a protest engendered by the very cogency of what Freud and then Lacan describe (it is the *effect* of that description).[87] And something of its position was certainly present in Lacan's earlier texts ('feminine sexuality ... as the effort of a *jouissance* wrapped in its own contiguity').[88] But Lacan came back to this response in the later texts, which can therefore be seen as a sort of reply, much as Freud's 1931 and 1933 papers on femininity addressed some of the criticisms which he had received.

---

[86] Montrelay attempts to resolve the 'Freud-Jones' controversy by making the two different accounts of femininity equal to *stages* in the girl's psychosexual development, femininity being defined as the passage from a concentric psychic economy to one in which symbolic castration has come into play. Access to symbolisation depends on the transition, and it is where it fails that the woman remains bound to a primordial cathexis of language as the undifferentiated maternal body. Montrelay should, therefore, be crucially distinguished from Irigaray at this point, since for her such a failure is precipitant of anxiety and is in no sense a concept of femininity which she is intending to promote.

[87] Note too the easy slippage from Irigaray's title *Ce sexe qui n'en est pas un*, 'This sex which isn't one', to Lacan's formula: 'This sex which isn't *one*'.

[88] 'Guiding Remarks', p. 97.

For Lacan, as we have seen, there is no pre-discursive reality ('How return, other than by means of a special discourse, to a pre-discursive reality?'),[89] no place prior to the law which is available and can be retrieved. And there is no feminine outside language. First, because the unconscious severs the subject from any unmediated relation to the body as such ('there is nothing in the unconscious which accords with the body'),[90] and secondly because the 'feminine' is constituted as a division in language, a division which produces the feminine as its negative term. If woman is defined as other it is because the definition produces her as other, and not because she has another essence. Lacan does not refuse difference ('if there was no difference how could I say there was no sexual relation'),[91] but for him what is to be questioned is the seeming 'consistency' of that difference — of the body or anything else — the division it enjoins, the definitions of the woman it produces.

For Lacan, to say that difference is 'phallic' difference is to expose the symbolic and arbitrary nature of its division as such. It is crucial — and it is something which can be seen even more clearly in the response to the later texts on femininity — that refusal of the phallic term brings with it an attempt to reconstitute a form of subjectivity free of division, and hence a refusal of the notion of symbolisation itself. If the status of the phallus is to be challenged, it cannot, therefore, be directly from the feminine body but must be by means of a different symbolic term (in which case the relation to the body is immediately thrown into crisis), or else by an entirely different logic altogether (in which case one is no longer in the order of symbolisation at all).

The demands against Lacan therefore collapse two different levels of objection — that the body should be mediated by language and that the privileged term of that mediation be male. The fact that refusal of the phallus turns out once again to be a refusal of the symbolic does not close, but leaves open as still unanswered, the question as to why that necessary symbolisation and the privileged status of the phallus appear as interdependent in the structuring and securing (never secure) of human subjectivity.

[89] *Encore*, p. 33.
[90] 'Seminar of 21 January, 1975', p. 165.
[91] *Les non-dupes errent*, 4, p. 18.

There is, therefore, no question of denying here that Lacan was implicated in the phallocentrism he described, just as his own utterance constantly rejoins the mastery which he sought to undermine. The question of the unconscious and of sexuality, the movement towards and against them, operated at exactly this level of his own speech. But for Lacan they function as the question of that speech, and cannot be referred back to a body outside language, a place to which the 'feminine', and through that, women, might escape. In the response to Lacan, therefore, the 'feminine' has returned as it did in the 1920s and 1930s in reply to Freud, but this time with the added meaning of a resistance to a phallic organisation of sexuality which is recognised as such. The 'feminine' stands for a refusal of that organisation, its ordering, its identity. For Lacan, on the other hand, interrogating that same organisation undermines any absolute definition of the 'feminine' at all.

Psychoanalysis does not produce that definition. It gives an account of how that definition is produced. While the objection to its dominant term must be recognised, it cannot be answered by an account which returns to a concept of the feminine as pre-given, nor by a mandatory appeal to an androcentrism in the symbolic which the phallus would simply reflect. The former relegates women outside language and history, the latter simply subordinates them to both.

Lacan's writing gives an account of how the status of the phallus in human sexuality enjoins on the woman a definition in which she is simultaneously symptom and myth. As long as we continue to feel the effects of that definition we cannot afford to ignore this description of the fundamental imposture which sustains it.

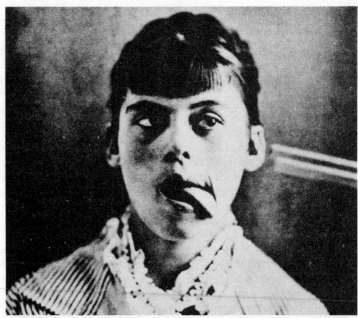

Tongue contraction produced in a hysteric in waking state through auricular reflex

Face and neck spasm of hysterical origin

Photographs from *Nouvelle iconographie photographique de la Salpêtrière*, P. Regnard Bourneville, Paris, 1876-78, courtesy of Joël Farges

3
Femininity and its Discontents

Is psychoanalysis a 'new orthodoxy' for feminism? Or does it rather represent the surfacing of something difficult and exceptional but important for feminism, which is on the verge (once again) of being lost? I will argue that the second is the case, and that the present discarding of psychoanalysis in favour of forms of analysis felt as more material in their substance and immediately political in their effects is a *return* to positions whose sensed inadequacy for feminism produced a gap in which psychoanalysis could — fleetingly — find a place.[1] What

[1] First published in *Feminist Review* 14, Summer 1983, pp. 5-21, this essay was originally requested by the editors of *Feminist Review* to counter the largely negative representation of psychoanalysis which had appeared in the journal, and as a specific response to Elizabeth Wilson's 'Psychoanalysis: Psychic Law and Order', *Feminist Review* 8, Summer 1981. (See also Janet Sayers, 'Psychoanalysis and Personal Politics: A Response to Elizabeth Wilson', *Feminist Review* 10, 1982.) As I was writing the piece, however, it soon became clear that Elizabeth Wilson's article and the question of *Feminist Review's* own relationship to psychoanalysis could not be understood independently of what has been — outside the work of Juliet Mitchell for feminism — a fairly consistent repudiation of Freud within the British Left. In this context, the feminist debate over Freud becomes part of a larger question about the importance of subjectivity to our understanding of political and social life. That this was in fact the issue became even clearer when Elizabeth Wilson and Angie Weir published an article 'The British Women's Movement' in *New Left Review* 148, November-December 1984, which dismissed the whole area of subjectivity and psychoanalysis from feminist politics together with any work by feminists (historians and writers on contemporary politics) who, while defining themselves as socialist feminists, nonetheless query the traditional terms of an exclusively

psychoanalysis offered up in that moment was by no means wholly satisfactory and it left many problems unanswered or inadequately addressed, but the questions which it raised for feminism are crucial and cannot, I believe, be approached in the same way, or even posed, from anywhere else. To ask what are the political implications of psychoanalysis for feminism seems to me, therefore, to pose the problem the wrong way round. Psychoanalysis is already political for feminism — political in the more obvious sense that it came into the arena of discussion in response to the internal needs of feminist debate, and political again in the wider sense that the repudiation of psychoanalysis by feminism can be seen as linking up with the repeated marginalisation of psychoanalysis within our general culture, a culture whose oppressiveness for women is recognised by us all.

Before going into this in more detail, a separate but related point needs to be made, and that is the peculiarity of the psychoanalytic object with which feminism engages. Thus to ask for effects from psychoanalysis in the arena of political practice is already to assume that psychoanalytic practice is a-political.[2] Recent feminist debate has tended to concentrate on theory (Freud's theory of femininity, whether or not psychoanalysis can provide an account of women's subordination). This was as true of Juliet Mitchell's defense of Freud[3] as it has been of many of the more recent replies. The result has been that psychoanalysis has been pulled away from its own practice. Here the challenge to psychoanalysis by feminists has come from alternative forms of therapy (feminist therapy and co-counselling). But it is worth noting that the way psychoanalysis is engaged with in much recent criticism already divests it of its practical effects at this level, or rather takes this question as settled in advance (the passing reference to the chauvinism of the psychoanalytic institution, the assumption that psychoanalysis depoliticises the woman analysand). In this context, therefore, the common theory/ practice dichotomy has a very specific meaning in that psychoanalysis can only be held accountable to 'practice' if it is assumed not to be one, or if the form of its practice is taken to have no purchase on political life. This assumes, for example, that there

class-based analysis of power.
[2] Wilson, p. 63.
[3] *Psychoanalysis and Feminism.*

is no politics of the psychoanalytic institution itself, something to which I will return.

Both these points — the wider history of how psychoanalysis has been placed or discarded by our dominant culture, and the detaching of psychoanalysis from its practical and institutional base — are related, in as much as they bring into focus the decisions and selections which have already been made about psychoanalysis before the debate even begins. Some of these decisions, I would want to argue, are simply wrong — such as the broad accusation of chauvinism levelled against the psychoanalytic institution as a whole. In this country at least, the significant impetus after Freud passed to two women — Anna Freud and Melanie Klein. Psychoanalysis in fact continues to be one of the few of our cultural institutions which does not professionally discriminate against women, and in which they could even be said to predominate. This is not of course to imply that the presence of women inside an institution is necessarily feminist, but women have historically held positions of influence inside psychoanalysis which they have been mostly denied in other institutions where their perceived role as 'carers' has relegated them to a subordinate position (eg. nursing); and it is the case that the first criticisms of Freud made by Melanie Klein can be seen to have strong affinities with later feminist repudiation of his theories.

For those who are hesitating over what appears as the present 'impasse' between feminism and psychoanalysis, the more important point, however, is to stress the way that psychoanalysis is being presented for debate — that is, the decisions which have already been made before we are asked to decide. Much will depend, I suspect, on whether one sees psychoanalysis as a new form of hegemony on the part of the feminist intelligentsia, or whether it is seen as a theory and practice which has constantly been relegated to the outside of dominant institutions and mainstream radical debate alike — an 'outside' with which feminism, in its challenge to both these traditions, has its own important forms of allegiance.

Components of the culture

In England, the relationship between the institution of psychoanalysis and its more general reception has always been complex, if not fraught. Thus in 1968, Perry Anderson could argue that major therapeutic and theoretical advances inside the psychoanalytic institution (chiefly in the work of Melanie Klein) had gone hand in hand with, and possibly even been the cause of, the isolation of psychoanalysis from the general culture, the slowness of its dissemination (until the Pelican Freud started to appear in 1974, you effectively had to join a club to read *The Standard Edition* of Freud's work), and the failure of psychoanalysis to effect a decisive break with traditions of empiricist philosophy, reactionary ethics, and an elevation of literary 'values', which he saw as the predominant features of our cultural life.[4] Whether or not one accepts the general 'sweep' of his argument, two points from that earlier polemic seem relevant here.

Firstly, the link between empiricist traditions of thought and the resistance to the psychoanalytic concept of the unconscious. Thus psychoanalysis, through its attention to symptoms, slips of the tongue and dreams (that is, to what *insists* on being spoken against what is *allowed* to be said) appears above all as a challenge to the self-evidence and banality of everyday life and language, which have also, importantly, constituted the specific targets of feminism. If we use the (fairly loose) definition which Anderson provided for empiricism as the unsystematic registration of things as they are and the refusal of forms of analysis which penetrate beneath the surface of observable social phenomena, the link to feminism can be made. For feminism has always challenged the observable 'givens' of women's presumed natural qualities and their present social position alike (expecially when the second is justified in terms of the first). How often has the 'cult of common sense', the notion of what is obviously the case or in the nature of things, been used in reactionary arguments against feminist attempts to demand social change? For Anderson in his article of 1968, this espousal of empiricist thinking provided one of the chief forms of resistance to Freud, so deeply committed is psychoanalysis to penetrating behind the surface and conscious manifestations of everyday experience.

Secondly, the relationship between this rejection of psychoanalysis and a *dearth* within British intellectual culture of a Marxism which could both theorise and criticise capitalism as a

[4] Perry Anderson, 'Components of the National Culture', *New Left Review* 50, July-August 1968.

social totality. This second point received the strongest criticism from within British Marxism itself, but what matters here is the fact that both Marxism *and* psychoanalysis were identified as forms of radical enquiry which were unassimilable to bourgeois norms. In the recent feminist discussion, however — notably in the pages of *Feminist Review* — Marxism and psychoanalysis tend to be posited as antagonistic; Marxism arrogating to itself the concept of political practice and social change, psychoanalysis being accused of inherent conservatism which rationalises and perpetuates the subordination of women under capitalism, or else fails to engage with that subordination at the level of material life.

In order to understand this, I think we have to go back to the earlier moment. For while the argument that Marxism was marginal or even alien to British thought was strongly repudiated, the equivalent observation about psychoanalysis seems to have been accepted and was more or less allowed to stand. This was perhaps largely because no-one on the Left rushed forward to claim a radicalism committed to psychoanalytic thought. *New Left Review* had itself been involved in psychoanalysis in the early 1960s, publishing a number of articles by Cooper and Laing,[5] and there is also a strong tradition, which goes back through Christopher Caudwell in the 1930s, of Marxist discussion of Freud. But the main controversy unleashed by Anderson's remarks centred around Marxism; in an earlier article Anderson himself had restricted his critique to the lack of Marxism and classical sociology in British culture, making no reference to psychoanalysis at all.[6] After 1968 *New Left Review* published Althusser's famous article on Lacan and one article by Lacan,[7] but for the most part the commitment to psychoanalysis was not sustained even by that section of the British Left which had orginally argued for its importance.

[5] David Cooper, 'Freud Revisited' and 'Two Types of Rationality', *New Left Review* 20, May-June 1963 and 29, January-February 1965; R. D. Laing 'Series and Nexus in the Family' and 'What is Schizophrenia?', *New Left Review* 15, May-June 1962 and 28, November-December 1964.

[6] Anderson, 'Origins of the Present Crisis'. *New Left Review* 23, January-February 1964; see also E.P. Thompson, 'The Peculiarities of the English', *Socialist Register* 1965.

[7] Louis Althusser, 'Freud and Lacan', tr. Ben Brewster, *New Left Review* 55, March-April 1969; Jacques Lacan, 'The Mirror Phase', tr. Jan Meil, *New Left Review* 51, September-October 1968.

Paradoxically, therefore, the idea that psychoanalysis was isolated or cut off from the general culture could be accepted to the extent that this very marginalisation was being *reproduced* in the response to the diagnosis itself. Thus the link between Marxism and Freudian psychoanalysis, as the twin poles of a failed radicalism at the heart of British culture, was broken. Freud was cast aside at the very moment when resistance to his thought had been identified as symptomatic of the restrictiveness of bourgeois culture. Juliet Mitchell was the exception. Her defence of Freud[8] needs to be seen as a redress of this omission, but also as a critique of the loss of the concept of the unconscious in the very forms of psychoanalysis (for example, Laing) sponsored by the British Left (the second problem as the cause of the first). In this context the case for psychoanalysis was part of a claim for the fundamentally anti-empiricist and radical nature of Freudian thought. That this claim was made via feminism (could perhaps *only* be made via feminism) says something about the ability of feminism to challenge the orthodoxies of both Left and Right.

Thus the now familiar duo of 'psychoanalysis and feminism' has an additional and crucial political meaning. Not just psychoanalysis *for* feminism or feminism *against* psychoanalysis, but Freudian psychoanalysis and feminism *together* as two forms of thought which relentlessly undermine the turgid resistance of common-sense language to all forms of conflict and political change. For me this specific sequence has been ironically or negatively confirmed (that is, it has been gone over again backwards) by the recent attempt by Michael Rustin to relate psychoanalysis to socialism through a combination of F. R. Leavis and Melanie Klein — the very figures whose standing had been taken as symptomatic of that earlier resistance to the most radical aspects of Freudian thought (Klein because of the confinement of her often challenging ideas to the psychoanalytic institution itself; Leavis beause of the inappropriate centrality which he claimed for the ethics of literary form and taste).[9] I cannot go into the details of Rustin's argument here, but its ultimate conservatism for feminism is at least clear; the advancement of 'mothering', and by

[8] Juliet Mitchell, 'Why Freud?', *Shrew,* November-December 1970, and *Psychoanalysis and Feminism.*

[9] Michael Rustin, 'A Socialist Consideration of Kleinian Psychoanalysis', *New Left Review* 131, January-February 1982.

implication of the role of women as mothers, as the psychic basis on which socialism can be built (the idea that psychoanalysis can *engender* socialism seems to be merely the flip side of the argument which accuses psychoanalysis of producing social conformity).

This history may appear obscure to many feminists who have not necessarily followed the different stages of these debates. But the diversion through this cultural map is, I think, important in so far as it can illustrate the ramifications of feminist discussion over a wider political spectrum, and also show how this discussion — the terms of the argument, the specific oppositions proposed — have in turn been determined by that wider spectrum itself.

Thus it will have crucial effects, for instance, whether psychoanalysis is discussed as an addition or supplement to Marxism (in relation to which it is then found *wanting*), or whether emphasis is laid on the concept of the unconscious. For while it is indeed correct that psychoanalysis was introduced into feminism as a theory which could rectify the inability of Marxism to address questions of sexuality, and that this move was complementary to the demand within certain areas of Marxism for increasing attention to the ideological determinants of our social being, it is also true that undue concentration on this aspect of the theory has served to cut off the concept of the unconscious, or at least to displace it from the centre of the debate. (This is graphically illustrated in Michèle Barrett's book, *Women's Oppression Today,* in which the main discussion of psychoanalysis revolves around the concept of ideology, and that of the unconscious is left to a note appended at the end of the chapter).[10]

Femininity and its Discontents

One result of this emphasis is that psychoanalysis is accused of 'functionalism', that is, it is accepted as a theory of how women are psychically 'induced' into femininity by a patriarchal culture, and is then accused of perpetuating that process, either through a practice assumed to be *prescriptive* about women's role (this is what women *should* do), or because the very effectiveness of the account as a *description* (this is what is demanded of women, what they are *expected* to do) leaves no possiblity of change.

[10] Michèle Barrett, *Women's Oppression Today,* London 1980, chapter 2, pp.80-83.

It is this aspect of Juliet Mitchell's book which seems to have been taken up most strongly by feminists who have attempted to follow through the political implications of psychoanalysis as a critique of patriarchy.

Thus Gayle Rubin, following Mitchell, uses psychoanalysis for a general critique of a patriarchal culture which is predicated on the exchange of women by men.[11] Nancy Chodorow shifts from Freud to later object relations theory to explain how women's childcaring role is perpetuated through the earliest relationship between a mother and her child, which leads in her case to a demand for a fundamental change in how childcare is organised between women and men in our culture.[12] Although there are obvious differences between these two readings of psychoanalysis, they nonetheless share an emphasis on the social exchange of women, or the distribution of roles for women, across cultures: 'Women's mothering is one of the few universal and enduring elements of the sexual division of labour'.[13]

The force of psychoanalysis is therefore (as Janet Sayers points out)[14] precisely that it gives an account of patriarchal culture as a trans-historical and cross-cultural force. It therefore conforms to the feminist demand for a theory which can explain women's subordination across specific cultures and different historical moments. Summing this up crudely, we could say that psychoanalysis adds sexuality to Marxism, where sexuality is felt to be lacking, and extends beyond Marxism where the attention to specific historical instances, changes in modes of production etc., is felt to leave something unexplained.

But all this happens at a cost, and that cost is the concept of the unconscious. What distinguishes psychoanalysis from socio-logical accounts of gender (hence for me the fundamental impasse of Nancy Chodorow's work) is that whereas for the latter, the internalisation of norms is assumed roughly to work, the basic premise and indeed starting-point of psychoanalysis is that it does not. The unconscious constantly reveals the 'failure' of identity. Because there is no continuity of psychic life, so there is no stability

---

[11] See Gayle Rubin, 'The Traffic in Women'; and for a critique of the use of Lévi-Strauss on which this reading is based, Elizabeth Cowie, 'Woman as Sign'.

[12] Nancy Chodorow, *The Reproduction of Mothering*.

[13] Ibid., p. 3.

[14] Sayers, p. 92.

of sexual identity, no position for women (or for men) which is ever simply achieved. Nor does psychoanalysis see such 'failure' as a special-case inability or an individual deviancy from the norm. 'Failure' is not a moment to be regretted in a process of adaptation, or development into normality, which ideally takes its course (some of the earliest critics of Freud, such as Ernest Jones, did, however, give an account of development in just these terms). Instead 'failure' is something endlessly repeated and relived moment by moment throughout our individual histories. It appears not only in the symptom, but also in dreams, in slips of the tongue and in forms of sexual pleasure which are pushed to the sidelines of the norm. Feminism's affinity with psychoanalysis rests above all, I would argue, with this recognition that there is a resistance to identity at the very heart of psychic life. Viewed in this way, psychoanalysis is no longer best understood as an account of how women are fitted into place (even this, note, is the charitable reading of Freud). Instead psychoanalysis becomes one of the few places in our culture where it is recognised as more than a fact of individual pathology that most women do not painlessly slip into their roles as women, if indeed they do at all. Freud himself recognised this increasingly in his work. In the articles which run from 1924 to 1931,[15] he moves from that famous, or rather infamous, description of the little girl struck with her 'inferiority' or 'injury' in the face of the anatomy of the little boy and wisely accepting her fate ('injury' as the *fact* of being feminine), to an account which quite explicitly describes the process of becoming 'feminine' as an 'injury' or 'catastrophe' for the complexity of her earlier psychic and sexual life ('injury' as its *price*).

Elizabeth Wilson and Janet Sayers are, therefore, in a sense correct to criticise psychoanalysis when it is taken as a general theory of patriarchy or of gender identity, that is, as a theory which explains how women wholly internalise the very mode of being which is feminism's specific target of attack; but they have missed out half the (psychoanalytic) story. In fact the argument seems to be circular. Psychoanalysis is drawn in the direction of a general theory of culture or a sociological account of gender because these seem to lay greater emphasis on the pressures of the

[15] Freud, 'The Dissolution of the Oedipus Complex' (1924); 'Some Psychical Consequences of the Anatomical Distinction Between the Sexes' (1925), SE XIX, PF 7; 'Female Sexuality' (1931).

'outside' world, but it is this very pulling away from the psychoanalytic stress on the 'internal' complexity and difficulty of psychic life which produces the functionalism which is then criticised.

The argument about whether Freud is being 'prescriptive' or 'descriptive' about women (with its associated stress on the motives and morals of Freud himself) is fated to the extent that it is locked into this model. Many of us will be familiar with Freud's famous pronouncement that a woman who does not succeed in transforming activity to passivity, clitoris to vagina, mother for father, will fall ill. Yet psychoanalysis testifies to the fact that psychic illness or distress is in no sense the prerogative of women who 'fail' in this task. One of my students recently made the obvious but important point that we would be foolish to deduce from the external trappings of normality or conformity in a woman that all is in fact well. And Freud himself always stressed the psychic cost of the civilising process for all (we can presumably include women in that 'all' even if at times he did not seem to do so).

All these aspects of Freud's work are subject to varying interpretation by analysts themselves. The first criticism of Freud's 'phallocentrism' came from inside psychoanalysis, from analysts such as Melanie Klein, Ernest Jones and Karen Horney who felt, contrary to Freud, that 'femininity' was a quality with its own impetus, subject to checks and internal conflict, but tending ultimately to fulfilment. For Jones, the little girl was 'typically receptive and acquisitive' from the outset; for Horney, there was from the beginning a 'wholly womanly' attachment to the father.[16] For these analysts, this development might come to grief, but for the most part a gradual strengthening of the child's ego and her increasing adaptation to reality, should guarantee its course. Aspects of the little girl's psychic life which were resistant to this process (the famous 'active' or 'masculine' drives) were defensive. The importance of concepts such as the 'phallic phase' in Freud's description of infantile sexuality is not, therefore, that such concepts can be taken as the point of insertion of patriarchy (assimilation to the norm). Rather their importance lies in the way that they indicate, through their very artificiality, that something

[16] Ernest Jones, 'The Phallic Phase', *IJPA* 14, Part 1, 1933, p. 265; Karen Horney, 'On the Genesis of the Castration Complex in Women' (1924), *Feminine Psychology,* London 1967, p. 53.

was being *forced,* and in the concept of psychic life with which they were accompanied. In Freud's work they went hand in hand with an increasing awareness of the difficulty, not to say impossibility, of the path to normality for the girl, and an increasing stress on the fundamental divisions, or splitting, of psychic life. It was those who challenged these concepts in the 1920s and 30s who introduced the more normative stress on a sequence of development, and coherent ego, back into the account.

I think we go wrong again, therefore, if we conduct the debate about whether Freud's account was developmental or not entirely in terms of his own writing. Certainly the idea of development is present at moments in his work. But it was not present *enough* for many of his contemporaries, who took up the issue and reinstated the idea of development precisely in relation to the sexual progress of the girl (her passage into womanhood).

'Psychoanalysis' is not, therefore, a single entity. Institutional divisions within psychoanalysis have turned on the very questions about the phallocentrism of analysts, the meaning of femininity, the sequence of psychic development and its norms, which have been the concern of feminists. The accusations came from analysts themselves. In the earlier debates, however, the reproach against Freud produced an account of femininity which was more, rather than less, normative than his own.

The politics of Lacanian psychoanalysis begin here. From the 1930s, Lacan saw his intervention as a return to the concepts of psychic division, splitting of the ego, and an endless (he called it 'insistent') pressure of the unconscious against any individual's pretension to a smooth and coherent psychic and sexual identity. Lacan's specific target was 'ego-psychology' in America, and what he saw as the dilution of psychoanalysis into a tool of social adaptation and control (hence the central emphasis on the concepts of the ego and identification which are often overlooked in discussions of his ideas). For Lacan, psychoanalysis does not offer an account of a developing ego which is 'not *necessarily* coherent',[17] but of an ego which is 'necessarily *not* coherent', that

---

[17] Wilson, 'Reopening the Case — Feminism and Psychoanalysis', opening seminar presentation in discussion with Jacqueline Rose, London 1982. This was the first of a series of seminars on the subject of feminism and psychoanalysis which ran into 1983; see articles by Parveen Adams, Nancy Wood and Claire Buck, *m/f* 8, 1983.

is, which is always and persistently divided against itself.

Lacan could therefore be picked up by a Marxist like Althusser not because he offered a theory of adaptation to reality or of the individual's insertion into culture (Althusser added a note to the English translation of his paper on Lacan criticising it for having implied such a reading),[18] but because the force of the unconscious in Lacan's interpretation of Freud was felt to undermine the mystifications of a bourgeois culture proclaiming its identity, and that of its subjects, to the world. The political use of Lacan's theory therefore stemmed from its assault on what English Marxists would call bourgeois 'individualism'. What the theory offered was a divided subject out of 'synch' with bourgeois myth. Feminists could legitimately object that the notion of psychic fragmentation was of little immediate political advantage to women struggling for the first time to find a voice, and trying to bring together the dissociated components of their life into a political programme. But this is a very different criticism of the political implications of psychoanalysis than the one which accuses it of forcing women into bland conformity with their expected role.

Psychoanalysis and History
The History of Psychoanalysis

What, therefore, is the political purchase of the concept of the unconscious on women's lived experience? And what can it say to the specific histories of which we form a part?

One of the objections which is often made against psychoanalysis is that it has no sense of history, and an inadequate grasp of its relationship to the concrete institutions which frame and determine our lives. For even if we allow for a moment the radical force of the psychoanalytic insight, the exclusiveness or limited availability of that insight tends to be turned, not against the culture or state which mostly resists its general (and publicly funded) dissemination,[19] but against psychoanalysis itself. The

[18] Althusser, 'Freud and Lacan', see publisher's note in *Lenin and Philosophy and Other Essays,* London 1971, pp.189-90.

[19] For a more detailed discussion of the relative assimilation of Kleinianism through social work in relation to children in this country, especially through the

'privatisation' of psychoanalysis comes to mean that it only refers to the individual as private, and the concentration on the individual as private is then seen as reinforcing a theory which places itself above history and change.

Again I think that this question is posed back to front, and that we need to ask, not what psychoanalysis has to say about history, but rather what is the history of psychoanalysis, that is, what was the intervention of psychoanalysis into the institutions which, at the time of its emergence, were controlling women's lives? And what was the place of the unconscious, historically, in that? Paradoxically, the claim that psychoanalysis is a-historical dehistoricises it. If we go back to the beginnings of psychoanalysis, it is clear that the concept of the unconscious was radical at exactly that level of social 'reality' with which it is so often assumed to have nothing whatsoever to do.

Recent work by feminist historians is of particular importance in this context. Judith Walkowitz, in her study of the Contagious Diseases Acts of the 1860s, shows how state policy on public hygiene and the state's increasing control over casual labour, relied on a category of women as diseased (the suspected prostitute subjected to forcible examination and internment in response to the spread of venereal disease in the port towns).[20] Carol Dyhouse has described how debates about educational opportunity for women constantly returned to the evidence of the female body (either the energy expended in their development towards sexual reproduction meant that women could not be educated, or education and the overtaxing of the brain would damage their reproductive capacity).[21] In the birth control controversy, the Malthusian idea of controlling the reproduction, and by implication the sexuality, of the working class served to counter the idea that poverty could be reduced by the redistribution of wealth.[22] Recurrently in the second half of the nineteenth century, in the period immediately prior to Freud, female sexuality became

Tavistock Clinic in London, see Rustin, p. 85 and note. As Rustin points out, the state is willing to fund psychoanalysis when it is a question of helping children to adapt, but less so when it is a case of helping adults to remember.

[20] Judith Walkowitz, *Prostitution and Victorian Society — Women, Class and the State*, London and New York 1980.

[21] Carol Dyhouse, *Girls Growing Up in Late Victorian and Edwardian England*, London 1981.

[22] Angus McLaren, *Birth Control in Nineteenth Century England*, London 1978.

the focus of a panic about the effects of industrialisation on the cohesion of the social body and its ability to reproduce itself comfortably. The importance of all this work (Judith Walkowitz makes this quite explicit) is that 'attitudes' towards women cannot be consigned to the sphere of ideology, assumed to have no purchase on material life, so deeply implicated was the concept of female sexuality in the legislative advancement of the state.[23]

Central to all of this was the idea that the woman was wholly responsible for the social well-being of the nation (questions of social division transmuted directly into the moral and sexual responsibility of subjects), or where she failed in this task, that she was disordered or diseased. The hysteric was either the overeducated woman, or else the woman indulging in non-procreative or uncontrolled sexuality (conjugal onanism), or again the woman in the lock hospitals which, since the eighteenth century, had been receiving categories refused by the general hospitals ('infectious diseases, "fever", children, maternity cases, mental disorders, as well as venereal diseases').[24] It was these hospitals which, at the time of the Contagious Diseases Acts, became the place of confinement for the diseased prostitute in a new form of collaborative relationship with the state.

This is where psychoanalysis begins. Although the situation was not identical in France, there are important links. Freud's earliest work was under Charcot at the Salpêtrière Clinic in Paris, a hospital for women: 'five thousand neurotic indigents, epileptics, and insane patients, many of whom were deemed incurable'.[25] The 'dregs' of society comprised the inmates of the Salpêtrière (psychoanalysis does not start in the Viennese parlour). Freud was working under Charcot whose first contribution to the study of hysteria was to move it out of the category of sexual malingering and into that of a specific and accredited neurological disease. The problem with Charcot's work is that while he was constructing the symptomatology of the disease (turning it into a respected object of the medical institution), he was reinforcing it as a special category of behaviour, visible to the eye, and the result of a degenerate hereditary disposition.

[23] Walkowitz, p. 69.
[24] Ibid., p. 59.
[25] Ilza Veith, *Hysteria: the History of a Disease,* London 1975, p. 229.

Freud's intervention here was two-fold. Firstly, he questioned the visible evidence of the disease — the idea that you could know a hysteric by looking at her body, that is, by reading off the symptoms of nervous disability or susceptibility to trauma. Secondly (and this second move depended on the first), he rejected the idea that hysteria was an 'independent' clinical entity, by using what he uncovered in the treatment of the hysterical patient as the basis of his account of the unconscious and its universal presence in adult life.

The 'universalism' of Freud was not, therefore, an attempt to remove the subject from history; it stemmed from his challenge to the category of hysteria as a principle of classification for certain socially isolated and confined individuals, and his shifting of this category into the centre of everybody's psychic experience: 'Her hysteria can therefore be described as an acquired one, and it presupposed nothing more than the possession of what is probably a very wide-spread proclivity — the proclivity to acquire hysteria'.[26] The reason why the two moves are interdependent is because it was only by penetrating behind the visible symptoms of disorder and asking what it was that the symptom was trying to *say*, that Freud could uncover those unconscious desires and motives which he went on to expose in the slips, dreams and jokes of individuals paraded as normal. Thus the challenge to the entity 'hysteria', that is, to hysteria *as* an entity available for quite specific forms of social control, relied on the concept of the unconscious. 'I have attempted', wrote Freud, 'to meet the problem of hysterical attacks along a line other than *descriptive*'.[27] Hence Freud's challenge to the visible, to the empirically self-evident, to the 'blindness of the seeing eye'.[28] (Compare this with Charcot's photographs offered as the evidence of the disease, some of which are reprinted here.) It is perhaps this early and now mostly forgotten moment which can give us the strongest sense of the force of the unconscious as a concept against a fully social classification relying on empirical evidence as its rationale.

The challenge of psychoanalysis to empiricist forms of reasoning was therefore the very axis on which the fully historical

[26] Freud, *Studies on Hysteria*, p.122; p.187.
[27] Freud, 'Preface and Footnotes to Charcot's Tuesday Lectures' (1892-94), SE I, p. 137.
[28] *Studies on Hysteria*, p. 117; p. 181.

intervention of psychoanalysis into late nineteenth-century medicine turned. The theories of sexuality came after this first intervention (in *Studies on Hysteria,* Freud's remarks on sexuality are mostly given in awkward footnotes suggesting the importance of sexual abstinence for women as a causal factor in the etiology of hysteria). But when Freud did start to investigate the complexity of sexual life in response to what he uncovered in hysterical patients, his first step was a similar questioning of social definitions, this time of sexual perversion as 'innate' or 'degenerate', that is, as the special property of a malfunctioning type.[29] In fact, if we take dreams and slips of the tongue (both considered before Freud to result from lowered mental capacity), sexuality and hysteria, the same movement operates each time. A discredited, pathological, or irrational form of behaviour is given its psychic value by psychoanalysis. What this meant for the hysterical woman is that instead of just being looked at or examined, she was allowed to *speak.*

Some of the criticisms which are made by feminists of Freudian psychoanalysis, especially when it is filtered through the work of Lacan, can perhaps be answered with reference to this moment. Most often the emphasis is laid either on Lacan's statement that 'the unconscious is structured like a language', or on his concentration on mental representation and the ideational contents of the mind. The feeling seems to be that the stress on ideas and language cuts psychoanalysis off from the materiality of being, whether that materiality is defined as the biological aspects of our subjectivity, or as the economic factors determining our lives (one or the other and at times both).

Once it is put like this, the argument becomes a version of the debate within Marxism over the different instances of social determination and their hierarchy ('ideology' versus the 'economic') or else it becomes an accusation of idealism (Lacan) against materialism (Marx). I think this argument completely misses the importance of the emphasis on language in Lacan and of mental representation in Freud. The statement that 'the unconscious is structured like a language' was above all part of Lacan's attempt to establish a continuity between the seeming disorder of the symptom or dream and the normal language through which we recognise each other and speak. And the

[29] Freud, *Three Essays on the Theory of Sexuality,* Part 1.

importance of the linguistic sign (Saussure's distinction between the signifier and the signified)[30] was that it provided a model internal to language itself of that form of indirect representation (the body speaking because there is something which cannot be said) which psychoanalysis uncovered in the symptomatology of its patients. Only if one thing can stand for another is the hysterical symptom something more than the logical and direct manifestation of physical or psychic (and social) degeneracy.

This is why the concept of the unconscious — as indicating an irreducible discontinuity of psychic life — is so important. Recognition of that discontinuity in us all is in a sense the price we have to pay for that earlier historical displacement.

Feminism and the Unconscious

It is, however, this concept which seems to be lost whenever Freud has been challenged on those ideas which have been most problematic for feminism, in so far as the critique of Freudian phallocentrism so often relies on a return to empiricism, on an appeal to 'what actually happens' or what can be *seen* to be the case. Much of Ernest Jones's criticism of Freud, for example, stemmed from his conviction that girls and boys could not conceivably be ignorant of so elementary a fact as that of sexual difference and procreation.[31] And Karen Horney, in her similar but distinct critique, referred to 'the manifestations of so elementary a principle of nature as that of the mutual attraction of the sexes'.[32] We can compare this with Freud: 'from the point of view of psycho-analysis the exclusive sexual interest felt by men for women is also a problem that needs elucidating and is not a self-evident fact based upon an attraction that is ultimately of a chemical nature'.[33] The point is not that one side is appealing to 'biology' (or 'nature') and the other to 'ideas', but that Freud's opening premise is to challenge the self-evidence of both.

---

[30] Ferdinand de Saussure, *Cours de linguistique générale* (1915), Paris 1972 (tr. Roy Harris, *Course in General Linguistics,* London 1983, pp.65-70.

[31] Jones, 'The Phallic Phase', p.15.

[32] Horney, 'The Flight from Womanhood' (1926), in *Feminine Psychology,* p. 68.

[33] *Three Essays,* p. 146n; p. 57n.

The feminist criticism of Freud has of course been very different since it has specifically involved a rejection of the evidence of this particular norm: the normal femininity which, in the earlier quarrel, Freud himself was considered to have questioned. But at this one crucial level — the idea of an unconscious which points to a fundamental division of psychic life and which therefore challenges any form of empiricism based on what is there to be observed (even when scientifically tested and tried) — the very different critiques are related. In *Psychoanalysis and Feminism,* Juliet Mitchell based at least half her argument on this point but it has been lost. Thus Shulamith Firestone, arguing in *The Dialectic of Sex* that the girl's alleged sense of inferiority in relation to the boy was the logical outcome of the observable facts of the child's experience, had to assume an unproblematic and one-to-one causality between psychic life and social reality with no possibility of dislocation or error.[34] The result is that the concept of the unconscious is lost (the little girl rationally recognises and decides her fate) and mothering is deprived of its active components (the mother is seen to be only subordinate and in no sense powerful for the child).[35] For all its more obvious political appeal, the idea that psychic life is the unmediated reflection of social relations locks the mother and child into a closed subordination which can then only be broken by the advances of empiricism itself:

> Full mastery of the reproductive process is in sight, and there has been significant advance in understanding the basic life and death process. The nature of ageing and growth, sleep and hibernation, the chemical functioning of the brain and the development of consciousness and memory are all beginning to be understood in their entirety. This acceleraton promises to continue for another century, or however long it takes to achieve the goal of Empiricism: total understanding of the laws of nature.[36]

Shulamith Firestone's argument has been criticised by feminists who would not wish to question, any more than I would, the importance of her intervention for feminism.[37] But I think it is

[34] Shulamith Firestone, *The Dialectic of Sex.*

[35] See Mitchell, 'Shulamith Firestone: Freud Feminised', *Psychoanalysis and Feminism*, Part 2, Section 2, chapter 5.

[36] Firestone, p. 170.

[37] Ibid., introduction by Rosalind Delmar.

important that the part of her programme which is now criticised (the idea that women must rely on scientific progress to achieve any change) is so directly related to the empiricist concept of social reality (what can be *seen* to happen) which she offers. The empiricism of the goal is the outcome of the empiricism at the level of social reality and psychic life. I have gone back to this moment because, even though it is posed in different terms, something similar seems to be going on in the recent Marxist repudiation of Freud. Janet Sayers's critique of Juliet Mitchell, for example, is quite explicitly based on the concept of 'what actually and specifically happens' ('in the child's environment' and 'in the child's physical and biological development').[38]

Utopianism of the Psyche

Something else happens in all of this which is probably the most central issue for me: the discarding of the concept of the unconscious seems to leave us with a type of utopianism of psychic life. In this context it is interesting to note just how close the appeal to biology and the appeal to culture as the determinants of psychic experience can be. Karen Horney switched from one to the other, moving from the idea that femininity was a natural quality, subject to checks, but tending on its course, to the idea that these same checks, and indeed most forms of psychic conflict, were the outcome of an oppressive social world. The second position is closer to that of feminism, but something is nonetheless missing from both sides of the divide. For what has happened to the unconscious, to that divided and disordered subjectivity which, I have argued, had to be recognised in us all if the category of hysteria as a peculiar property of one class of women was to be disbanded? Do not both of these movements make psychic conflict either an accident or an obstacle on the path to psychic and sexual continuity — a continuity which, as feminists, we recognise as a myth of our culture only to reinscribe it in a different form on the agenda for a future (post-revolutionary) date?

Every time Freud is challenged, this concept of psychic cohesion as the ultimate object of our political desires seems to return. Thus the French feminist and analyst, Luce Irigaray,

[38] Sayers quoted by Wilson in 'Reopening the Case'.

challenges Lacan not just for the phallocentrism of his arguments, but because the Freudian account is seen to cut women off from an early and untroubled psychic unity (the primordial state of fusion with the mother) which feminists should seek to restore. Irigaray calls this the 'imaginary' of women (a reference to Lacan's idea of a primitive narcissism which was for him only ever a fantasy). In a world felt to be especially alienating for women, this idea of psychic oneness or primary narcissism has its own peculiar force. It appears in a different form in Michèle Barrett's and Mary McIntosh's excellent reply to Christopher Lasch's thesis that we are witnessing a regrettable decline in the patriarchal family.[39] Responding to his accusation that culture is losing its super-ego edge and descending into narcissism, they offer the particularly female qualities of mothering (Chodorow) and a defense of this very 'primary narcissism' in the name of women against Lasch's undoubtedly reactionary lament. The problem remains, however, that whenever the 'feminine' comes into the argument as a quality in this way we seem to lose the basic insight of psychoanalysis — the failure or difficulty of femininity for women, and that fundamental psychic division which in Freud's work was its accompanying and increasingly insistent discovery. If I question the idea that psychoanalysis is the 'new orthodoxy' for feminists, it is at least partly because of the strong political counterweight of this idea of femininity which appears to repudiate both these Freudian insights together.

To return to the relationship between Marxism and psychoanalysis with which I started, I think it is relevant that the most systematic attack we have had on the hierarchies and organisation of the male Left[40] gives to women the privilege of the personal in a way which divests it *(has* to divest it) of complexity at exactly this level of the conflicts and discontinuities of psychic life. Like many feminists, the slogan 'the personal is political' has been central to my own political development; just as I see the question of sexuality, as a political issue which *exceeds* the province of Marxism ('economic', 'ideological' or whatever), as one of the most important defining characteristics of feminism

[39] Michèle Barrett and Mary McIntosh, 'Narcissism and the Family: A Critique of Lasch', *New Left Review* 135, September-October 1982.

[40] Sheila Rowbotham, Lynne Segal and Hilary Wainright, *Beyond the Fragments — Feminism and the Making of Socialism,* London 1979.

itself. But the dialogue between feminism and psychoanalysis, which is for me the arena in which the full complexity of that 'personal' and that 'sexuality' can be grasped, constantly seems to fail.

In this article, I have not answered all the criticisms of psychoanalysis. It is certainly the case that psychoanalysis does not give us a blueprint for political action, or allow us to deduce political conservatism or radicalism directly from the vicissitudes of psychic experience. Nor does the concept of the unconscious sit comfortably with the necessary attempt by feminism to claim a new sureness of identity for women, or with the idea of always conscious and deliberate political decision-making and control (psychoanalysis is *not* a voluntarism).[41] But its challenge to the concept of psychic identity is important for feminism in that it allows into the political arena problems of subjectivity (subjectivity *as* a problem) which tend to be suppressed from other forms of political debate. It may also help us to open up the space between different notions of political identity — between the idea of a political identity for feminism (what women require) and that of a feminine identity for women (what women are or should be), expecially given the problems constantly encountered by the latter and by the sometimes too easy celebration of an identity amongst women which glosses over the differences between us.

Psychoanalysis finally remains one of the few places in our culture where our experience of femininity can be spoken as a problem that is something other than the problem which the protests of women are posing for an increasingly conservative political world. I would argue that this is one of the reasons why it has not been released into the public domain. The fact that psychoanalysis cannot be assimilated directly into a political programme as such does not mean, therefore, that it should be discarded, and thrown back into the outer reaches of a culture which has never yet been fully able to heed its voice.

[41] Sayers, pp. 92-93.

4

George Eliot and
the Spectacle of the Woman

Two moments of horror stand out in *Daniel Deronda* for the way
they echo each other across the text, a horror which resides as
much in the fact of their repetition as in the story they tell. In the
first, Gwendolen Harleth plays a game of charades and, suddenly
confronted by a picture of a dead face and a fleeing figure in a
panel, she freezes into an image of terror 'like a statue into which a
soul of Fear had entered'.[1] Much later in the book, Gwendolen
is brought to the jetty after the drowning of her husband,
Grandcourt, and, rising from the boat 'pale as one of the sheeted
dead', 'seemed to shrink with terror'.[2] The second episode fulfils
the image of the first: Grandcourt becomes the dead face
('a dead face — I shall never get away from it'/'his
dead face is there and I cannot bear it'/'I cannot bear
his dead face'[3]) and Gwendolen the figure who flees. The
repetition therefore has a moral purpose; it signals that
the moment could have been anticipated as the fulfillment
of a moral judgement, one to which Gwendolen will
increasingly submit: 'as if she had waked up in a world where some

[1] George Eliot, *Daniel Deronda*, London 1876, Harmondsworth 1967, p. 91 (all
references to the Penguin edition). This essay, written for this collection, was
presented in February 1986 at Oxford University as part of a series of lectures for a
new course, 'Women's Writing 1780-1980', introduced into the Oxford English
degree this year.
[2] Ibid., p. 750.
[3] Ibid., p. 753, 758.

judgement was impending'.[4]

The two moments also echo each other in the form of their physicality, the image of the crazed woman which they produce: 'her pallid lips were parted; her eyes, usually narrowed under their long lashes, were dilated and fixed',[5] 'shivering, with wet hair streaming, a wild amazed consciousness in her eyes'.[6] Gwendolen's eyes are at the centre of a spectacle which is met in turn by the controlling gaze of the man: Herr Klesmer in the first instance and then Daniel Deronda himself ('her wandering eyes fell on Deronda ... as if she had been expecting him and looking for him').[7] Thus Gwendolen's fear 'terrifying in its terror'[8] is received by the male spectator and completes itself in the place of the one who looks. The overlap between the fear and the spectacle (fear as spectacle) is then given a further twist in the first episode when Gwendolen, seeking to impress Herr Klesmer with her art, tries to pass off the crisis as part of the performance, as something merely presented for the benefit of the watching man.

In the charade, Gwendolen plays the role of Hermione in *The Winter's Tale*. It is at the point where the statue steps down from the imitation of death into life that Gwendolen freezes back in terror into the image of a statue herself ('like a statue into which a soul of Fear had entered'[9]). The moment works like a reverse-motion shot in the cinema which will be developed half a century later as a central technique of the special effect. In the episode with Gwendolen, the technique of reversal allows the character, like Shakespeare's Hermione, to pass back and forwards between the state of the living and the dead. Likewise, when Gwendolen appears to Deronda on the jetty, alive after her husband's death, she rises in the boat 'pale like one of the sheeted dead'.[10] Spectacle becomes a life-and-death matter in which the distinction between the two states of being is lost: Hermione returning from the dead, Gwendolen surviving the drowning of her husband but as a ghost. Who is guilty in these moments? These near murders produce an effect of doubling which — alongside the apparent certainty of

[4] Ibid., p. 750.
[5] Ibid., p. 91.
[6] Ibid., p. 750.
[7] Ibid.
[8] Ibid., p. 91.
[9] Ibid.
[10] Ibid., p. 750.

judgement — leaves the question of responsibility in suspense. Rather it is the dramatic staging, the spectacle itself, to which the story seems ineluctably to return.

In both of these episodes, George Eliot contradicts her own commentary at an earlier point in the book: 'For Macbeth's rhetoric about the impossibility of being many opposite things in the same moment referred to the clumsy necessities of action and not to the subtler possibilities of feeling. We cannot speak a loyal word and be meanly silent, we cannot kill and not kill in the same moment; but a moment is room wide enough for the loyal and mean desire, for the outlash of a murderous thought and the sharp backward stroke of repentance.'[11]

To kill and not kill in a clumsy, necessitous action fairly describes the drama of *The Winter's Tale* as much as the drowning of Grandcourt. Unlike Hermione, Grandcourt dies. Gwendolen does not kill him, but she does not save him and, along the lines of the finest discrimination, that is enough — in her judgement at least — to condemn her.

This is not the first time that George Eliot has taken her strange commandment ('we cannot kill and not kill in the same moment') and staged it. In chapter 15 of *Middlemarch*, the narrator offers to 'make the new settler Lydgate better known to anyone interested in him than he could possibly be even to those who had seen the most of him since his arrival in Middlemarch'.[12] Better knowledge is ultimately hidden knowledge, the story of Lydgate's early passion for the stage actress Madame Laure whom he would 'go and look at' for his 'only relaxation', 'just as he might have thrown himself under the breath of the sweet south on a bank of violets for a while'.[13] The sweetness of that breath and that look turn sour, however, when Madame Laure, whose husband plays the part of the lover she kills in the play, 'veritably stabbed her husband, who fell as death willed'.[14] Vindicated by the courts, she is then pursued with increasing passion by Lydgate to the point of her confession: '*I meant to do it*'.[15] Gwendolen also confesses to Deronda: 'I saw

[11] George Eliot, *Middlemarch,* London 1871-72, Harmondsworth 1965, p. 72 (all references to the Penguin edition).

[12] Ibid., pp. 170-171.

[13] Ibid., p. 180.

[14] Ibid.

[15] Ibid., p. 182.

my wish outside me'.[16] The narrator comments: 'a question as to the outward effectiveness of a criminal desire dominant enough to impel even a momentary act, cannot alter our judgement of the desire', but Deronda himself 'shrinks' from that question. He decides that it is only Gwendolen's remorse after the fact which so brutally gives the character of a 'decisive action' to the 'inappreciably instantaneous glance of desire'.[17]

Stabbing and drowning — what is instantaneous in the glance of desire is the violence of an act, an act which resides only, or so purely, in its intention. The 'glance of desire' stands for that fleeting moment, which suspends and decides the character's relation to the event, while also receiving its other meaning from the gaze of the male onlooker who, in each of these episodes, comes to meet it. Only in the first episode from *Middlemarch* does the spectacle assign to the man and the woman the transparent roles of a historical sexual division — the woman actress and the infatuated man of science — but the same structure persists in the episodes of Eliot's later book. From the professional stage to the charade of the drawing room to the final tragic event, the spectacle works its way insidiously into the body of the narrative. In *Middlemarch* it carries its secret shamefully on the outskirts of the story as a performance which, like Lydgate, we as readers take time out to see. But it returns in *Daniel Deronda* to the heart of the central female character's experience.

The scrutiny of the woman and her guilt which all three episodes have in common clearly bears the weight of another question. 'To kill and not kill' evokes another predicament, that of knowing and not knowing, that is, the predicament of a knowledge which can never be complete. This is the dilemma expressed at the start of that same chapter 15 of *Middlemarch* when the narrator offers a better, truer knowledge of Lydgate to the reader, while also recognising that a man is most often 'only a cluster of signs for his neighbour's false suppositions'.[18] Only a fictional character can be totally known. But if knowledge is of the order of fiction, then the certainty of knowledge itself starts to fail. The relentless scrutiny of the woman and her guilt can then be seen as a type of logical response to this failing. Guilty or not guilty, the

---

[16] *Daniel Deronda*, p. 761.
[17] Ibid., p. 762.
[18] *Middlemarch*, p. 171.

question of the woman's sexuality transposes the problem of the limits of knowledge into the form of a judgement.

Freud will later give a name to this problem of knowledge by identifying it as nothing less than the division of being itself. Fräulein Elizabeth von R., the first full-length analysis of a hysteria undertaken by Freud, is in the 'peculiar situation of knowing and at the same time not knowing'.[19] Recognition of this mechanism in the genesis of the hysterical symptom leads Freud to the concept of the unconscious which first appears here as the repository of (guilty) sexual feelings but which shifts in the course of this work to the more formal sign of a division, or *Spaltung,* at the heart of consciousness itself. To not know one's sexual history, to not want to know it, indicates a crime that the hysteric has *not* in fact committed other than in the 'glance of desire'. But desire itself now stands for a conflict of affect and knowledge which no moral judgement can resolve. If Freud's move is from the sexuality of the woman to the necessary failure of a knowledge or consciousness which would control either the woman or itself, George Eliot's move can be seen as logically going back in the opposite direction: from a problem of knowing at the heart of language and fiction to the drama of a woman's sexual crime.

In his attempt to describe the 'strange state of mind in which one knows and does not know a thing at the same time', Freud writes of the 'blindness of the seeing eye'.[20] The act of looking which is so central to the investigation of the woman in these moments of Eliot's writing is put into crisis by psychoanalysis which sees the immediately visible as a lure or seduction — a seduction embodied by the woman in the story of Madame Laure in *Middlemarch* and of which she finds herself accused. After the episode, which was in any case only a moment out for Lydgate from his study of galvanism ('Lydgate's only relaxation now was to go and look at this woman ... without prejudice to his galvanism, to which he would presently return'[21]), Lydgate resolves to take a 'strictly scientific view of woman'.[22] The lure of the visible is countered by the vision of science which knows and therefore controls its object. Lydgate will in fact be mistaken again

[19] Freud, *Studies on Hysteria,* p. 16.
[20] Ibid., p.117; p. 181.
[21] *Middlemarch,* p. 180.
[22] Ibid., p. 183.

in his judgement of a woman, but that failure is charted by Eliot as a fall from his true status and vocation as a visionary man of science. The woman stands, therefore, for a corruption of the visible and a degradation of the scientific pursuit of truth. The woman deceives, but she is *easy*: 'hidden actresses are not so difficult to find as some other hidden facts'.[23]

In chapter 15 of *Middlemarch*, Eliot shows how the question of female sexuality and the question of science are implicated in each other. For if that link can be read backwards now through Freud, it belongs even more to the scientific models which precede him. Lydgate's science is part of the new anatomical pathology derived from Bichat which, instead of seeing bodies as 'federal' associations of organs to be studied individually or apart, sought out a 'fundamental knowledge of structure' from the primary webs or tissues out of which the organs are made. This primary web, together with the painstaking quest through the 'threads of investigation' which leads to it, is the model for George Eliot's writing (the 'woven and interwoven' threads of 'human lots') as well as for her conception of character itself ('for character too is a process and an unfolding').[24] The unfolding of the moral self historically associated with her form of the novel is lifted in part from the paradigm of the new nineteenth-century science.[25] Lydgate's research follows this paradigm: 'he was ambitious above all to contribute towards enlarging the scientific, rational basis of his profession'.[26] But the very chapter which most clearly states this ambition — of character and writer alike — also reveals its opposite, that is, a form of looking at the woman that suddenly tips over into complicity with a sexual crime. Chapter 15 of *Middlemarch* suggests, therefore, that the controlling knowledge of science is threatened, but also guaranteed — upheld even — by the image of a female sexuality gone wild.

In *Daniel Deronda* too, there is the same quest, the same search after a true knowledge, which runs alongside the gradual

[23] Ibid., p. 181.

[24] Ibid., pp. 170-178.

[25] For a full discussion of George Eliot's relationship to nineteenth-century science, specifically Social Darwinism, see Gillian Beer, *Darwin's Plots: Evolutionary Narrative in Darwin, George Eliot and Nineteenth Century Fiction*, London 1983.

[26] *Middlemarch*, p. 177.

emergence of the guilt of a woman. Gwendolen learns from that guilt and grows through it, at the same time as Deronda uncovers his true history, which means the founding of an organic centre for all cultures (compare Lydgate: 'what was the primitive tissue?')[27] and the securing of his patrilineal descent. The two progressions, of the man and the woman, mimic each other in reverse (it has often been pointed out that he seems to get the better deal). But this later narrative merely gives a more moralised and refined version of the link between male truth and a woman's failing revealed so starkly and symptomatically in the earlier book. With this difference, that in *Daniel Deronda* it is the degeneracy of the whole social body that is now in need of repair.

The wider culture sees the same relationship between the sexual morality of the woman and social decay. It displays the same link between the scrutiny of female sexuality and the authority of the new forms of social investigation and science. For this was the period when anxiety about social cohesion and class difference was expressed in the emergent language of sanitation, social hygiene and moral reform. A generalised moralisation of the political sphere which found its natural and inevitable focus in the woman. The supremacy of the woman's moral nature and her potential degeneracy were the twin poles of a representation which had already transposed a panic about the social body — its ordered regulation and self-reproduction — into moral terms. And to the extent that female sexuality was answerable for that regulation as much as for its demise, so the image of the woman's moral purity always harboured within it that of female vice.

The most blatant example of this process were the Contagious Diseases Acts of the 1860s which allowed for the arrest, medical inspection and confinement of any woman suspected of being a prostitute in the port towns.[28] A piece of unmistakeable legal discrimination against women, the acts were publicly fought and finally repealed. As a form of systematic policing, the acts brought whole areas of unorganised labour under the surveillance of the state. As a historic collaboration between the legislature and medical institutions, they gave that surveillance — through their focus on the woman — the most concrete and grotesque of

[27] Ibid., p. 178.
[28] See Judith Walkowitz, *Prostitution and Victorian Society.*

physical shapes. William Acton, leading medical and social reformer, demonstrates most clearly the sexual fantasy underpinning the new emphasis on moral investigation and reform: 'It is time to burst through the veil of that artificial bashfulness which has injured the growth, while it has affected the features of genuine purity. Society has suffered from that spurious modesty which lets fearful forms of vice swell to rank luxuriousness, rather than point at their existence — which coyly turns its head away from the "wounds and putrefying sores" that are eating into our system, because it would have to blush at the exposure.'[29]

Something has to be looked at which has not been looked at before, vice must be rooted out, and the woman must be inspected, because — according to a seemingly logical sequence — it is the woman who is the immediate and visible cause of social decay ('the law cannot deal with remote causes ... whether man's vice or woman's is the cause that prostitution exists is a very wide question ... prostitutes are the direct, *visible* cause of the prevalence of syphilis'.)[30] The prostitute therefore becomes the publicly sanctioned image against which society measures its moral consciousness of self. But if morality is a sexual matter, it is not just because of the reference to the prostitute and the explicit discourse of purity and vice. It is also because of the sexual fantasy, the relentless and punishing scrutiny of the woman, which supports it. In the second half of the nineteenth century, morality makes a spectacle of itself.

Across a range of discourses this spectacle repeats itself, each time calling attention to a sexualisation which resides in the very act of looking, at the precise point where that sexuality is being most rigorously stamped out or denied. The pornographer royal, Henry Ashbee, merely gives the most dramatic inflation of that scenario when he compares his own activity as a collector of the literary taboo with the forms of investigation legitimated by the new science: 'As little, it is my belief, will my book excite the passions of my readers, as would the naked body of a woman, extended on the dissecting table, produce concupiscience in the

[29] William Acton, *A Practical Treatise on Diseases of the Urinary and Generative Organs,* 2nd ed., London 1851, p. 2.
[30] Acton, *The Contagious Diseases Act — Shall the Contagious Diseases Act be applied to the civilian population,* London 1870, pp. 31-32.

minds of the students assembled to witness the operation performed upon her.'[31]

The same perversion of the look, which sanitises and sanctifies itself with reference to the new science.

In this context, George Eliot's implication in nineteenth-century social discourse takes on a special significance, one not adequately covered by the idea of erudition (that breadth of learning and awareness most often used to counter any assumed deficiency of the female writer). For the discourses of medicine and the law which surface in the body of George Eliot's texts are not sexually innocent. They bring with them specific consequences at the level of sexual representation, in much the same way as Matthew Arnold's writings on culture, which are also latent in her writing, have their own (largely reactionary) political objectives and effects. More than a question of influence however (the idea of a simple determination which passes to the literary from its outside), what is at issue here is the manifestation in literary and non-literary writing alike of an imaginary structure which constitutes the woman as its stake. Whether symptomatically in the drama of Madame Laure or centrally in the dilemma of Gwendolen Harleth, George Eliot's writing reveals that same scenario which focuses its anxiety on the sexuality of the woman and makes her the privileged object of investigation and control. The moral examination of female psychology — in which we classically locate the depth of George Eliot's fully human perception — is therefore doubly contaminated. By the sexual fantasy which supports it as well as by all the questions about social inequality and misery which this attention directed at the woman serves to displace. We can recall Brecht's criticism of the nineteenth-century novel — that it concentrated a whole history in the moral consciousness of an individual as if this was the place where history was best examined or resolved — and add to that criticism a sexual question or gloss. For in whose consciousness, historically, has that morality been invested? Or, more precisely, whose morality, that of the man or the woman, has been seen as the *sum total* of their history, making them answerable for, yet also sharply excluded from, the vaster expanses of historical time? Gwendolen's moral journey, Deronda's historical quest, not only mime a classic sexual paradigm or distribution of identities, they

---

[31] Henry S. Ashbee, *Index librorum prohibitorum*, London 1877, p. 1xx.

also show the sexual division which lies at the heart of morality itself.

At the same time, we can recognise the other side of the stereotype — the sanctity which is so close to its counter-image of degeneracy and potential vice. For the line which runs from culpability to moral self-awareness is a fully sexual trajectory which can be crossed in either direction. Even the prostitute can be described in terms of moral self-sacrifice, even a criminal sexuality can be evoked in the image of the religious devotee: 'There is in the warm fond heart of a woman a strange and sublime unselfishness, which men too commonly discover only to profit by, — a positive love of self-sacrifice, — an active, so to speak, an *aggressive* desire to show their affection, by giving up to those who have won it something they hold very dear. It is an unreasoning and dangerous yearning of the spirit, precisely analogous to that which prompts the surrenders and self-tortures of the religious devotee.'[32]

This could be a descripton of the spiritual yearnings of a Dorothea Brooke. More strongly still, the prostration of the woman offered here once again so blatantly as spectacle prefigures the '*attitudes passionelles*' of Charcot's hysterical patients whose images will be frozen and immortalised half a century later in the *Iconographie photographique de la Salpêtrière*.[33] Saint Theresa was the patron saint of hysteria (the analogy with Dorothea Brooke is made explicit by the narrator of *Middlemarch* in the preface to the book). But when Freud and Breuer point this out in 1895, they will have turned their attention away from the seduction of the image, away from the morality it was used to enshrine, to the problem of sexual and linguistic identity which the emphasis on image and morality together covers over and denies.

For if spectacle is stereotype, it is equally, and perhaps even more crucially, language and narrative form. The morality which aims to control its (female) object can only ever speak from the

[32] Acton, *Prostitution, considered in its moral, social and sanitary aspects, in London and other large cities, with proposals for the mitigation and prevention of its attendant evils*, London 1857, p.20. Acton's image of the woman shifted neatly across to the other side of the stereotype in response to later agitation to repeal the Acts: 'It is not liberty, but wanton licence. It is not freedom, but lawless indulgence', *The Contagious Diseases Act*, p. 32.

[33] P. Regnard Bourneville, *Iconographie photographique de la Salpêtrière*, (Service de M. Charcot), Paris 1876-78 (see Huberman, *Invention de l'hysterie, Charcot et l'iconographie photographique de la Salpêtrière*, Paris 1982).

place where total knowledge is assumed to be possible, which meant for so many of the dominant writers of this moment the increasingly unstable but still hegemonic language of the bourgeoisie. What was being asked of the woman therefore was that sexuality and language should be refined. At moments the controversy over female sexual license seemed to resolve itself into a debate about the proper linguistic form. When a Mr. Taylor published a pamphlet defending women against the Contagious Diseases Acts, it was attacked by Acton not for its argument but for its style:

> On the Contagious Diseases Act —
> WOMEN NOT ANIMALS
> showing how the new act debases women,
> debauches men, destroys the liberty of the subject,
> and tends to increase Disease.
>
> How strangely do these frantic sentences compare with the extract I have already quoted from the last report of the House of Commons: 'Prostitution appears to have diminished, its worst features to have been softened, and its physical evils abated'.[34]

The corruption of female sexuality and the corruption of the language went together; they leant each other support. The cohesion of the moral body requires the cleaning up of language and of the woman at the same time. Female sexuality becomes answerable, therefore, for something which is felt as a sexual and linguistic debasement. Not by chance Freud will remove the moral indictment of the woman at the same moment that he asks what it means to constitute oneself with such unswerving certainty in language, whether public discourse or everyday speech.

It is in terms such as these that I think it makes sense to talk of the hysterisation of the body of the woman in the second half of the nineteenth century, at that moment when George Eliot published her last novel only ten years before the earliest writings of Freud. It is generally recognised that George Eliot is a transitional writer, especially with reference to *Daniel Deronda* in which the narrative cohesion of a work like *Middlemarch* founders in mimicry of the social disintegration at the heart of English culture. That

---

[34] *The Contagious Diseases Act*, p. 19.

disintegration throws up a Gwendolen who could perhaps be defined as the original literary hysteric, but the spectacle and scrutiny of the woman was already there in *Middlemarch* in the shape of Madame Laure, and running alongside it at the very centre of the novel, the reference to hysteria was already present, albeit in a muted form, in the shape of Dorothea Brooke. But if Dorothea is saved from the worst violence of this scenario, that might be because Madame Laure is there to save her, to siphon off the real anxiety around the woman, the vanishing-point of tension in the text. Only to have it return — spectacularly — in the troubled and troubling figure of Gwendolen Harleth: 'Was she beautiful or not beautiful? and what was the secret of form or expression which gave the dynamic quality to her glance? Was the good or evil genius dominant in those beams?'[35]

From the very opening lines of the narrative in *Daniel Deronda,* the reader is implicated, with no possibility of distance, in a panic about the meaning of the woman. The disintegration of Gwendolen, the breakdown of the novel's own form, start *together* at the moment when the reader is constituted as spectator vis-à-vis a woman whose ultimate decipherment could be said to be the overriding objective of the book. The disturbance of the feminine is bound into the very form of the narrative as the narrator starts by taking up the place of the man, miming perhaps,[36] inflating certainly, the voyeurism which constitutes the woman as spectacle. The first lines of *Daniel Deronda* show the moral categories of good and evil emerging in response to a *need* for judgement, a judgement which might settle the disturbance posed by the woman to the one who looks. As if desire lights upon its object, finds itself disarmed and then punishes the woman for the upset produced. Only a woman whose charm leaves the onlooker's own identity intact can escape the weight of a condemnation which has been decided almost before the question has been put: 'Probably the evil; else why was the effect that of unrest rather than of undisturbed charm? Why was the wish to look again felt as coercion and not as a longing in which the whole being

---

[35] *Daniel Deronda*, p. 35.

[36] Mary Jacobus discusses Eliot's implication in negative images in terms of miming and mimicry in 'The Question of Language: Men of Maxims and *The Mill on the Floss*', in Elizabeth Abel ed., *Writing and Sexual Difference,* Chicago and Brighton 1982.

consents?'[37]

Deronda's restlessness, his search for a historic fulfillment and completion in which his 'whole being' could 'consent' is already projected onto a woman who, long before the revelation of the Princess Halm-Eberstein, is made answerable for a disturbance of male equipoise. The hysterisation of the woman resides in this scenario, generated by the very form of the narrative itself.

The transition from *Middlemarch* to *Daniel Deronda*, so often commented on as a breakdown or relinquishment of the more coherent novel form, turns therefore on a shift in the representation of the woman at the level of narrative voice. Eliot discards the distance of 'history': 'Miss Brooke had that sort of beauty which seems to be thrown into relief by poor dress' (the first lines of the narrative of *Middlemarch*), for a form of 'discourse' which implicates the narrator in the story: 'Was she beautiful or not beautiful?'. But the narrator who has lost that safe distance only to become entangled in the web of the story is a man, and the fall from narrative omnipotence is caused by a woman who will later be compared by one of her spectators to a serpent: 'Woman was tempted by a serpent: why not man?'.[38] The tale of temptation and loss of grace is latent to the process of the writing. In these famous opening lines of *Daniel Deronda*, George Eliot could be seen as bringing to fruition a structure of fantasy which greatly exceeds the domain of the novel, in which the man and the woman are distributed between the two poles of spectacle and the tale of female sexuality becomes the ultimate story to be told because — as is so clear in this instance — she has already been made the cause of a crisis in the act of telling itself.

Gwendolen's psychic distress, something which can be catalogued in relation to this novel as a list of her symptoms, comes in response to this structure which is given from the very opening lines of the book. The woman is by definition troubled because the category of female sexuality has *already* been constituted as disturbance at this level of narrative form.

---

[37] *Daniel Deronda*, p. 35.

[38] Ibid., p. 41; the narrator qualifies: 'The remark that Gwendolen wound her neck about more than usual this evening was true. But it was not that she might carry out the serpent idea more completely: it was that she watched for any chance of seeing Deronda, so that she might inquire about this stranger, under whose measuring gaze she was still wincing'. (pp. 41-42.)

Gwendolen's poetry and criminality ('As if all the most poetic criminals were not women!'); her agoraphobia (her tremor when alone and 'there came some rapid change in the light'; her sense of helplessness in response to 'solitude in any wide scene'); her aversion ('I can't love people. I hate them'); the hysteria of intensity with which she responds to Lydia Glasher's curse ('screamed again and again with hysterical violence') — all of these gradually accumulate into the image of a frozen terror which exceeds any one cause the narrative might offer and which simply receives its sharpest physical image in the charade and on the jetty.[39] As if George Eliot were distending the spectacle of the woman to the logical point of its most total horror and underscoring its perversion. 'What is being asked of the woman?' — the query reveals itself behind the more obvious question charted by this, and so many other, narratives: 'What does a woman want?'

In all of this, the narrator's own position is as divided as the impossible injunction ('kill and not kill') on which the narrative drama finally turns (the opening identification with the man simply makes that more clear). That passage about contradiction comes precisely at the end of a dilemma of assessment vis-à-vis the woman, a lengthy discussion of how to judge a woman (Gwendolen) whose 'potent charm' affects all who see her. But that same charm is immediately suspect, and in the middle of the paragraph, after celebrating it for the reader, the narrator veers to the other side. Charm turns to a coercion which stems from the 'inborn energy of egoistic desire' and 'power of inspiring fear'.[40] It is this problem of fixing the identity of a woman, of judging the origins of her power, that then drives the narrator headlong into the realm of violent contraries — 'to kill and not kill' — which the story will finally enact. Rather than argue that George Eliot is criticising or merely reproducing a set of stereotyped images of femininity, we should perhaps notice the undecideability, the oscillation at the level of narrative identity itself which the problem of assessing the woman, of positioning oneself in relation to her representation, seems to provoke. If mastery and hysteria go together, with the second unleashed by the overcontrolled assertion of the first, then to insist on the coherence of George

[39] Ibid., pp. 85, 94-95, 115, 407.
[40] Ibid., pp. 71-72.

Eliot's own position in relation to these images is to repeat the very mechanism which engenders the disturbance of Gwendolen Harleth in the book.

But the same observation raises problems for a form of assessment which would now celebrate the internal self-deconstruction of the text.[41] For the tension between certainty and failure of judgement, as it reveals itself emblematically in the passage about Gwendolen, is a tension in which the issue of female sexuality is at stake. The division between Gwendolen's and Deronda's story is a false one, not just because the moralism of the second is challenged by the irony or rhetoric of the first, but also because the search for a sureness of identity relies on the disturbance of the woman to give it form. The incompatibility of the two halves can be heralded as the collapse of self-knowledge of the (any) text, but they lock back into each other at the point of sexual division. Gwendolen's hysteria serves to halt, even as it exposes, the ceaseless dispersal of the text. Thus what has so often been recognised as the tension of the writing can only be grasped with reference to a structure of fantasy in which all the basic terms of knowledge, mastery and hysteria, later to be theorised by Freud, already play themselves out. If this text performs, it does so *sexually*, calling up in that process a whole history of representation which weaves its way back and forwards across the literary and the non-literary text. This is why the image of a woman subjected to a panic-stricken and ceaseless scrutiny seems to me to be of such central importance. Because it reveals so-called historical discourse to be implicated in a fantasy at the heart of literary form, and literature itself to be caught up in the most pernicious of social images and codes in the very process of writing. Gwendolen Harleth is there as the price of a breakdown felt within these two orders, of representation and culture, together. If George Eliot's last novel can only resolve that felt crisis by a journey off the edge of English culture (Deronda's quest), she is not alone in looking back to the woman and asking her to make good that other social degeneration through a renewal of the moral self.

A question remains about the 'illness' of the woman in this late

[41] See, in particular, Cynthia Chase, 'The Decomposition of the Elephants: Double-Reading *Daniel Deronda*', *PMLA* 93:2, March 1978.

nineteenth-century text, about where it leaves George Eliot as a writer and us as readers of the text. In the anthology *Writing and Sexual Difference,* Elaine Showalter discusses this problem of the negative representation of women found in so many nineteenth-century texts: 'The nineteenth century woman inscribed her own sickness, her madness, her anorexia, her agoraphobia, and her paralysis in her texts'.[42] The reference is to Gilbert and Gubar's *The Madwoman in the Attic,*[43] but Showalter's point is that there is a danger of complicity between a strategy of reading which identifies these instances of disturbance and a damaging image of femininity itself. This moment in the article expresses a type of crisis in feminist criticism which looks to women's writing for the signs of a revolt against this condition (the assertion of another femininity) or else can only repeat that condition as a truth about women of which the wider culture is then accused. The sickness of the woman in George Eliot's writing seems, however, to break against both of these models, offering itself as neither complicity nor transcendent judgement, since the hysteria of the woman is given as a fantasy of the man at the same time as George Eliot qua narrator implicates herself so directly in the perversity, and even pleasure, of its process. We seem to sanitise the very concept of fantasy when we allow to the woman who writes only two positions — subordination to the stereotype or release into the freedom of writing from its weight. Yet could it not also be — and at the risk of troubling the concept of an *écriture feminine* — that, suspending her relation to the very fact of sexual identity, the woman equally uses writing to *masquerade*?[44]

To ask George Eliot to be a woman or a man in this context (which has also been described as the question of the hysteric) is impossible for reasons which go way beyond the question of the

[42] Elaine Showalter, 'Feminist Criticism in the Wilderness' in *Writing and Sexual Difference,* p. 25.

[43] Sandra Gilbert and Susan Gubar, *The Madwoman in the Attic,* New Haven 1979.

[44] The key psychoanalytic text here would be Joan Rivière's 'Womanliness as Masquerade'. The crucial text by George Eliot herself is *The Lifted Veil,* which has just been reprinted by the feminist publishing house, Virago (London 1985). First brought to attention by Gilbert and Gubar in *The Madwoman in the Attic,* it is written in the voice of a first person male narrator who recounts retrospectively how he telepathised his own destruction by the woman who is the object of his desire.

pseudonym through which Marian Evans — partly, one can assume, for merely functional reasons — expressed the ambiguity of her role. For the question of sexual identity is seen to founder in the very place of the narrator in this problematic late nineteenth-century text. The attendant fantasy of a patriarchal lineage regained, in all its desperation, has been criticised for its incredibility as writing as much as for the irreality of its project and even split off from the rest of the book.[45] Yet that very desperation (the extravagent boldness of resolution and critical reaction alike) merely testifies to its own impossibility, at the same time as we have to recognise that it is in some sense sponsored, not to say heralded, by the overall drive of the book.

We cannot decide George Eliot's position as a writer in this scenario, any more than we can place her definitively on the side of the novel's attempts at self-assertion or its undoing. But the formal question carries a more explicitly feminist question when we see that the divisions of the writing in its own relationship to itself work across the paradigm of sexual difference and have an image of femininity so centrally at stake. This question is nothing less than the question of our own implication as readers in a structure and images which we challenge even as they bear down upon, and at moments seduce, us all.

Showalter argues for the difference of women's writing (women's writing *as* different) and opposes this to the myth of a 'serenely undifferentiated universality of texts', suggesting that the fact of women's experience should be set against the utopian notion of a writing where there would be no difference left at all — that fantasy of universality which has always turned out historically to leave women in second place.[46] But to problematise the category of women's experience in writing is not to slip back into a universalist (masculine) domain. Rather it is to show how writing in itself undermines, even as it rehearses at its most glaring, the very model of sexual difference itself. In this context, the category of sexual difference is not a 'code word for post-feminism' or a 'reason for not talking about women'.[47] It refers

[45] F.R. Leavis's famous move in *The Great Tradition,* London 1948.

[46] 'Feminist Criticism in the Wilderness', p. 35.

[47] Elaine Showalter, 'Shooting the Rapids: Feminist Criticism in the Mainstream', paper presented to the third Theory and Text Conference, *Sexual Difference,* Southampton University 1985, *Oxford Literary Review* 8:1-2, 1986, p. 222.

neither to a realm untouched by sexual division, nor to one in which the identity of a woman would guarantee her relation to the text. Rather it belongs to that part of feminism which sees it as crucial to ask of George Eliot, and by implication ourselves, the question generated but not answered by her writing: what it means to assert oneself unequivocally as either a woman or a man.

5
Hamlet —
the 'Mona Lisa' of Literature

It does not seem to have been pointed out that T. S. Eliot's famous concept of the 'objective correlative', which has been so influential in the assessment of literature and its values, was originally put forward in 1919 in the form of a reproach against the character of a woman.[1] The woman in question is Gertrude in Shakespeare's *Hamlet*, and the reproach Eliot makes is that she is not good enough aesthetically, that is, *bad* enough psychologically, which means that in relationship to the affect which she generates by her behaviour in the chief character of the drama — Hamlet himself — Gertrude is not deemed a sufficient *cause*.

The question of femininity clearly underpins this central, if not indeed *the* central, concept of Eliot's aesthetic theory, and this is confirmed by the fact that Eliot again uses an image of femininity — and by no means one of the most straightforward in its own representation or in the responses it has produced — to give us the measure of the consequent failure of the play. *Hamlet* the play, Eliot writes, is 'the Mona Lisa of literature',[2] offering up in its essentially enigmatic and indecipherable nature something of that

[1] T. S. Eliot, *'Hamlet'* (1919), in *Selected Prose of T. S. Eliot,* ed. Frank Kermode, London 1975. This essay was first presented as a talk at the Pembroke Center for Teaching and Research on Women, Brown University, 1984; printed in *Critical Quarterly,* Autumn 1986; a different version appeared as 'Sexuality in the reading of Shakespeare: *Hamlet* and *Measure for Measure'* in *Alternative Shakespeares,* ed. John Drakakis, London and New York 1985.

[2] *'Hamlet'*, p. 47.

maimed or imperfect quality of appeal which characterises Leonardo's famous painting. The aesthetic inadequacy of the play is caused by the figure of a woman, and the image of a woman most aptly embodies the consequences of that failure. Femininity thus becomes the stake, not only of the internal, but also of the critical drama generated by the play.

Equally important, however, is the fact that femininity has been at the heart of the psychoanalytic approach to *Hamlet*, from Ernest Jones onwards — a fact which has again been overlooked by those who have arrested their attention at the famous Oedipal saga for which his reading of the play is best known. 'Hamlet was a woman'[3] is just one of the statements about *Hamlet* which Jones quotes as indicating the place of the 'feminine' in a drama which has paradoxically been celebrated as the birth of the modern, post-Renaissance, conception of man. In this essay, I will try to focus what I see as the centrality of this question of femininity to an aesthetic theory which has crucially influenced a whole tradition of how we conceptualise literary writing, and to the psychoanalytic theory which was being elaborated at exactly the same time, at the point where they converge on the same object — Shakespeare's *Hamlet* — described by Freud as an emblem of 'the secular advance of repression in the emotional life of mankind'.[4]

I

To start with T. S. Eliot's critique of *Hamlet*. T. S. Eliot in fact sees his reading of the play as a move away from psychological approaches to *Hamlet* which concentrate too much on the characters to the exclusion of the play itself: '*Hamlet* the play is the primary problem, and Hamlet the character only secondary'.[5] Eliot therefore makes it clear that what he has to say exceeds the fact of the dramatic personae and strikes at the heart of aesthetic form itself. The problem with *Hamlet* is that there is something in the play which is formally or aesthetically unmanageable: 'like the *Sonnets*' (another work by Shakespeare in which a question of sexual ambivalence has always been recognised) '*Hamlet* is full of

---

[3] Ernest Jones, *Hamlet and Oedipus* (1949), New York 1954, p. 88.

[4] Freud, *The Interpretation of Dreams*, p. 264; p. 366.

[5] '*Hamlet*', p. 45.

some stuff that the writer could not drag to light, contemplate, or manipulate into art'.[6] Eliot then describes the conditions, as he sees it, of that in which *Hamlet* fails — the successful manipulation of matter into artistic form. It is here that he produces the concept of the 'objective correlative' for the first time: 'The only way of expressing emotion in the form of art is by finding an 'objective correlative'; in other words, a set of objects, a situation, a chain of events which shall be the formula of that *particular* emotion; such that when the external facts ... are given, the emotion is immediately evoked .... The artistic 'inevitability' lies in this complete adequacy of the external to the emotion'.[7]

Emotion, or affect, is therefore only admissable in art if it is given an external object to which it can be seen, clearly and automatically, to correspond. There must be nothing in that emotion which spills over or exceeds the objective, visible (one could say conscious) facts, no residue or trace of the primitive 'stuff' which may have been the original stimulus for the work of art. This is where *Hamlet* fails: Hamlet the man is dominated by an emotion which is inexpressible, because it is in *excess* of the facts as they appear. And that excess is occasioned by Gertrude who precipitates Hamlet into despondency by her 'o'er hasty' marriage to his dead father's brother and successor, who turns out also to have been the agent of the former king's death. For Eliot, Gertrude is not an adequate equivalent for the disgust which she evokes in Hamlet, which 'envelopes and exceeds her'[8] and which, because she cannot adequately contain it, runs right across the fabric of the play. Gertrude is therefore disgusting, but not quite disgusting *enough*. Eliot is, however, clear that he is not asking for a stronger woman character on the stage, since he recognises that it is in the nature of the problem dealt with in this play — a son's feelings towards a guilty mother — that they should be in excess of their objective cause. On this count, Gertrude's inadequacy turns around and becomes wholly appropriate: 'it is just *because* her character is so negative and insignificant that she arouses in Hamlet the feeling which she is incapable of representing'.[9]

What is at stake behind this failing of the woman, what she fails

6 Ibid., p. 48.
7 Ibid.
8 Ibid.
9 Ibid., pp. 48-49.

to represent, therefore, is precisely unrepresentable — a set of unconscious emotions which, *by definition,* can have no objective outlet and which are therefore incapable of submitting to the formal constraints of art. What we get in *Hamlet* instead is 'buffoonery' — in Hamlet himself the 'buffoonery of an emotion which can find no outlet in action', for the dramatist the 'buffoonery of an emotion which he cannot express in art'.[10] Such 'intense', 'ecstatic' (Gertrude uses the word 'ecstasy' to describe Hamlet's madness in the bedchamber scene of the play) and 'terrible' feeling is for Eliot 'doubtless a subject of study for the pathologist' and why Shakespeare attempted to express the 'inexpressibly horrible' we cannot ever know, since we should have finally 'to know something which is by hypothesis unknowable and to understand things which Shakespeare did not understand himself'.[11]

Today we can only be struck by the extraordinary resonance of the terms which figure so negatively in Eliot's critique — buffoonery, ecstasy, the excessive and unknowable — all terms in which we have learnt to recognise (since Freud at least) something necessarily present in any act of writing (*Hamlet* included) which only suppresses them — orders them precisely into form — at a cost. Eliot's criticism of *Hamlet* can therefore be turned around. What he sees as the play's weakness becomes its source of fascination or even strength.

In this context, the fact that it is a woman who is seen as cause of the excess and deficiency in the play and again a woman who symbolises its aesthetic failure starts to look like a repetition. Firstly, of the play itself — Hamlet and his dead father united in the reproach they make of Gertrude for her sexual failing ('O Hamlet what a falling off was there'), and *horror* as the exact response to the crime which precedes the play and precipitates its drama ('O horrible! O horrible! most horrible!').[12] Secondly, a repetition of a more fundamental drama of psychic experience itself as described by Freud, the drama of sexual difference in which the woman is seen as the cause of just such a failure in representation, as something deficient, lacking or threatening to

[10] Ibid., p. 49.
[11] Ibid..
[12] William Shakespeare, *Hamlet*, 1,v, 47 and 1,v, 80. All references to the Arden Shakespeare unless otherwise specified.

the system and identities which are the precondition not only of integrated artistic form but also of so-called normal adult psychic and sexual life. Located by Freud at the point where the woman is first seen to be different,[13] this moment can then have its effects in that familiar mystification or fetishisation of femininity which makes of the woman something both perfect and dangerous or obscene (obscene if *not* perfect). And perhaps no image has evoked this process more clearly than that of the 'Mona Lisa' itself, which at almost exactly this historical moment (the time of Freud and Eliot alike) started to be taken as the emblem of an inscrutable femininity, cause and destination of the whole of human mystery and its desires: 'The lady smiled in regal calm: her instincts of conquest, of ferocity, all the heredity of the species, the will to seduce and to ensnare, the charm of deceit, the kindness that conceals a cruel purpose — all this appeared and disappeared by turns behind the laughing veil and buried itself in the poem of her smile. Good and wicked, cruel and compassionate, graceful and feline she laughed.'[14]

By choosing an image of a woman to embody the inexpressible and inscrutable context which he identified in Shakespeare's play, Eliot ties the enigma of femininity to the problem of interpretation itself: 'No one has solved the riddle of her smile, no one has read the meaning of her thoughts', 'a presence ... expressive of what in the way of a thousand years men had come to desire'.[15] Freud himself picks up the tone in one of his more problematic observations about femininity when he allows that critics have recognised in the picture 'the most perfect representation of the contrasts which dominate the erotic life of women; the contrast between reserve and seduction, and between the most devoted tenderness and a sensuality that is ruthlessly demanding — consuming men as if they were alien beings'.[16]

What other representation, we might ask, has so clearly produced a set of emotions without 'objective correlative', that is, in excess of the facts as they appear? T. S. Eliot's reading of *Hamlet*

[13] Freud 'The Dissolution of the Oedipus Complex'; 'Some Psychical Consequences of the Anatomical Distinction Between the Sexes'.

[14] Angelo Conti, cit. Freud, 'Leonardo da Vinci and a Memory of his Childhood' (1910), SE 11, p. 109; PF 14, p. 201.

[15] Muther and Walter Pater, cit. in ibid., pp. 108, 110; pp. 200, 202.

[16] Ibid., p. 108; p. 200.

would therefore seem to suggest that what is in fact felt as inscrutable, unmanageable or even horrible (ecstatic in both senses of the term) for an aesthetic theory which will only allow into its definition what can be controlled or managed by art is nothing other than femininity itself.

At the end of Eliot's essay, he refers to Montaigne's 'Apologie of Raymond Sebond' as a possible source for the malaise of the play. Its discourse on the contradictory, unstable and ephemeral nature of man has often been seen as the origin of Hamlet's suicide soliloquy; it also contains an extraordinary passage anticipating Freud where Montaigne asks whether we do not live in dreaming, dream when we think and work, and whether our waking merely be a form of sleep.[17] In relation to the woman, however, another smaller essay by Montaigne — 'Of Three Good Women' — is equally striking for the exact reversal which these three women, models of female virtue, represent vis-à-vis Gertrude herself in Shakespeare's play, each one choosing self-imposed death at the point where her husband is to die.[18] The image is close to the protestations of the Player Queen in the Mousetrap scene of *Hamlet* who vows her undying love to her husband; whereupon Gertrude, recognising perhaps in the Player Queen's claims a rebuke or foil to her own sexual laxness, comments 'The lady doth protest too much'[19] (a familiar cliché now for the sexual 'inconstancy' of females). So what happens, indeed, to the sexuality of the woman, when the husband dies, who is there to hold its potentially dangerous excess within the bounds of a fully social constraint? This could be seen as one of the questions asked by *Hamlet* the play and generative of its terrible effect.

Before going on to discuss psychoanalytic interpretations of *Hamlet*, it is worth stressing the extent to which Eliot's theory is shot through with sexuality in this way and its implications for recent literary debate. Taking their cue from psychoanalysis, writers like Roland Barthes and Julia Kristeva have seen the very stability of the sign as index and pre-condition for that myth of linguistic cohesion and sexual identity which we must live by but

[17] John Florio, tr., *The Essays of Michael, Lord of Montaigne* (1603), London and New York 1885, pp. 219-310.
[18] Ibid., pp. 378-382.
[19] *Hamlet*, III, ii, 225.

under whose regimen we suffer.[20] Literature then becomes one of the chief arenas in which this struggle is played out. Literary writing which proclaims its integrity, and literary theory which demands that integrity (objectivity/correlation) of writing, merely repeat that moment of repression when language and sexuality were first ordered into place, putting down the unconscious processes which threaten the resolution of the Oedipal drama and of narrative form alike. In this context, Eliot's critical writing, with its stress on the ethical task of writer and critic, becomes nothing less than the most accomplished (and influential) case for the interdependency and centrality of language and sexuality to the proper ordering of literary form. Much recent literary theory can be seen as an attempt to undo the ferocious effects of this particularly harsh type of literary super-ego — one whose political repressiveness in the case of Eliot became more and more explicit in his later allegiance to Empire, Church and State.

Eliot himself was aware of the areas of psychic danger against which he constantly brushed. He was clear that he was touching on 'perilous' issues which risk 'violating the frontier of consciousness', and when he talks of writing as something 'pleasurable', 'exhausting', 'agitating', as a sudden 'breakdown of strong habitual barriers', the sexuality of the writing process which he seeks to order spills over into the text.[21] And Eliot's conception of that order, what he sees as proper literary form, is finally an Oedipal drama in itself. In his other famous essay 'Tradition and the Individual Talent', which was written in the same year as the '*Hamlet*' essay, Eliot states that the way the artist can avoid his own disordered subjectivity and transmute it into form is by giving himself up to something outside himself and surrendering to the tradition that precedes and surrounds him. Only by capitulating to the world of dead poets can the artist escape his oppressive individuality and enter into historical time: 'Set [the artist] for

---

[20] See, in particular, Roland Barthes, 'La mythologie aujourd'hui', *Esprit* 1971 (tr. Stephen Heath, 'Change the Object itself', *Image, Music, Text,* London 1977) and *S/Z*, Paris 1970 (tr. Richard Miller, *S/Z,* London and New York 1974); Julia Kristeva, *La révolution du langage poétique,* Paris 1974 (excerpts from Part I of this book have been translated in *The Kristeva Reader,* ed. Toril Moi, forthcoming Oxford 1986).

[21] T. S. Eliot, 'The Use of Poetry and the Use of Criticism' (1933), in *Selected Prose,* pp. 92, 89.

contrast and comparison among the dead' for 'the most individual parts of his work are those in which the dead poets, his ancestors, assert their immortality most vigourously'.[22] Thus, just as in the psychoanalytic account, the son pays his debt to the dead father, symbol of the law, in order fully to enter his history, so in Eliot's reading the artist pays his debt to the dead poets and can only become a poet by that fact. Eliot's conception of literary tradition and form could therefore be described as a plea for appropriate mourning and for the respecting of literary rites — that mourning whose shameful inadequacy, as Jacques Lacan points out in his essay on *Hamlet*,[23] is the trigger and then constant refrain of the play: the old Hamlet cut off in the 'blossom' of his sin; Polonius interred 'hugger mugger'; Ophelia buried wrongly — because of her suicide — in consecrated ground.

In Eliot's reading of *Hamlet*, therefore, the sexuality of the woman seems to become the scapegoat and cause of the dearth or breakdown of Oedipal resolution which the play ceaselessly enacts, not only at the level of its theme, but also in the disjunctions and difficulties of its aesthetic form. Much has been made of course of the aesthetic problem of *Hamlet* by critics other than Eliot, who have pondered on its lack of integration or single-purposiveness, its apparent inability to resolve itself or come to term (it is the longest of Shakespeare's plays), much as they have pondered on all these factors in the character of Hamlet himself.

Hamlet poses a problem for Eliot, therefore, at the level of both matter and form. Femininity is the image of that problem; it seems in fact to be the only image through which the problem can be conceptualised or thought. The principal danger, femininity thus becomes the focus for a partly theorised recognition of the psychic and literary disintegration which can erupt at any moment into literary form.

One more example, and perhaps the most graphic, can serve to illustrate how far femininity is implicated in this aesthetic theory — the lines which Eliot uses from Tourneur's *The Revenger's Tragedy* to describe the artist surrendering to his inspiration before ordering it into form:

[22] T. S. Eliot, 'Tradition and the Individual Talent' (1919), in ibid., p. 38.
[23] Lacan, 'Desire and the interpretation of desire in *Hamlet*' in Felman ed., *Literature and Psychoanalysis*.

And now methinks I could e'en chide myself
For doating on her beauty, though her death
Shall be revenged after no common action.
Does the silkworm expend her yellow labours
For thee? For thee does she undo herself?
Are lordships sold to maintain ladyships
For the poor benefit of a bewildering minute?
Why doth yon fellow falsify highways,
And put his life between the judge's lips,
To refine such a thing — keeps horse and men
To beat their valours for her?[24]

For a play that has also been discussed as excessive and perhaps even more than *Hamlet,* this moment gives the strongest measure of that excess. The speech is made by Vindice, the Revenger, to the skull of his former mistress who was poisoned by the Duke for resisting his advances. His revenge takes the form of wrapping this skull in the full bodied attire of the woman and dowsing its mouth with poison so that the Duke will first be seduced and then poisoned in its embrace. In this crazed image, the woman appears at once as purity and lust, victim and destroyer, but the split representation shows how the feminine can serve as a receptacle for a more fundamental horror of sexuality and death. Femininity becomes the place in which man reads his destiny, just as the woman becomes a symptom for the man.[25]

Likewise in *Hamlet*, these two themes — of death and sexuality — run their course through the play, both as something which can be assimilated to social constraint and as a threat to constraint and to the social altogether. For *Hamlet* can be seen as a play which turns on mourning and marriage — the former the means whereby death is given its symbolic form and enters back into social life, the latter the means whereby sexuality is brought into the orbit of the law. When *Hamlet* opens, however, what we are given is *too much* of each (perhaps this is the excess) — too much mourning (Hamlet wears black, stands apart, and mourns beyond the natural term) and too much marriage (Gertrude passes from one husband to another too fast). As if these two regulators of the furthest edges of social and civil life, if they become overstated, if there is too much of them, tip over into their opposite and start to look like what

[24] Tourneur, cit. in 'Tradition and the Individual Talent', p. 42.
[25] Lacan, 'Seminar of 21 January, 1975', p. 168.

they are designed to hold off. Eliot's essay on *Hamlet*, and his writing on literature in general, gives us a sense of how these matters, which he recognises in the play, underpin the space of aesthetic representation itself and how femininity figures crucially in that conceptualisation.

II

If Eliot's aesthetic theories move across into the arena of sexuality, Ernest Jones's psychoanalytic interpretation of *Hamlet* turns out also to be part of an aesthetic concern. His intention is to use psychoanalysis to establish the integrity of the literary text, that is, to uncover factors, hidden motives and desires, which will give back to rational understanding what would otherwise pass the limits of literary understanding and appreciation itself: 'The perfect work of art is one where the traits and reactions of the character prove to be harmonious, consistent and intelligible when examined in the different layers of the mind'.[26] Jones's reading, therefore, belongs to that psychoanalytic project which restores to rationality or brings to light, placing what was formerly unconscious or unmanageable under the ego's mastery or control. It is a project which has been read directly out of Freud's much contested statement '*Wo Es war, soll Ich werden*', translated by Strachey 'Where id was, there ego shall be'.[27] Lacan, for whom the notion of such conscious mastery is only ever a fantasy (the fantasy of the ego itself) retranslates or reverses the statement: 'There where it was, so I must come to be'.[28]

For Jones, as for Eliot, therefore, there must be no aesthetic excess, nothing which goes beyond the reaches of what can ultimately be deciphered and known. In this context, psychoanalysis acts as a key which can solve the enigma of the text, take away its surplus by offering us as readers that fully rational understanding which Shakespeare's play — Jones recognises like Eliot — places at risk. The chapter of Jones's book which gives the Oedipal reading of *Hamlet*, the one which tends to be included in

[26] '*Hamlet*', p. 49.

[27] Freud, 'The Dissection of the Psychical Personality', *New Introductory Lectures* (1932), SE 22, p. 80; PF 2, p. 112.

[28] Lacan, 'The Agency of the Letter in the Unconscious', p.171 (translation modified).

the anthologies of Shakespeare criticism, is accordingly entitled 'The psychoanalytic solution'.[29] Taking his reference from Freud's comments in *The Interpretation of Dreams*,[30] Jones sees Hamlet as a little Oedipus who cannot bring himself to kill Claudius because he stands in the place of his own desire, having murdered Hamlet's father and married his mother. The difference between Oedipus and Hamlet is that Oedipus unknowingly acts out this fantasy, whereas for Hamlet it is repressed into the unconscious revealing itself in the form of that inhibition or inability to act which has baffled so many critics of the play. It is this repression of the Oedipal drama beneath the surface of the text which leads Freud to say of *Hamlet*, comparing it with Sophocles's drama, that it demonstrates the 'secular advance of repression in the emotional life of mankind'.[31]

But Jones's book and the psychoanalytic engagement with *Hamlet* does not stop there and it is finally more interesting than this Oedipal reading which, along with Jones's speculations on Hamlet's childhood and Shakespeare's own life, has most often been used to discredit them. For while it is the case that Jones's account seems to fulfil the dream of any explanatory hypothesis by providing an account of factors which would otherwise remain unaccountable, a closer look shows how this same reading infringes the interpretative and sexual boundaries which, like Eliot, it seems to be putting into place.

The relationship of psychoanalysis to *Hamlet* has in fact always been a strange and repetitive one in which Hamlet the character is constantly given the status of a truth, and becomes a pivot for psychoanalysis and its project, just as for Eliot *Hamlet* is the focal point through which he arrives at a more general problem of aesthetic form. For Freud, for instance, Hamlet is not just Oedipus, but also melancholic and hysteric, and both these readings, problematic as they are as diagnoses of literary characters, become interesting because of the way they bring us up against the limits of interpretation and sexual identity alike. The interpretative distinction between rationality and excess, between normality and abnormality, for example, starts to crumble when

---

[29] See, for example, Laurence Lerner ed., *Shakespeare's Tragedies, An Anthology of Modern Criticism*, Harmondsworth 1963.

[30] *The Interpretation of Dreams*, pp. 264-266; pp. 364-368.

[31] Ibid., p. 264; p. 366.

the melancholic is defined as a madman who also speaks the truth. Freud uses *Hamlet* with this meaning in 'Mourning and Melancholia' written in 1915: 'We only wonder why a man has to be ill before he can be accessible to a truth of this kind. For there can be no doubt that if anyone holds an opinion of himself such as this (an opinion which Hamlet holds of himself and of everyone else) he is ill, whether or not he is speaking the truth or whether he is being more or less unfair to himself.'[32]

Taken in this direction, *Hamlet* illustrates not so much a failure of identity as the precarious distinction on which this notion of identity rests. In 'Psychopathic Characters on the Stage', Freud includes *Hamlet* in that group of plays which rely for their effect on the neurotic in the spectator, inducing in her or him the neurosis watched on stage, crossing over the boundaries between onstage and offstage and breaking down the habitual barriers of the mind.[33] A particular *type* of drama, this form is nonetheless effective only through its capacity to implicate us *all*: 'A person who does not lose his reason under certain conditions can have no reason to lose'.[34] Jones makes a similar point and underscores its fullest social import when he attributes the power of *Hamlet* to the very edge of sanity on which it moves, the way that it confuses the division which 'until our generation (and even now in the juristic sphere) separated the sane and the responsible from the irresponsible insane'.[35] T. S. Eliot also gave a version of this, but from the other side, when he described poetry in 'Tradition and the Individual Talent' as an escape from emotion and personality, and then added 'but, of course, only those who have personality and emotion can know what it means to want to escape from these things'.[36] So instead of safely diagnosing Hamlet, his Oedipal drama, his disturbance, and subjecting them to its mastery and control, the psychoanalytic interpretation turns back onto spectator and critic, implicating the observer in those forms of irrationality and excess which Jones and Eliot in their different ways seek to order into place.

Calling Hamlet a hysteric, which both Freud and Jones also

[32] Freud, 'Mourning and Melancholia' (1915), SE 14, pp. 246-247; PF 11, p. 255.

[33] Freud, 'Psychopathic Characters on the Stage' (1905 or 1906), SE 7.

[34] Lessing, cit. in ibid., p. 30n.

[35] Jones, p. 70.

[36] '*Hamlet*', p. 43.

do,[37] has the same effect in terms of the question of sexual difference, since it immediately raises the question of femininity and upsets the too tidy Oedipal reading of the play. Freud had originally seen the boy's Oedipal drama as a straightforward desire for the mother and rivalry with the father, just as he first considered the little girl's Oedipal trajectory to be its simple reverse. The discovery of the girl's pre-Oedipal attachment to the mother led him to modify this too easy picture in which unconscious sexual desires in infancy are simply the precursors in miniature of the boy's and the girl's later appropriate sexual and social place.[38] We could say that psychoanalysis can become of interest to feminism at the point where the little girl's desire for the father can no longer be safely assumed. But equally important is the effect that this upset of the original schema has on how we consider the psychic life of the boy. In a section called 'Matricide' normally omitted from the anthologies, Jones talks of Hamlet's desire to kill, not the father, but the mother.[39] He takes this from Hamlet's soliloquy before he goes to his mother's bedchamber in Act III, scene ii of the play:

> Let not ever
> The soul of Nero enter this firm bosom;
> Let me be cruel, not unnatural.
> I will speak daggers to her, but use none.[40];

and also from Gertrude's own lines 'What wilt thou do? Thou wilt not murder me? Help! Ho!'[41] (the murder of Polonius is the immediate consequence of this). Thus desire spills over into its opposite and the woman becomes guilty for the affect which she provokes.

This is still an Oedipal reading of the play since the violence towards the mother is the effect of the desire for her (a simple passage between the two forms of excess). But the problem of desire starts to trouble the category of identification, involving

[37] Freud, *The Origins of Psychoanalysis,* letters to Wilhelm Fliess, Drafts and Notes, 1887-1902, ed. Marie Bonaparte, Anna Freud and Ernst Kris, London 1954, p. 224; Jones, p. 59.
[38] Freud, 'Female Sexuality'.
[39] Jones, chapter 5, pp. 105-114.
[40] *Hamlet*, III, ii, 384-387.
[41] Ibid., III, iv, 20-21.

Jones in a discussion of the femininity in man (not just desire *for* the woman but identification *with* her), a femininity which has been recognised by more than one critic of the play.[42] Thus on either side of the psychoanalytic 'solution', we find something which makes of it no solution at all. And Hamlet, 'as patient as the female dove',[43] becomes Renaissance man only to the extent that he reveals a femininity which undermines that fiction. Femininity turns out to be lying behind the Oedipal drama, indicating its impasse or impossibility of resolution, even though Freud did himself talk of its dissolution, as if it suddenly went out of existence altogether. But this observation contradicts the basic analytic premise of the persistence of unconscious desire.

The point being not whether Hamlet suffers from an excess *of* femininity, but the way that femininity itself functions *as* excess — the excess of this particular interpretative schema (hence presumably its exclusion from the summaries and extracts from Jones), and as the vanishing-point of the difficulties of the play. And in this, Ernest Jones outbids T. S. Eliot vis-à-vis the woman: 'The central mystery [of Hamlet] has well been called the Sphinx of modern literature'.[44] The femininity of Hamlet is perhaps finally less important than this image of the feminine which Jones blithely projects onto the troubled and troubling aesthetic boundaries of the play.

III

If the bad or dangerous woman is aesthetic trouble, then it should come as no surprise that the opposite of this disturbance — an achieved aesthetic or even creativity itself — then finds its most appropriate image again in femininity, but this time its reverse: the good enough mother herself. As if completing the circuit, André

---

[42] Jones, pp. 88, 106. The concept of femininity in relation to Hamlet's character appears again in Marilyn French, *Shakespeare's Division of Experience*, London 1982, p. 149 and in David Leverenz, 'The Woman in *Hamlet*: an interpersonal view', in *Representing Shakespeare, New Psychoanalytic Essays*, eds. Murray M. Schwarz and Coppélia Kahn, Baltimore and London 1980.

[43] *Hamlet*, V,i,281. The image of the female dove was objected to by Knight as a typographical error in the Variorum edition of the play, ed. H. H. Furness, 15th ed., Philadelphia 1877, Part 1, p. 410n.

[44] Jones, pp. 25-26.

Green turns to D.W. Winnicott's concept of the maternal function as the basis for his recent book on *Hamlet*.[45] Femininity now appears as the very principle of the aesthetic process. Shakespeare's Hamlet forecloses the femininity in himself, but by projecting onto the stage the degraded and violent image of a femininity repudiated by his character, Shakespeare manages to preserve in himself that other femininity which is the source of his creative art: 'Writing *Hamlet* had been an act of exorcism which enabled its author to give his hero's femininity — cause of his anxieties, self-reproaches and accusations — an acceptable form through the process of aesthetic creation .... By creating *Hamlet,* by giving it representation, Shakespeare, unlike his hero, managed to lift the dissociation between his masculine and feminine elements and to reconcile himself with the femininity in himself.'[46]

The reading comes from Winnicott's paper 'Creativity and its Origins', which ends with a discussion of Shakespeare's play.[47] It is a fully psychological reading of the author, but its interest once again lies in the way that femininity moves and slips across the different levels of the text and the analytic process — the enigma and source of the analysis as of the play. More clearly and explicitly for Winnicott than for the other writers discussed so far, it is aesthetic space itself that is conceptualised in terms of sexual difference and the place of femininity within that. Creativity *per se* (the creativity in all of us — so this is not just the creativity of the artist) arises for Winnicott out of a femininity which is that primordial space of being which is created by the mother alone. It

[45] In *Hamlet et HAMLET*, Paris 1982, André Green continues the work he began in *Un oeil en trop*, Paris 1969, (tr. Alan Sheridan, *Tragic Effect: Oedipus Complex and Tragedy*, Cambridge 1979) on the psychoanalytic concept of representation in relation to dramatic form, and argues that, while the explicit themes of *Hamlet* (incest, parricide, madness) have the clearest links with the concerns of psychoanalysis, the play's central preoccupation with theatrical space and performance also falls within the psychoanalytic domain through the concept of psychic representation and fantasy. Green examines the way that theatricality, or show, and femininity are constantly assimilated throughout the play (I, ii, 76ff, II, ii, 581ff, III, i, 50ff). In the remarks which follow, I concentrate on the concept of femininity which he sets against this negative assimilation in his final section on Shakespeare's creative art (pp. 25-62).

[46] *Hamlet et HAMLET*, p. 256.

[47] D. W. Winnicott, 'Split-off male and female elements found clinically in men and women' (1966), *Psychoanalytic Forum*, ed. J. Linden, New York 1972.

is a state of being which is not yet a relationship to the object because there is as yet no self, and it is, as Green defines it, *'au-dela de la représentation'*, the other side of representation, before the coming of the sign (this comes very close to French feminists such as Luce Irigaray on femininity and language[48]). But it is worth noting how the woman appears at the point either where language and aesthetic form start to crumble or else where they have not yet come to be. 'Masculinity does, femininity is' is Winnicott's definition. It took a sceptical analyst in the audience when Winnicott first presented the paper to point to its fully literary and mythical origin; it transpires that Winnicott had been reading Robert Graves' 'Man does, Woman is', but the observation from the floor was not included when Winnicott's famous paper was subsequently published in his book.[49]

Winnicott's definition, like Green's, and like that of Eliot before them, once again starts to look like a repetition (one might ask what other form of analysis can there be?) which reproduces or repeats the fundamental drama of *Hamlet*, cleaving the image of femininity in two, splitting it between a degradation and an idealisation which, far from keeping each other under control (as Green suggests), set each other off, being the reverse sides of one and the same mystification. And like Eliot, Green also gets caught in the other face of the idealisation, the inevitable accusation of Gertrude: 'Is the marriage of Gertrude consequence or cause of the murder of Hamlet's father? I incline towards the cause (*Je pencherai pour la cause*)'.[50] And at the end of his book he takes off on a truly wild speculation which makes Gertrude the stake in the battle between the old Fortinbras and the old Hamlet before the start of the play.

But the fact that *Hamlet* constantly unleashes an anxiety which

[49] See especially Luce Irigaray, *Speculum of the Other Woman,* and Michèle Montrelay, 'Inquiry into Femininity'.

[49] Winnicott first presented this paper to the British Psycho-Analytic Society in 1966 under the title 'Split-off male and female elements found clinically in men and women: theoretical inferences' (see note 47 above). It was then included in *Playing and Reality,* London 1971. The discussion of sexual difference in the paper as a whole is far more complex and interesting than the final descent (ascent) into mythology which is addressed here, although it is this concept of femininity, with its associated emphasis on mothering, which has recently been imported directly into psychoanalytic readings of Shakespeare (see especially Leverenz and the whole anthology in which the article appears).

[50] *Hamlet et HAMLET,* p. 61.

returns to the question of femininity tells us above all something about the relationship of aesthetic form and sexual difference, about the fantasies they share — fantasies of coherence and identity in which the woman appears repeatedly as both wager and threat. 'Fantasy in its very perversity' is the object of psychoanalytic interpretation,[51] but this does not mean that psychoanalysis might not also repeat within its own discourse the fantasies, or even perversions, which it uncovers in other forms of speech.

In Lacan's own essay on *Hamlet*, he puts himself resolutely on the side of the symbolic, reading the play in terms of its dearth of proper mourning and the impossibility for Hamlet of responding to the too literal summons of the dead father who would otherwise represent for the hero the point of entry into his appropriate symbolic place (the proximity between this essay and Eliot's 'Tradition and the Individual Talent' is truly striking). Lacan therefore places the problem of the play in the symbolic, on the side of the father we might say; Green in the 'before' of representation where the mother simply *is*. The difference between them is also another repetition, for it is the difference between the law of the father and the body of the mother, between symbol and affect (one of Green's best known books in France was an account of the concept of 'affect' in Freud and a critique of Lacan's central premise that psychic life is regulated by the exigencies of representation and the linguistic sign).[52] But it is a difference with more far-reaching implications, which reconnect with the question of the fantasy of the woman and her guilt with which this essay began. For the concentration on the mother, on her adequacies and inadequacies, was the development in psychoanalytic theory itself which Lacan wanted to redress, precisely because, like *Hamlet*, it makes the mother cause of all good and evil, and her failings responsible for a malaise in all human subjects, that is in men *and* in women, which stems from their position in the symbolic order of culture itself. The problem of the regulation of subjectivity, of the Oedipal drama and the ordering of language and literary form — the necessity of that regulation and its constant difficulty or failing — is not, to put it at its most simple, the woman's fault.

[51] Lacan, 'Desire and the interpretation of desire in *Hamlet*', p. 14.
[52] Green, *Le discours vivant, le concept psychanalytique de l'affect,* Paris 1973.

Finally, therefore, a question remains, one which can be put to André Green when he says that Shakespeare saved his sanity by projecting this crazed repudiation of the feminine onto the stage, using his art to give it 'an acceptable form'.[53] To whom is this acceptable? Or rather what does it mean to us that one of the most elevated and generally esteemed works of our Western literary tradition should enact such a negative representation of femininity, or even such a violent repudiation of the femininity in man? I say 'esteemed' because it is of course the case that Eliot's critique has inflated rather than reduced *Hamlet*'s status. In 'Tradition and the Individual Talent', Eliot says the poet must 'know' the mind of Europe;[54] *Hamlet* has more than once been taken as the model for that mind. Western tradition, the mind of Europe, Hamlet himself — each one the symbol of a cultural order in which the woman is given too much and too little of a place. But it is perhaps not finally inappropriate that those who celebrate or seek to uphold that order, with no regard to the image of the woman it encodes, constantly find themselves up against a problem which they call femininity — a reminder of the precarious nature of the certainties on which that order rests.

[53] *Hamlet et HAMLET,* p. 256.
[54] 'Tradition and the Individual Talent', p. 39.

6
Julia Kristeva — Take Two

In an article published in 1975, Julia Kristeva wrote: 'The symbolic order is assured as soon as there are images which secure unfailing belief, for belief is in itself the image: both arise out of the same procedures and through the same terms: *memory, sight and love...*'.[1] The article appeared in a special issue of *Communications* on *Psychoanalysis and the Cinema* which marked a type of turning-point within semiotics when psychoanalysis was brought to bear on the cultural analysis of the sign. Cinema was central to that shift because it so clearly rested on the twin axes of identification and fantasy — mechanisms built into the very structure of the apparatus and then merely given their most appropriate and predictable content, bodied forth as it were, in Hollywood's endless sagas of love. Writing on identification, Freud had put love and hypnosis together because of the idealisation, subjection, compliance and sapping of initiative which they are capable of inducing in the

[1] Julia Kristeva, 'Ellipse sur la frayeur et la séduction spéculaire', *Communications,* special issue *Psychanalyse et Cinéma,* 23, 1975, p. 77, (my italics) (tr. Dolores Burdick, 'Ellipsis on Terror and The Specular Seduction', *Wide Angle* 3: 2, 1979). This essay was first presented as a paper at the 'Feminism/Theory/Politics' Conference held at the Pembroke Center for Teaching and Research on Women, Brown University, in March 1985; it will also be published in the papers of the Conference. It was written in part as a response to Ann Rosalind Jones, 'Kristeva on Femininity: The Limits of a Semiotic Politics', *Feminist Review* 18, November 1984.

subject.[2] In view of which, Julia Kristeva's latest book — *Histoires d'amour (Histories of Love* or *Love Stories)* — which takes a cinematic image, that of *ET,* as the truth of a culture suffering a dearth of love and idealisation, appears as something of an ironic twist.[3] What has happened? How can we best understand this move? Where has Julia Kristeva been and gone?

This question can only be posed, I believe, historically and psychoanalytically, which means tracing out a conceptual movement and context which, for Kristeva at least, has constantly been informed by psychoanalysis — a movement which then turns back on itself in so far as psychoanalysis provides many of the terms through which it can itself be understood. Kristeva is also a self-diagnostician, and the psychic drive or investment of much of her writing can often be lifted straight out of her texts. 'I desire the Law', she writes in a key chapter of this latest book,[4] voicing a panic which — psychoanalysis itself might have anticipated — was bound to be the ultimate effect of that earlier onslaught on the securing identity of the image, which Kristeva and the *Tel Quel* group had castigated throughout the 1970s as little more than bourgeois deceit.

Julia Kristeva's work belongs to that semiotic tradition most closely identified with the work of Roland Barthes, in which the analysis of the structure of language rapidly became a critique of the stabilising illusion of the sign, and of those forms of writing, in particular the nineteenth-century novel, which were seen to embody and guarantee that illusion for a bourgeois society binding its subjects into the spurious unity of a culture inaccessible to change. The unity of the culture and the psychic unity of subjects went together, with the second as pre-condition of the first, complementary facades which bound over the psychic and social divisions beneath. Kristeva now argues that this dual emphasis set her apart from the pitfalls of structuralism and of what became for many the predominant strand of 'post-

---

[2] Sigmund Freud, *Group Psychology and the Analysis of the Ego* (1921), SE 18, pp. 111-116; PF 12, pp. 141-147.

[3] Kristeva, *Histoires d'amour*, Collection 'Infini', Paris 1983.

[4] Kristeva, 'Stabat Mater' in *Histoires d'amour,* p. 237; this chapter first appeared as 'Hérethique d'amour', *Tel Quel* 77, Winter 1974 (tr. in *The Kristeva Reader*).

structuralism' alike: 'For some the important task was to 'deconstruct' phenomenology and structuralism as a minor form of metaphysics unaware of being so. For others, amongst whom I count myself, it was indispensable to give the structure its 'dynamic' by taking into consideration, on the one hand the speaking subject and his or her unconscious experience, and, on the other, the pressures of other social structures.'[5]

The point was made by Kristeva in 1974: 'Crude grammatology abdicates the subject ... uninterested in symbolic and social structures, it has nothing to say in the face of their destruction or renewal.'[36]

It is worth noting already therefore that the appeal to the unconscious was part of a move to bring back history and social structures into that form of 'structuralism and after' which, in direct proportion to its repudiation of metaphysics, was seen by Kristeva as increasingly locked within its terms.

From that original diagnosis, Julia Kristeva then set herself a wager — which she herself has defined as exorbitant[7] — to confront language at the point where it undoes itself, pushing against that illusion of safety through which alone it can function, uncovering the psychic forces which sustain that illusion but which equally put it at risk. From among the *Tel Quel* group with whom she was associated from the late 1960s, Kristeva could be seen as the only writer who took to its limits the engagement between psychoanalysis and semiotics (already in 1969 she was calling her work a *'sémanalyse')*[8], an engagement which had in many ways seemed to stall at the concepts of 'identification', 'interpellation' and 'the subject's position in language' which had been brought in, via Lacanian psychoanalysis, to buttress Althusser's theory of ideology and the state.

In a move whose force and difficulty can perhaps only be fully understood now, Kristeva chose to drive that engagement with language and the sign into the most violent depths of their own process, where the dangers for psychic coherence, and indeed for the social (Kristeva's previous book, *Pouvoirs de l'horreur,* could be

---

[5] Kristeva, 'Mémoires', *Infini* 1, 1983, p. 44.

[6] Kristeva, *La révolution du langage poétique,* Paris 1974, p. 130

[7] Kristeva, *Desire in Language,* ed. Leon S.Roudiez, tr. Thomas Gora, Alice Jardine and L. Roudiez, Oxford 1984, preface, p.x.

[8] Kristeva, *Semeiotikè: Recherches pour une sémanalyse,* Paris 1969.

seen as her book about fascism)[9] made that earlier concept of subjectivity and its illusions look as comforting and facile as the literary forms which had been the object of its critique.

'Site of maximum abjection', the only place where the 'savagery' of the speaking being can be heard,[10] psychoanalysis became for Kristeva the means of taking that shift to subjectivity and the unconscious at its word (body and letter) through a clinical engagement with the acquisition, dissolution and pathology of language, all of which had lain beneath the earlier analysis of literary form and style. The more explicit psychoanalytic project followed directly therefore from the investigation of avant-garde writing. It reflected the need to confront speech in the throes of a pathology otherwise in danger of being restricted to its aesthetic mode. There is also an important historical link between psychoanalysis and the literary avant-garde in France through the surrealists. Against a medical institution largely unsympathetic to psychoanalysis which addressed madness 'from the place of reason' with a prophylactic aim, the surrealists had tried in the 1920s and 30s to speak of madness 'from the place of madness itself'.[11]

I 'Only the superego must see the light of day'[12]

That such a wager (such a speech) should finally be impossible is in fact given in advance by Kristeva's early writing. Kristeva's work has become best known for the concept of the 'semiotic' which she defines as the traces of the subject's difficult passage into the proper order of language (the symbolic or 'thetic' instance). It inherits Freud's concept of the primary processes as well as that of the drive — aspects of subjectivity which are only ever partially bound into the norms of psychic and sexual life. It then inflects these concepts through Lacan's account of subjectivity which gives language, or representation, central importance as the

[9] Kristeva, *Pouvoirs de l'horreur: essai sur l'abjection*, Paris 1980 (tr. Leon Roudiez, *Powers of Horror*, New York 1982).

[10] 'Mémoires', pp. 45, 53.

[11] Elisabeth Roudinesco, 'Histoire de la psychanalyse en France', *Infini* 2, 1983, p. 66.

[12] *La révolution du langage poétique*, p. 477.

means through which these norms are vehiculed into place. Disorders of psychic identity and linguistic disorders are tied into each other, a link which is permitted by the psychoanalytic emphasis on the centrality — and fragility — of speech. But if Kristeva concentrates on the signs of that fragility (troubles of phonological, syntactic and enunciating laws), she can only do so in terms of the order of language against which they break. The 'semiotic' can never wholly displace the 'symbolic' since it relies on that very order to give to it its, albeit resistant, shape.

In Kristeva's analysis of Mallarmé's poetry, for example, she describes the sound patterns of the language in terms of the basic mechanisms of the drive (explosion, implosion), drawing on Roman Jakobson's famous article 'Why Mama and Papa?' which traced the consonant opposition to the primary vocal gestures and needs of the infant.[13] But even if these oppositions can evoke once again these earliest affective processes, they can only do so now by underscoring the phonological patterns which form the ground rules of ordinary speech. They are also immediately caught up in — and cannot operate without — the semantic content which is made explicit by the text, as well as being held in check by a syntax, disrupted but still recognisable, which Mallarmé himself referred to as his 'sole guarantee'.[14] Kristeva talks of Mallarmé's use of syntax as at once a 'supercompetence' and a 'risk' for the subject.[15] In the section of *La révolution du langage poétique* on 'The semiotic apparatus of the text', she concentrates on the shifters (the movement of the first person pronoun across the text), allusions to other texts (the place of the text in a history of writing) and syntax (transformations and their rules) as much as on the phonological patterns of the language which are all too easily assimilated to the idea of a body at play. On this Kristeva is explicit: the body can only ever be *signified*, it is never *produced. Après-coup,* rather than regression, this is neither a pure body in process nor a total disintegration of speech.

Furthermore, the extent to which the 'semiotic' is confined to the expression and celebration of its heterogeneity and disruptive charge alone is the index not only of its psychic, but also of its

[13] Roman Jakobson, 'Why Mama and Papa?' (1959), *Studies on Child Language and Aphasia,* Hague 1971.
[14] Cit. in *La révolution du langage poétique,* p. 29.
[15] Ibid., p. 270.

political limitations. This is a point which has been overlooked in most commentaries on Kristeva's writing.[16] In *La révolution du langage poétique,* Lautréamont and Mallarmé are chosen by Kristeva because of the sexual and linguistic scandal which they represented for bourgeois moral and literary forms — an excess confined to marginal expression by a repressive culture and state (we can recognise in this analysis the project of the later Russian Formalists — 'A Slap in the Face of Public Taste' — to which Kristeva adds a psycho-sexual emphasis).[17] But in so far as these writers fail to move back in the opposite direction and to take up the recognisable social institutions and meanings from which they have been banned, so they fall prey to aestheticism, mysticism and anarchy. In a later article on dissidence Kristeva will talk of the *'verve anarchiste'* of the Paris Commune against 'power, institutions and beliefs',[18] but there has never been a promotion of anarchy as such. For Kristeva, to abdicate symbolic norms — to enact that abdication — opens the way to psychosis: 'The way to psychosis — foreclusion of the thetic instance — remains open ... and this situation translates the ideological limitations of the avant-garde.'[19]

For Kristeva, as far back as 1974 therefore, the 'logical, thetic, binding, instance' (also called meaning or *'sens'*) was the *'sine qua non'* of practice'.[20] Mallarmé's refusal of politics, Lautréamont's silence on sexual and familial ideologies, were the direct consequence of a failure to re-engage that instance, even though it is the crisis to which they so relentlessly subject it which constitutes the value of their work. The question therefore becomes not how to disrupt language by leaving its recognisable forms completely *behind,* but how to articulate the psychic processes which language normally glosses over *on this side of* meaning or sense. The avant-garde text, like the speech of the psychotic and the neurotic symptom, speaks a truth in a form which is too easily banished.

Despite the apparent dualism of that semiotic/symbolic division, there is therefore no strict demarcation between them.

[16] See, for example, Terry Eagleton, *Literary Theory,* pp. 190-191.

[17] First manifesto of the Cubo-futurists issued in 1912 and signed by Mayakovsky, Burlyuk, Khlebnikov and Kruchyonykh.

[18] Kristeva, 'Un nouveau type d'intellectuel: le dissident', *Tel Quel* 74, Winter 1977, p. 4 (tr. 'A New Type of Intellectual: the Dissident' in *The Kristeva Reader).*

[19] *La révolution du langage poétique,* p. 169.

[20] Ibid., p. 616.

There cannot be if the semiotic is to find articulation and if the symbolic is to feel its effects. The symbolic is not, as has been argued, a rigid, monolithic stucture,[21] but unstable and shifting. Kristeva's recognition of this is simply the other side of her acknowledgement that the semiotic has to work through the very order of language it defies. Their relationship is one of a 'dynamic'. 'Complete repression (were such a thing possible) would entail consequences preventing the symbolic function'.[22] It is in fact a tenet of Freudian psychoanalysis that repression can never be absolute. If it were, the very concept of repression could not be thought.

It is worth stressing these points simply because they show how closely Kristeva's concept of social transformation, as early as 1974, already approximated to the idea of the analytic *cure*. Kristeva has often been criticised for inadequately posing her appeal to semiotic heterogeneity in terms of social practice, although this was in fact her own criticism of the avant-garde text. But that criticism, advanced by Kristeva herself, relied in turn on the notion that resistance must finally be articulated in a voice which can be heard, and this necessarily involves, as it does in the analytic setting, a partial re-integration of speech. Paradoxically, the very aspect of the theory which stopped Kristeva's writing from spinning off into the gratuitous celebration of noise is the aspect now criticised for its psychically normative implications; as if 'being an analyst' (the opening words of Kristeva's own statement on the back of this latest book), and working towards an at least partial symbolisation of the repressed meant, by definition, abdicating any commitment to social change. In the 1970s, Kristeva herself criticised psychoanalysis on exactly these grounds,[23] but a closer look shows that some form of 'integration' was always seen by her as the pre-condition of any effectivity in the social; it is the concept of what that effectivity should aim for which has altered. This fact suggests to me at least that Kristeva's discarding of Marxism can hardly be laid at the door of her increasing involvement with psychoanalysis. From the very beginning, the psychoanalytic insight and the concept of practice

[21] Jones, p. 68.

[22] *La révolution du langage poétique*, p. 148.

[23] Ibid., p. 493 and Kristeva, 'Sujet dans le langage et pratique politique', *Tel Quel* 58, Summer 1974, p. 27.

together acted as a check on that original critique of the subject as a purely ideological lure. Psychosis — we can be thankful — was never offered as a revolutionary ideal.

The problems raised by Kristeva's challenge to language and identity can perhaps be recognised as another version of a more familiar political question: how to effect a political transformation when the terms of that transformation are given by the very order which a revolutionary practice seeks to change. The presence of 'revolution' in the title of that early book was never, it should be stressed, part of a suggestion that psychic or aesthetic disruption could substitute for other forms of politics. But it did aim at this larger issue of the conditions, and limits, of revolutionary change. In 1974, Kristeva located this logical 'impasse', or bind, in the Marxist theory of a class whose abolition, along with that of class itself, will emerge out of the same historical conditions which produced it. The proletariat has a privileged consciousness of a social totality tending towards its own elimination, which also means eliminating the very class and consciousness which had grasped its totality as such.[24] It is a concept of self-negation which, in a less quoted but central chapter of *La révolution du langage poétique,* Kristeva then carries over into her discussion of the subject's relation to language and psychic life. In his paper on 'Negation', Freud had made the negative instance the pre-condition of logical thought — the subject expels part of itself in order that it may come to be.[25] This description of loss as the founding moment of subjectivity then forms the basis, via Lacan, of Kristeva's concept of psychic life. But equally important, it already bears the weight of that other question — whose difficulty has become more and more pressing — of a transformation which will finally mean relinquishing the very forms of self-recognition through which it was first desired. The classic opposition between revolution and reform takes on another meaning when what is involved is the subject's very ability to hold itself together in speech.

The problem was perhaps bound to emerge as soon as the question of identity (psychic and sexual) was introduced into the analysis of how a specific social order is upheld. The turn to subjectivity and sexuality had originally been part of a rejection of

[24] *La révolution du langage poétique,* pp. 386-387.
[25] Freud, 'Negation' (1925), SE 19; PF 11.

those forms of economism or traditional Marxist analysis which excluded these questions from politics or else seemed to relegate them to second place. This was central to *Tel Quel*'s commitment to Maoist China and the concept of a cultural revolution in the seventies. But in so far as the conception of sexuality was a psychoanalytic one, so it rapidly touched on aspects of subjectivity which cannot be 'managed' even by more progressive institutional and familial forms. Although *Tel Quel* prefaced their Summer 1974 issue with a quotation from Reich on the socially liberating power of sexuality, it was clear from the outset that, unlike Reich, their idea of sexuality was not that of a quantity to be released but of processes which unsettle the most fundamental self-definition of the subject. No priority, therefore, to 'psychic liberation',[26] first because the psychic was always the *non-sufficient* condition of genuine social transformation, second because it was precisely not 'liberation' that was at stake. For that very reason, the psychoanalytic move immediately found itself hedged in on both sides: by an appeal back and away from questions of sexuality to the politics of a purely class opposition which it had been the crucial intention to shift,[27] or else by a call from off the very edge of language. It could be argued — and was argued by Kristeva — that by ignoring language, or not seeing language as an issue, the first of these positons firmly entrenches itself within its laws. Kristeva herself has said over and again that her own aim is to avoid both of these alternatives: no absolutism of the 'thetic' which then gets erected as a theological law, but no denial of the 'thetic' which brings with it the fantasy of 'an irrationalism in pieces'.[28]

In assessing the changes in Kristeva's work, we need therefore to distinguish a number of different levels.

Firstly, what appears to me as an increasing recognition on Kristeva's part that there can be no direct politicisation of the unconscious since this is to confuse political and psychic resistance or, more simply, struggle and symptomatic distress.

Secondly, a discarding on Kristeva's part of revolutionary politics (Marxist and then Maoist), and, since 1977, of any political

---

[26] Jones, p. 61.

[27] One of the clearest examples of this tendency is the article by Peter Dews, 'The *Nouvelle Philosophie* and Foucault', *Economy and Society* 8: 2, May 1979.

[28] *La révolution du langage poétique*, p. 80.

discourse which totalises the social, in favour of a highly individualistic conception of dissidence and worth.[29] Kristeva has set the latter against all politics — including feminism — but this does not necessarily follow; the critique of totalities, for example, could be related to recent feminist criticism of the monolithic language and organisation of the Left.[30] To this extent, Kristeva's image of feminism as a political movement in these moments is drawn from only one half of the description which she herself gives of it in 'Women's Time'.[31]

Thirdly, a continuing focus on questions of psycho-sexual identity whose basic insight has not changed: that identity is necessary but only ever partial and therefore carries with it a dual risk — the wreck of all identity, a self-blinding allegiance to psychic norms. To hold onto both sides of this dynamic is, Kristeva argues, almost impossible, although one is in fact always implicated in both. Certainly Kristeva sees psychoanalysis as one of the few places in our culture where this dynamic is fully allowed to speak, at the same time as her work also veers from one side to the other of the divide.

Clearly these are related, but we collapse the levels into each other at a price. To say that the unconscious cannot be politicised does not necessarily entail setting up psychoanalysis as an alternative to all politics. To argue that questions of sexuality are not — in a one-to-one relation — managed or exhausted by traditional political discourse or transformation does not mean that we have to discard these questions from political understanding and debate. The fact that Kristeva now seems to withdraw the analytic insight from the directly political arena does not mean that it was always and necessarily asocial from the start. Nor can psychoanalysis be seen, in a simple way, as the sole cause and determining factor in the political shift. Kristeva's abandonment of that earlier concept of revolution can also be

[29] Kristeva, 'La littérature dissidente comme refutation du discours de gauche', *Tel Quel* 76, Summer 1978 and *'Histoires d'amour* — Love Stories', in *Desire*, ed. Lisa Appignanesi, Institute of Contemporary Arts Documents, London 1983.

[30] Sheila Rowbotham *et al.*, *Beyond the Fragments*.

[31] Kristeva, 'Le temps des femmes', *34/44: Cahiers de recherche de science de textes et documents* 5, Winter 1979 (tr. Alice Jardine and Harry Blake, 'Women's Time', in N. O. Keohane *et al.*, *Feminist Theory: A Critique of Ideology*, Chicago 1981, Brighton 1982; also in *The Kristeva Reader*).

related to changes — some of which have been welcomed by feminism — in the field of politics itself. It would be possible to argue, for example, that some form of political pluralism, case for local initiatives, and multiple political strategies, follows more logically from the rejection of revolutionary Marxism which, for *Tel Quel* and their subsequent journal *Infini*, has been accompanied by an unmistakeable shift to the right. It was, after all, feminism which first argued that subjectivity (the 'personal') was a political stake. Kristeva's move can in fact be turned back on itself, since she herself has never discarded the attempt to understand the different and changing forms of social articulation through which identities are moved in — and out of — place.

II 'A freudful mistake'[32]

I do not think we should be surprised, therefore, nor too comfortably critical or dismissive, when Kristeva proceeds to fall, at various points throughout her work, into one or other side of the psychic dynamic which she herself describes. The latest book, with its appeal to the 'father of individual pre-history', can certainly be seen, as I have already suggested, as a race back into the arms of the law. But Kristeva's own work, and responses to Kristeva, have equally been marked by the opposite impulse, notably around the concept of the semiotic which has acquired something of an existence of its own, outside the realm of meaning without which, strictly, it does not make sense. The attraction of the theory was always that it pointed to aspects of language which escaped the straitjacket of symbolic norms. But this has also made the theory vulnerable to some very archaic notions of the content of the repressed. Variously, and at times conjointly, Kristeva has attributed to the semiotic: femininity, colour, music, body and affect — concepts whose oppressive lyricism has at times been welcomed by feminism but which feminism has also been the quickest to reject. It is also through these concepts that Kristeva takes her leave of Lacan. The concept of 'affect', for example, comes through André Green, a member of the *Association Psychanalytique de France* founded when its members split with Lacan in 1964 (Kristeva trained as an analyst with this school).

[32] Joyce, cit. in *La révolution du langage poétique*, p. 504.

Published in 1973, one year before *La révolution du langage poétique*, Green's book *Le discours vivant* developed the concept of affect in Freud as part of a critique of Lacan's central premise that psychic life is ruled by the exigencies of representation and the linguistic sign.[33] In an article published in the journal of the *Association* in 1979, Kristeva reiterated Green's critique of Lacan — that Lacan's concept of language assimilates into itself and absorbs 'what the dualism of Freudian thought holds to be strangely irreducible: drive, affect' — although she immediately qualifies: 'Is there any need to recall that the position which takes the semiotic as heterogeneous does not arise from a concern to integrate some alleged concreteness, brute corporality, or energy-in-itself into a language suspected of being too abstract .... This semiotic is without primacy and has no place as origin.'[34]

There is no doubt, however, that the push here is against language itself, even though Kristeva herself is again the best analyst of the dangers this might imply. In an interview in 1977 on the United States, Kristeva praised the 'non-verbal' aspects of modern American culture which draw more 'radically and profoundly than in Europe' on the realms of 'gesture, colour and sound', but then she asked whether that same non-verbalisation might not also be the sign of a resistance, the almost psychotic hyper-activity of a violent and overproductive culture incessantly on the go.[35] Even if we do not accept the representation of American culture, Kristeva's own check on the celebration of a place beyond language is worthy of note.

It is, however, almost impossible not to assign the status of origin to the semiotic once it is defined as beyond language in this way. Elsewhere Kristeva defines heterogeneity as the 'archaisms of the semiotic body', 'logically and chronologically prior to the institution of the symbolic', 'genetically detected in the first echolalias of infants'. And it is this concept of priority which lies behind Kristeva's psychoanalytic interest in the acquisition of language and in object relations theory which concentrates on the

---

[33] André Green, *Le discours vivant*, op. cit.

[34] Kristeva, 'Il n'y a pas de maître à langage', *Nouvelle Revue de Psychanalyse, Regards sur la psychanalyse en France*, 20, Autumn 1979, pp. 130-131.

[35] Kristeva, with Philippe Sollers and Marcelin Pleynet, 'Pourquoi les Etats Unis?', *Tel Quel* 71-73, Autumn 1977, pp. 4, 19 (tr. 'The US Now: A Conversation', *October* 6, Fall 1978; also in *The Kristeva Reader*).

interaction between the mother and child. But the emphasis on this relationship immediately produces a split between the order of the mother and of the father, giving to the first the privilege of the semiotic and separating it out from the culture in which it is inscribed. Juliet Mitchell has discussed how in the 1920s and 30s attention was focused on this relationship because it was felt to hold the key to the pre-oedipal sexuality of the female child. She also argues that the effect of this was to close off the question of sexual difference — of the symbolically produced and only ever partial division between men and women, masculinity and femininity, a division which this theory takes for granted and thus helps to reproduce.[36] Lacan's emphasis on the symbolic was first of all developed against this tendency. It represented an attempt to return to the larger questions of cultural determination figured in Freud's myth of the beginnings of culture in *Totem and Taboo*.[37] In Kristeva's case, the attention to the mother does not ignore these wider issues but becomes part of a more general question about the place of the mother-child relation in the constitution of cultural taboos (see below). But as soon as Kristeva gives to this relation the status of origin — psychic or cultural, or both — it is handed over to the realm of the senses, outside of all history and form. Kristeva uses this quotation from Freud to support the identification of the semiotic with an essentially maternal domain: 'It [an advance in intellectuality] consists, for instance, in deciding that paternity is more important than maternity, although it cannot, like the latter, be established by the evidence of the senses.'[38]

For Kristeva, this relinquishing of the maternal is loss, as much as advance, and it is never complete, but this does not alter the fully ideological division between maternal and paternal, senses and ideation, which it serves to reinforce.

But the problematic nature of this tendency in Kristeva's thought is perhaps best illustrated by the very term of the semiotic itself, which Kristeva calls 'chora' or receptacle after Plato's cosmology (*The Timaeus*), where it stands for the mediating instance in which the copies of the eternal model receive their

[36] Juliet Mitchell, 'Introduction I', *Feminine Sexuality*, pp. 19-20.

[37] Freud, *Totem and Taboo* (1913), SE 13; PF 12.

[38] Freud, *Moses and Monotheism* (1938-39), SE 23, p. 118; PF 13, p. 365, cit. in *La révolution du langage poétique*, p. 445n.

shape. Plato himself describes the 'chora' as maternal, and from the beginning Kristeva based the link to Freud on this: 'this rhythmic space without thesis or position, the process where *significance* comes to be, Plato indicates as much when he designates this receptacle nursing, maternal'.[39] But if Plato did so, it was because the mother was seen as playing no part in the act of procreation, a receptacle or empty vessel *merely* for the gestation of the unborn child.[40]

III 'I hate Maria and when I see her portrait I go down on my knees'[41]

It seems to me now that the concept of the semiotic, especially in those formulations which identify it with the mother and place it beyond language, is the least useful aspect of Kristeva's work, even though it is the concept for which she is best known. For what happens to this maternally connoted and primitive semiotic is that it is first defined as the hidden underside of culture (we can recognise the proximity of this to the classical demonic image of femininity) and then idealised as something whose value and exuberance the culture cannot manage and has therefore had to repress (a simple reverse of that first image which makes femininity the ideal excluded instance of all culture).

Kristeva herself charts these dramatic reversals from idealisation of the woman to degradation and back again throughout her discussion of the writings of Mallarmé and Céline. But she does so by analysing them as *fantasies* whose violent oscillations, especially in the case of Céline, bring greater and greater violence in their train. Furthermore, as Kristeva has constantly insisted, idealisation of the semiotic in itself involves a denial or cover up of the psychic pain and violence which in fact characterises the early interaction between the mother and child. This is why Kristeva is able at one and the same time to lay out the horrors of the fantasmatic structure which underpins the writings

[39] Ibid., pp. 24-25, p. 579n.
[40] Francis MacDonald Cornford, *Plato's Cosmology, The Timaeus*, tr. and with a running commentary, London and New York 1937, p. 187.
[41] Stephane Mallarmé, Lettre à Cazalis, *Correspondance*, 1, p. 77, cit. in *La révolution du langage poétique*, p. 453.

of an author like Céline, while at the same time praising that writing for exposing a psychic drama which — with massive social repercussions — is constantly denied, projected onto the other, and then played out by the culture at large.[42] Céline's writing is a *symptom.* It reveals *horror* as a matter of *power* — the power of fascination when we are confronted with the traces of our own psychic violence, the horror when that same violence calls on social institutions for legitimation, and receives it.

In *Pouvoirs de l'horreur,* Kristeva takes up the question with which she ended *La révolution du langage poétique:* 'How can negativity, or the reject be articulated in the social?',[43] returning to a mostly forgotten emphasis of that earlier book — the negativity or reject, horror or abjection as she now calls it, which characterises the semiotic realm. She then charts the way that different religious cultures have drawn up the boundaries (soiling, abomination, sin) of what they can — bodily — contain. It is another version of the problem which has run right through her writing — of what can be articulated on this side of culture without breaking its limits, — only the account of what needs to be spoken has got considerably worse.

Kristeva could also be seen here as feeding back the issue of pre-oedipal sexuality into the theorisation of cultural origins which Freud — following his changed account of femininity — had himself failed to do. She makes the point that discussions of the incest taboo have concentrated on the place of the father together with the forms of disorder (obsessional neurosis and paranoia) associated with his prohibitory role, leaving the mother precisely as the idealised relic of what comes to be forbidden, a kind of lost territory which says nothing of the psychic ambivalence of that early relation, nor of the disorders (psychosis and phobia) with which it can be clinically linked. Kristeva's increasing interest in those analysts who concentrate on the most difficult aspects of that early relation (Rosenfeld, Bion) stems from this critique. If this is object-relations theory, therefore, it is with a difference, since there is no concept of 'adequacy' at stake. Rather it seems that, in response to an idealisation latent in her own formulations, Kristeva was replying that the semiotic is no 'fun'.

For what does it mean, we can ask, to place the mother at the

---

[42] *Powers of Horror.*
[43] *La révolution du langage poétique,* p. 545.

source and fading-point of all subjectivity and language — a point which, as Kristeva herself has argued, threatens the subject with collapse? Surely this is already the effect of an idealisation which barely conceals the reproach, felt threat and feared loss of identity fermenting underneath?

As soon as Kristeva asks this question, then the whole of her work seems to turn on itself, implicating her own concepts in the fantasies, ambivalence and projections which she describes. Kristeva had criticised Mallarmé for the way that he targets, or fixates onto the woman the disruptions of language played out in his writing, making the woman the bearer of their eternal secret, mystifying them and thus depriving them of what might otherwise be their more unsettling social effects.[44] And in *Pouvoirs de l'horreur,* she describes the way in which Céline fantasises his own mortality as feminine and projects it onto the woman who then appears as a persecutor, for the life she not only gives, but denies. Much of this book is about the way in which the limits of language and its dissolution are constantly thought in terms of sexual difference, the way that cultures define and secure their parameters by relegating the woman to their outer edge.

Yet, in a twist which gives back to these same fantasies the weight of a primordial truth, Kristeva asks whether they may not find their basis in a femininity whose over powerful and physical reality effectively places cultures at risk. Is the repudiation of this power of the mother ('maleficent in its power to give mortal life') indeed the pre-condition of symbolic identity on which all cultures rest? Is this same power *'historic or fantasmatic'*, *'attributed'* to the woman, or is the early relation to the mother its *'unconscious base'?*[45] Kristeva says that her question is not about primacy or cause and effect, although at one point she does describe the taboo on the mother as the 'primary mytheme' of all culture,[46] which seems to give the psychic a primacy and brings her uncomfortably close to the form of argument advanced against Malinowski in the 1920s and 30s by Ernest Jones. In fact Kristeva oscillates, but in the process she has turned a much older debate about the relationship between psychic and social determination in the production of social forms into a query about the origins and persistence (not

[44] Ibid., pp. 468, 474.
[45] *Powers of Horror,* pp. 158, 91, 100, 106 (translations modified).
[46] Ibid., p. 106.

least of all in her own writing) of some of the most disturbing images of femininity in our culture.

Kristeva's work splits on a paradox, or rather a dilemma: the hideous moment when a theory arms itself with a concept of femininity as different, as something other to the culture as it is known, only to find itself face to face with, or even entrenched within, the most grotesque and fully cultural stereotypes of femininity itself. Unlike some of her most virulent detractors,[47] however, Kristeva at least knows that these images are not so easily dispatched. It is not by settling the question of their origins that we can necessarily dismantle their force.

IV Feminism and its fantasies

Kristeva's relationship to these highly charged and ambivalent images, and the way that she works at the limits of psychic identity, explains, I think, the strength but also the tension of her writing for feminism. Kristeva has never fully identified with feminism and it has never been the place from which she has chosen to speak, although she does describe her place as a woman as central to her overall project: 'It was necesssary perhaps to be a woman to attempt to take up that exorbitant wager of carrying the rational project to the outer borders of the signifying ventures of men.'[48]

Kristeva has, however, been attractive to feminism because of the way that she exposes the complacent identities of psycho-sexual life. But as soon as we try to draw out of that exposure an image of femininity which escapes the straitjacket of symbolic forms, we fall straight into that essentialism and primacy of the semiotic which is one of the most problematic aspects of her work. And as soon as we try to make of it the basis for a political identity, we turn the concept inside out, since it was as a critique of identity itself that it was originally advanced. No politics without identity, but no identity which takes itself at its word. The tension is captured in

---

[47] Jennifer Stone, 'The Horrors of Power: A Critique of Julia Kristeva', *The Politics of Theory*, Proceedings of the Essex Conference in the Sociology of Literature, July 1982, Colchester 1983; Peter Gidal, 'On Julia Kristeva', *Undercut* (Journal of the London Filmmakers Cooperative) 12, 1984.

[48] *Desire in Language*, preface, p. x.

the title of one of Kristeva's best known articles — 'D'une identité l'autre' — which has been translated as 'From One Identity to Another', but which is also aimed at the opposite: 'identity and its other' — that is, the other of identity itself.[49] This is why Kristeva has increasingly distanced herself from a feminism which she has described as 'too existentialist'[50] (this relates specifically to psychoanalysis and echoes Juliet Mitchell's 1974 critique of feminist rejection of Freud[51]), and which she sees — wrongly as far as I am concerned — as a monolithic entity which, in its claim for identity and power (identity as power), repeats and reinforces the rigidity of the culture which produced it.[52]

At its most simple, therefore, the question becomes: what could it mean to construct a political identity out of processes heralded as the flight of identity itself? Especially given that recognition of the aberrant nature of those processes was, in a sense, the price we paid for moving out of a psychic functionalism which had underlain the earlier accounts of the subject's ideological place.

At the same time, Kristeva gives to women the privilege of the central dilemma caught by her writing: how to challenge the very form of available self-definition without losing the possibility of speech. Against the offered and familiar alternatives of bureaucracy and madness, it is women for Kristeva who know the necessity of, and demand, a place on the historical stage, while also calling the bluff of a psychic and sexual order of things which they pass through and across: 'traverser', a word central to Kristeva's writing, implies that you go *through* certainly, but also *out*.[53]

Of these two directions — towards identity and its other side — Kristeva calls the second 'negativity', which recalls the negativity of the semiotic and underlines the psychic difficulty at stake. It can be summarised as a refusal: 'Ce n'est jamais ça' — 'No, it's not

---

[49] Kristeva, 'D'une identité, l'autre', *Tel Quel* 62, Summer 1975 (tr. 'From One Identity to Another', *Desire in Language*).

[50] *Histoires d'amour,* p. 242.

[51] Juliet Mitchell, *Psychoanalysis and Feminism*, op. cit.

[52] 'Sujet dans le langage et pratique politique', p. 26; 'La femme, ce n'est jamais ça'. *Tel Quel* 59, Autumn 1974, p. 24 (tr. Marilyn August, 'Woman Can Never Be Defined', *New French Feminisms,* ed. Elaine Marks and Isabelle de Courtivron, Brighton 1981, p. 141); *Powers of Horror,* p. 208.

[53] Kristeva, 'Polylogue', *Tel Quel* 57, Spring 1974; tr. in *Desire in language,* p. 164, as 'experience'.

that' or 'That won't do' which, taken together with the translation 'Woman Can Never Be Defined', make the woman the subject as well as the object of the statement.[54] The other side of this negativity, Kristeva calls the 'ethics' of femininity, or women's commitment to an ethics which saves them, as she puts it, from a 'Nietzschean rage'.[55] Criticised recently for linking this to women's experience of motherhood,[56] Kristeva is nonetheless echoing a longstanding feminist demand that this aspect of femininity should be allowed a voice in constructing the priorities of the political domain. And while this may seem to come close to a history of oppressive discourses which have given to women as mothers the privilege of the ethical (and not a great deal else), for Kristeva *ethics* has nothing whatsoever to do with *duty* or the idea that women should people the race. No ethics *without* maternity, but not mothering as ethical *duty* or *role:* 'The ethical which aims for a negativity is opposed to ethics understood as the observation of laws'.[57] Ethics plus (as) negativity describes a subjective position which avoids conformity (the first without the second) and esoterism or marginality (the second without the first), capturing alternatives which have historically presented themselves to feminism: between an equality which risks absorption into the law, and an absolute difference which can only defy it.

But perhaps even more difficult in relation to feminism, and less commented on, is this issue of the negative aspects that Kristeva identifies in the semiotic which feminism has at times been tempted to claim as its own special realm. Difficult precisely because Kristeva has not stopped at the positive aspects of this process but has gone over to the other side, dredging up archaic images of the mother which, for all their status as fantasy (because of their status as fantasy), are not without their effects. If we stop at the critique of identity — the celebration of a heterogeneity which it is too easy politically to rebuff — we avoid this more troubling area which consists of the psychic ambivalence of the drives. But if we follow this through, then we find ourselves having to relinquish an idealised vision of the lost maternal continent which we have often and so fiercely wished to protect: 'Death

---

[54] 'Woman Can Never Be Defined'.
[55] Ibid., p.138 (tr. modified).
[56] Jones, p. 62.
[57] *La révolution du langage poétique,* p. 102.

explodes inside the peace we thought to have absorbed (nirvana, intoxication, silence)'.[58] But once that has been said, it becomes impossible to avoid talking about fantasy, not just by men of women, but also amongst women, and even within feminism itself: 'to extol a centripetal, becalmed and softened feminine sexuality, only to to exhume most recently, under the cover of idylls amongst women, the sado-masochistic ravages beneath.'[59]

A question, or image, of feminine paranoia? In what appears to me as one of the most powerful moments of self-diagnosis in her text, Kristeva certainly says so[60] (the structure of paranoia was already there in the article I started with on the hallucinatory power of film). But since Freud at least we have ceased to use diagnosis as a cause for dismissal, still less as a category of abuse. Rather it is the moment when Kristeva recasts *for* women the problem of identity to which she has constantly returned. For what could be a simple love between women, since identity is always in opposition *to*? And yet what could be a place without identity, other than a falling into the realm of the unnameable, body without language, a realm to which women have often and so oppressively been confined? Even between women (that mother-daughter relationship of which politically we have asked so much), the act of differentiation-recognition of the other leads — if not to violence — then at least, and of necessity, to psychic pain.

V 'The King is with the body'[61]

This latest book (*Histoires d'amour*) is therefore no idyll since 'hatred ... underpins, carries, determines' the identity it now pleads for and the love whose history it describes.[62] 'Narcissus in troubled waters' — one of the chapter headings of the previous book — is there to caution us against a return to identity, narcissism and idealisation which, at first glance, bears all the signs of a retreat. Kristeva now outlines the precondition for a psychic identity which neither the abjection of the mother nor the punishing imago

[58] *Histoires d'amour,* p. 81.
[59] Ibid., p. 349.
[60] Ibid., pp. 242-244.
[61] Shakespeare, *Hamlet,* IV, iii, 26.
[62] *Histoires d'amour,* p. 121.

of the oedipal father can ground, repair or sustain. She finds this pre-condition in a primary identification with a non-oedipal 'father of individual pre-history': 'pre-history' because, it seems, Kristeva is still searching for an ideal and prior psychic instance now lost on the side of the mother (too abject for words), 'non-oedipal' because she still wants to save this idealisation from the tyranny of the symbolic in which ideals are shaped.

Yet again, we can ask what separation (or splitting) this is. For although Freud does refer to the child's early identification with such a pre-oedipal father, there is ambivalence (abjection?) in this identification *from the very first*, and in a key passage from *Group Psychology and the Analysis of the Ego* to which Kristeva refers, he describes this identification as a derivative of the oral drive which assimilates and annihilates its object.[63] Kristeva calls this identification the advent of the psychic and a deferring of the oral drive, but she has been asked whether this imaginary father and the phallic mother might not be one and the same thing.[64] In fact Kristeva's concept seems at times to come close to Maud Mannoni's attempt to ground psychic identity in the paternal genealogy of the child.[65] It is worth noting, however, that it is only those moments in Kristeva's own writing where she too rigidly demarcates identity and drive, symbolic and semiotic, conscious and unconscious, and distributes them between the realms of the father and the mother, that allows for this paternal return.

It is nonetheless a striking move from Kristeva's early assertion that paternal power will symbolically flourish wherever the question of sexuality is not specifically and critically posed.[66] An assertion which echoed the belief within feminism that the key to women's subordination lay in the symbolic enshrinement and perpetuation of patriarchal law. For even if we now recognise that the passage from symbolic system to the concrete instances of women's subordination cannot be made so easily or so fast,[67] the analysis holds surely still as a castigation of the values in which a culture embodies its own worth. At the same time it must be said,

[63] Freud, *The Ego and the Id*, pp. 31-32; pp. 370-371; *Group Psychology and the Analysis of the Ego*, p. 105; pp. 134-135; *Histoires d'amour*, pp. 31-32.

[64] Louise Burchill, 'The Last Word of this Adventure: Interview with Julia Kristeva', *On the Beach*, 1984, p. 26.

[65] Maud Mannoni, *L'enfant, sa 'maladie' et les autres*, op. cit.

[66] *La révolution du langage poétique*, p. 452.

[67] Rosalind Coward, *Patriarchal Precedents*, London 1982.

however, that once the precise connections between symbol and concrete power have been questioned or opened up for debate, then we cannot say what political effects will follow from a recognition of the father and his place in the psychic life of the child.

Nor is it a simple idealisation which is being promoted here, the idea of a paternally grounded identity which simply receives and comforts the subject. Kristeva criticises interpretations of Judaic writing which uncover the latent violence of its rhetoric and celebrate part object without identity, or letter without the law, but she nonetheless knows that the risk awaiting those who obey the law of the father is the paranoia of the chosen.[68]

As I understand it, what is most clearly at stake is a psychic necessity: at its most simple, the confrontation of the therapist with the pain of a fragmentation without identity or place. For even the one who plays with language through writing has of course come through to the other side: 'The writer: a phobic who succeeds at metaphor so as not to die of fear but to resuscitate through signs'.[69]

I do not think that Kristeva should be criticised therefore for her commitment to the concept of psychic identity, nor for her increasingly analytically informed aim to understand the processes through which it is produced — a commitment which does not have to imply a collusion with the way that identity is paraded in the culture at large. Since, far from this involving a denial of the other psychic forces which have been at the centre of her writing, it could be seen as the only place from which they can be known. This recognition was there from the outset and, as I have tried to argue, it was this, paradoxically, which saved Kristeva's writing from the anarchy of its own terms. Nor do I think that Kristeva should be dismissed for her analysis of love as a strategy which allows individual subjects to negotiate the troubled psychic waters which she herself so graphically describes. To which we could add that this love does not have to be incompatible with politics. Did not Kristeva herself say that without love of women there was no point in going to China in 1974?[70]

In this latest book, Kristeva pleads for love in response to what

[68] *Histoires d'amour*, p. 69.
[69] *Powers of Horror*, p.38 (tr. modified).
[70] 'Woman Can Never Be Defined', p.139.

she sees as a dearth of idealisation in our culture (shades of Christopher Lasch?), a dearth which is precipitating an abolition of psychic space which gives nothing but abjection the reign. 'I plead for the Imaginary as antidote to the crisis'.[71] But then, as is so often the case, Kristeva provides the self-diagnosis: 'doubtless a Cartesian deformation to dream of such a pre-Cartesian subject in love'; the critique: 'only for mirrors infatuated with stable images do crises exist'; and the caution: 'we lack today an amatory code, but it would be an imposture to propose new ones'.[72]

Finally, one can also point to the overall consistency of Kristeva's project in which this latest book has its place. In 1983 Kristeva argued, against an easy misreading of the title of *Tel Quel*'s new journal *Infini*, that for her at least it does not represent the return of a 'religious psychology or ideology' but rather the 'never abandoned effort to take transcendence seriously and to track down its premises into the most hidden recesses of language. My prejudice is that of believing that God is analysable. Infinitely'.[73]

For me Kristeva's work remains important because of the way it is poised on that interface of politics/psychoanalysis/feminism. In response to the demand for an attention to sexuality, some forms of Marxism will argue for a return to the politics of class. In response to the questions of psychic identity raised by sexuality, feminism seems at moments to come close to dropping the psychoanalytic understanding of sexuality itself, or at least Julia Kristeva who, it should also be said, has too long served as an ideal. But sexuality — the crucial ways it determines and structures our lives — cannot be understood without acknowledging the importance of fantasy, and fantasy in turn reveals aspects of subjectivity which crush the splendour of our (conscious) dreams.

Kristeva's reversals from celebration of the semiotic to abjection and back to a (now paternal) ideal reveal the instability of fantasy itself. They also underscore the problem which arises when political discourse turned on the category of identity and its illusions and accused it of upholding or of being the pre-condition of all other social norms — recognising in that moment that if

[71] *Histoires d'amour,* p. 354.
[72] Ibid., pp. 168, 348; *'Histoires d'amour* — Love Stories', p. 21.
[73] 'Mémoires', pp. 46-47.

sexuality was so intractable, it is because it strikes at the heart of identity itself. And having once gained that insight, we cannot just drop the question of identity and its impasses from the debate.

Kristeva was not the first to bring these issues onto the political stage. They are already there in the confrontation with violence, in the debates about the limits of censorship, about sado-masochism, pornography and the law. Kristeva writes across (*'traverser'*) these problems and has pushed them to (her own) breaking-point. Her work gives us the measure of the difficulties when politics tries to open itself up to the ravages of the unconscious mind.

Part Two
The Field of Vision

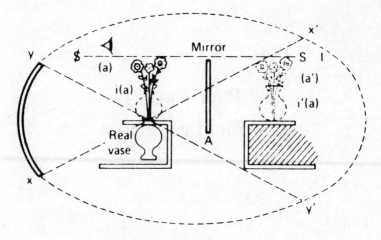

FIG. 1
Experiment of the inverted vase

7
The Imaginary

I cannot urge you too strongly to meditate on the science of optics ... peculiar in that it attempts by means of instruments to produce that strange phenomenon known as *images*, unlike the other sciences which carry out on nature a division, a dissection, or anatomical breakdown.

> Lacan, *Le séminaire I: Les écrits techniques de Freud* (1953-54), Paris 1975, p. 90.

...in so far as it is an optical schema, the model is precisely unable to indicate that the look, as a partial object *a*, is deeply hidden and unattainable to the same extent as I am unable to see myself from the place where the Other is looking at me.

> 'Le clivage du sujet et son identification', *Scilicet* 2-3, 1970, p.120.

This essay attempts to do three things: (1) to place the concept of the Imaginary as used in recent papers on film theory back in its psychoanalytic context; (2) to show how the psychoanalytic literature from which it has been drawn has itself undermined the concept as an original reference to an autonomous psychic instance; (3) to suggest that this partial collapsing of the Imaginary throws into question the use of the concept to delineate or explain some assumed position of plenitude on the part of the spectator in the cinema.[1]

[1] This essay, originally presented as a British Film Institute Educational Paper in 1975, was published in *The Talking Cure: Essays in Psychoanalysis and Language,*

The proliferation of references to psychoanalysis in literature on the cinema is probably exceeded only by the number of references to the camera and geometrical optics in the literature of psychoanalysis itself. These references could be said to fall broadly into two main categories:

1. The relationship between the observer and the camera/mirror/screen/microscope, taken as the model for the psychic apparatus; in which case the stress is on 'virtuality', referring either:

(a) to positions within the apparatus:

> we should picture the instrument which carries out our mental functions as resembling a compound microscope or a photographic apparatus, or something of the kind. On that basis, psychical locality will correspond to a point inside the apparatus at which one of the preliminary stages of an image comes into being. In the microscope and telescope, as we know, these occur in part at ideal points, regions in which no tangible component of the apparatus is situated.[2]

(b) to the status of the object to be recorded in relation to that of the apparatus:

> When you see a rainbow, you are seeing something purely subjective. You can see it at a certain distance where it joins the surrounding scenery. It is not there. It is a subjective phenomenon. And yet, thanks to a photographic apparatus, you will be able to record it quite objectively ... Is it not true to say that the photographic apparatus is a subjective apparatus constructed

ed. Colin MacCabe, London 1981, pp. 132-161. It was written in response to a specific demand — for some clarification of the concept of the Imaginary which was being fairly loosely imported into certain areas of literary, and specifically film, criticism at a time when works by Jacques Lacan, from which it had been taken, were relatively unavailable in English. The main body of the article is therefore an exposition of the concept in psychoanalytic theory. At the same time as it was being written, Christian Metz wrote his important article 'The Imaginary Signifier' on the pertinence of the concept for the study of cinema ('Le signifiant imaginaire', *Communications* 23, 1975, trs. Celia Britton, Annwyl Williams, Ben Brewster and Alfred Gazetti, *Psychoanalysis and Cinema: The Imaginary Signifier*, London 1983). Some of Metz's arguments are taken up in a final brief section of the article published here; see also 'The Cinematic Apparatus: Problems in Current Theory' and 'Woman as Symptom' in this collection.

[2] Freud, *The Interpretation of Dreams*, p. 536.

entirely through the assistance of an x and y which inhabit the domain in which the subject lives, that is the domain of language?[3]

(c) or to the status of the image itself:

> What I have called *the mirror stage* is interesting in that it manifests the affective dynamism by which the subject originally identifies himself with the visual *Gestalt* of his own body ... an ideal unity, or salutary *imago*.[4]

In each of these cases, the virtual nature of image, object, or apparatus seems to be displaceable; the experiment of the 'inverted vase' can be used to produce a virtual image of an upright real image of a real object, which is in fact upside down and out of sight (cf. pp. 178-179 for explanation of the stages of the experiment).

2. The subject as producer of symptoms, taken as the metaphors for a repressed signifier, where the emphasis on the visual image can refer to:

(a) complete foreclosure of symbolic or verbal representation, as in the case of hallucination;

(b) scenic substitution, as in the case of the screen memory;

(c) regression through the mental apparatus during sleep to the visual cathexis of mnemic traces as immediate perceptions. (In this last case, the comparison with the symptom only becomes legitimate if the visual cathexis of the image is related to its latent content, and hence to the dream as compromise-formation.)

Any appeal to these references by film theory has to ask whether they are simply generalisable as references to the subject's constitutional drive towards fabrication, or whether they can act as the point of a more precise dialogue between psychoanalysis and analysis of the cinema, in which the relationship of spectator to film could be seen as the formal microcosm, and reiteration, of this fictional insertion of the subject into its world. The conflation of the optical language of projection and identification as specified in Lacan's concept of the Imaginary with the looser connotation of the term as some form of fictional narrative has made this concept the nodal point of such an encounter; 'identification' again often being used loosely to refer to the assumed compliance of the film with the desire of the spectator

---

[3] *Les écrits techniques de Freud*, p. 91.
[4] Lacan, 'The mirror stage', pp. 18-19.

(also assumed).

The foundations of Lacan's concept of the Imaginary first appear in his paper 'The Mirror Stage' which takes as its major reference point Freud's 1914 paper 'On Narcissism — an Introduction'.[5] 'On Narcissism' will therefore form the (belated) starting-point of this discussion, the myth of Narcissus being especially apt to delineate that moment in which an apparent reciprocity reveals itself as no more than the return of an image to itself.

I

In 1914, Freud's original postulate of an opposition between sexual libido and ego or self-preservative interest had been challenged by a body of psychic disorders, loosely called schizophrenia or *dementia praecox,* and which Freud preferred to call paraphrenia to cover both *dementia praecox* and paranoia, in which the sexual libido withdrawn from objects of the external world and redirected on to objects of phantasy in neurosis, was simply displaced on to the subject's ego with no intermediary substitutes. The presence of what appeared to be purely ego-directed libido, with the corresponding shift of emphasis to this question of direction, veered dangerously close to the Jungian concept of libido as a pure energic reservoir distinguishable only according to the direction of its moments. It was in order to anticipate and forestall this interpretation of ego-libido that Freud makes his crucial distinction, in the paper on narcissism, between auto-erotic instincts (the child derives its first sexual satisfaction auto-erotically, that is, from its own body) and the ego as a separate function: 'The auto-erotic instincts, however, are there from the very first; so there must be something added to auto-eroticism — a new psychical action — in order to bring about narcissism'.[6]

For Lacan, it is this moment which sets up the ego as an **imaginary instance:**

The *Urbild,* which is a unit comparable to the ego, is constituted at a

[5] Freud 'On Narcissism: An Introduction' (1914), SE 14; PF 11.
[6] 'On Narcissism', p. 77; p. 69.

specific moment in the subject's history, from which the ego begins to take up its functions. In other words the human ego is constituted on the foundations of the imaginary relation. The function of the ego, Freud writes, must have *eine neue psychische...Gestalt.* In the development of the psychic organism, some thing new appears whose function it is to give shape to narcissism. Surely this marks the imaginary origin of the ego-function?[7]

— a specific *Urbild* or construct, therefore, which from then on functions as the instance of the Imaginary, commanding both the illusory nature of the relationship between the subject and the real world, and the relationship between the subject and the identifications which form it as 'I'. The confusion at the basis of an 'ego-psychology' would be to emphasise the relationship of the ego to the perception-consciousness system over and against its role as fabricator and fabrication, designed to preserve the subject's precarious pleasure from an impossible and non-compliant real. The various shifts in Freud's own use of the concept from *Studies on Hysteria* where it is presented as an ideational mass, to its complete delineation as a separate function in the final topography *(The Ego and the Id)*[8] partially lend themselves to such a confusion. Lacan grafts his concept of the Imaginary on to the moment at which the fortification of the ego is conjoined with the possibility of deceptive self-reference in the concept of narcissism. In the 1936 paper 'The Mirror Stage', the relationship between narcissism and ego-formation 'reverses': the ego itself becomes the reflection of a narcissistic structure grounded on the return of the infant's image to itself in a moment of pseudo-totalisation. In Section II of the *Ecrits*, narcissism will be taken as the starting-point for three constitutive moments — that of the ego, of the function of recognition in its capacity to engender a potentially infinite number of objects in the world, and of the correlative functions of aggressivity and libidinal object-choice.

What does Lacan mean, therefore, when he states that the ego is an imaginary function? In what way is his concept of the Imaginary distinct from the point, stressed as early as 1895 by Freud in his *Project for a Scientific Psychology*,[9] that the

[7] *Les écrits techniques de Freud,* p. 133.
[8] Freud, *Studies on Hysteria* and *The Ego and the Id.*
[9] *Project for a Scientific Psychology,* pp. 295-297.

establishment of perceptual identity by the ego allows reality to be set up only to the satisfaction of the pleasure principle?

In his seminar of 1954, Lacan introduces the case-history of a six-year-old boy, named as Robert, as relevant to the psychoanalytic distinction between neurosis and psychosis. The case is presented by Rosine Lefort, who describes her patient as he first appeared to her at the age of three years and nine months in a state of hyper-agitation aggravated by complete motor and linguistic inco-ordination. I will not go into the details of the child's development through analytic treatment, but will stop at one of the first behavioural manifestations of the patient to be presented by the analyst: 'Unco-ordinated prehension — the child would throw out his arm to grasp an object and if he missed it, he would not be able to rectify his movement, but had to start it again from scratch'.[10] Lacan seizes on this factor as revealing that the subject's control of objects is not dependent on its visual capacity, but on the *synthesis* of this with the sense of distance, their co-ordination dependent on its ability to conceptualise its body as total; the rectification of the child's motor inco-ordination during analysis is taken to demonstrate the relation 'between strictly sensori-motor maturation and the subject's functions of imaginary control'.[11] The early emphasis by Lacan on *Gestalt,* on the child's ability to represent its body to itself, is, therefore, not simply a notion of some comforting if illusory poise, but is directly linked at this stage in his theory to its ability to control its world in a physical sense. In fact, one of the key factors of the mirror-stage is that the child is in a state of nursling dependency and relative motor inco-ordination and yet the image returned to the child is fixed and stable, thereby anticipating along the axis of maturation. Robert's incapacity is therefore a type of regressive paradigm of the mirror-stage where the absence of image leads to a failure in the function of bodily co-ordination. What is important here is the relationship between control, and an auto-synthesis based on a projected image of the subject, a relationship confirmed by the behavioural phenomenon of transitivism, in which the child imitates and completes the action of the other child in play: 'those gestures of fictitious actions by which a subject reconducts the imperfect effort of the other's gesture by confusing

---

[10] *Les écrits techniques de Freud*, p. 108.
[11] Ibid., p. 122.

their distinct application, those synchronies of spectacular captation that are all the more remarkable in that they precede the complete co-ordination of the motor apparatuses that they bring into play'.[12]

Taking off from the behavioural confirmations of the mirror-stage, Lacan then reads it back into a structure of subjectivity, whose basic relation is that between a fragmented or inco-ordinate subject and its totalising image (the structural equivalent of the metonymic relation, part for whole). In order to vehicle the image, the subject's own position must be fixed (in the first stage of the inverted vase experiment — cf. Fig. 1. — the eye must be inside the cone formed by a generating line joining each point of the image i(a) to the surface of the spheric mirror). It is from this fixity, and the images that are thus produced, that the subject is able to postulate objects of permanence and identity in the world.[13]

The mirror stage is, therefore, the focus for the interdependency of image, identity and identification: 'We have only to understand the mirror stage *as an identification,* in the full sense that analysis gives to the term: namely, the transformation that takes place in the subject when he assumes an image'.[14] As a result of identifying itself with a discrete image, the child will be able to postulate a series of equivalencies between the objects of the surrounding world, based on the conviction that each has a recognisable permanence. Identification of an object world is therefore grounded in the moment when the child's image was alienated from itself as an imaginary object and sent back to it the message of its own subjecthood. It is the process of enumeration and exchange which sets off from this point that will inform Lacan's later concept of linguistic insistence, defined as a process whch starts off from this position of a signifier which was primarily evicted from its own place.

The narcissistic mode of identification has as its corollary both the libidinal object-tie and the function of aggressivity. Lacan refers to Weissman's theory of the germ-plasm as confirmation of Freud's distinction between the subject as individual ego and the

[12] 'The mirror stage', p. 18.
[13] Note that Janet (quoted by Lacan) compared the formal stagnation of the images thus produced to the frozen gestures of actors when a film is halted in mid-projection (i.e. when it is not a film).
[14] 'The mirror stage', p. 2.

subject as the member of a species whose sexual function it is to privilege the type, and stresses that sexual drive depends on a recognition of appropriateness or typicality (rarely is sexual drive aroused by a member of another species).

In Freud's 1914 paper, narcissism became the prototype of a form of object choice based on the subject's own image(s) and was opposed to the anaclitic, where sexual desire was attached to self-preservative interest and hence selected its object according to the image of provider or protector. Lacan's emphasis places narcissism not only in opposition to the anaclitic form of object choice, but actually at the root of the minimal recognition necessary to ensure the subject's sexual engagement. Thus libido, far from being an energic or substantialist concept, is constitutionally bound to the Imaginary: 'We call libidinal investment that which makes an object desirable, that is, what leads to its confusion with the image we carry within us, diversely, and more or less, structured'.[15] What this means simply is that access to the object is only ever possible through an act of (self-) identification.[16] At the same time this relation of the libidinal object-tie to identification reveals perhaps at its clearest the paradox that the subject finds or recognises itself through an image which simultaneously alienates it, and hence, potentially, *confronts* it. This is the basis of the close relationship between narcissism and aggressivity, and Lacan turns to Klein for confirmation of the aggressive component of the original imaginary operation. The child expels objects which it fears as dangerous: 'Why dangerous? For exactly the same reason as it is dangerous for them. Precisely *en miroir,* the child reflects onto them the same destructive capacities which it feels itself to contain'.[17] It then turns to other objects, distinguished from and related to the first by means of an imaginary equation:

> Different objects from the external world, more neutralised, will be posed as the equivalents of the first, will be related to them by an equation which, note, is imaginary. Thus the symbolic equation [faeces — urine] which we rediscover between these objects arises

[15] *Les écrits techniques de Freud,* p. 162.

[16] Cf. Freud on identification in relation to love and hypnosis, *Group Psychology and the Analysis of the Ego,* chapter 8, 'Being in Love and Hypnosis', pp. 111-116.

[17] *Les écrits techniques de Freud,* p. 96.

from an alternating mechanism of expulsion and introjection, of projection and absorption, that is to say, from an imaginary game.[18]

Lacan goes on to make a distinction between projection and introjection, which will be discussed later. The point here is that the expulsion and absorption of objects in a Kleinian sense acts as the aggressive counterpart of the subject's discovery of itself in an alienated and alienating image which presents itself as dangerous and hence potentially as a rival. The final Oedipal identification of the subject with her or his rival (the parent of the same sex) is only made feasible by this primary identification which places the subject in a position of auto-rivalisation. The death instinct can be reformulated at this stage by Lacan as stemming not only from the submission of the individual to factor x of 'eternal life', but also from the libido's obligatory passage through the Imaginary, where it is subjected to a master image, and ultimately to the image of the master (the Oedipus complex).

Two factors emerge from this preliminary delineation of the Imaginary — the factor of aggression, rivalry, the image as alienating on the one hand, and the more structurally oriented notion of a fundamental mis-recognition as the foundation of subjectivity, with the image as salutary fiction, on the other. The division is in a sense arbitrary, and the two are bound by the concept of the ego as the instance of negation, presented by Freud in his 1925 paper of that title as the symbolic equivalent of the original expulsion mechanism whereby the subject builds itself and its world.[19] The mirror-phase demonstrates this process whereby the subject negates itself and burdens/accuses/attacks (*charger*) the other, and this has its corollary in the analytic setting where inclination towards the imaginary relation between analyst and analysand is always the sign of a resistance to signification:

> it is to the extent that the being's admission fails to reach its destination that the utterance carries over to the axis where it latches onto the other ... The subject latches onto the other because what is struggling for utterance fails. The blocking of the utterance, in so far as something perhaps makes it fundamentally impossible, is the pivot where, in analysis, speech tips over entirely onto its

[18] Ibid.,p. 96.
[19] Freud, 'Negation'.

original aspect and is reduced to its function of relating to the other.[20]

The emphasis on verbal communication[21] belongs here to Lacan's distinction between the Imaginary and the Symbolic, in their relationship to the third category, the Real. Before discussing these categories, it is necessary to show how the concepts which have so far emerged from that of narcissism can be further broken down into ideal ego and ego ideal on the one hand, and into the three types of identification put forward by Freud in chapter 7 of *Group Psychology and the Analysis of the Ego*[22] on the other, since it is on to these further distinctions that the Lacanian triptych will be charted.

In his paper on narcisssism, Freud goes on to discuss the relationship of the ego to repression, in that the ego becomes the guardian of that narcissistic self-regard lost with the insertion of the infant into a social world, and hence only retrievable by the setting-up of an image on which the subject will model itself. It is in the paragraph which describes this process, through which the subject conforms to an image which is, and can make it, the centre of its world, that the distinction between ideal ego and ego ideal appears: 'The subject's narcissism, makes its appearance displaced on to this new ideal ego, which, like the infantile ego,

---

[20] *Les écrits techniques de Freud,* pp. 59-60.

[21] Certain points should perhaps be clarified here. At this stage in Lacan's work the relation between the Imaginary and the Symbolic was often posed as a sequence — from the image (fixed, stable) to language or the word (the means of intersubjective communication). Since language is properly the domain of psychoanalysis, it is easy to see the relation between this and analytic practice. Resistance has two meanings here — as a reference to the stranglehold of the imaginary relation (hostility, rivalry, etc.) and as the refusal of the subject to relinquish that position and enter the domain of language. Language is therefore conceived of as a (potentially full) speech which breaks the impasse of the imaginary relation (hostility, rivalry, etc.) and as the refusal of the subject to distinction between ideal ego and ego ideal (the speech of the Other) discussed below, undergoes a crucial alteration in Lacan's own work, which also affects that between the terms Imaginary and Symbolic. At the point where language ceases to be a potentially full speech and is seen as a structure or set of differences based on a primary absence, there can no longer be a simple progression from the Imaginary (mis-recognition) to the Symbolic (mediation, recognition), since the emphasis is now on the 'splitting' which is constitutive of language itself. It is this conceptual shift which the essay goes on to describe in Part II.

[22] Freud, *Group Psychology and the Analysis of the Ego,* pp. 105-110; pp. 134-140.

finds itself possessed of every perfection that is of value ... He is not willing to forego the narcissistic perfection of his childhood ... he seeks to recover it in the new form of an ego ideal'.[23]

The distinction would seem to correspond to choice *(b)* and *(c)* of the four alternative narcissistic object choices:

(a) what he himself is (i.e. himself);
(b) what he himself was;
(c) what he himself would like to be;
(d) someone who was once part of himself [24]

— the ideal ego corresponding to what 'he himself was', and the ego ideal to what 'he himself would like to be', at the moment at which they can be identified as disjunct. The ideal ego would therefore be a projected image with which the subject identifies, and comparable to the imaginary captation of the mirror-phase; the ego ideal would be a secondary introjection whereby the image returns to the subject invested with those new properties which, after the 'admonitions of others', and the 'awakening of his own critical judgement'[25] are necessary for the subject to be able to retain its narcissism while shifting its 'perspective'.

The distinction here is that between projection as related to *Gestalt,* and introjection as invariably accompanied by the speech of the Other,[26] that is, to introjection as a symbolic moment, and the basis on which the further social investment necessary for the formation of the super ego will intervene. Significantly, when Freud introduces category *(c),* he adds the proviso that it will not be justified until a later stage in the discussion, the point at which he introduces the concept of the super ego.

The ideal ego will therefore be what the subject once was, the ego ideal what it would like to be in order to retrieve what it was,

[23] 'On Narcissism', p. 94; p. 88.
[24] Ibid.,p. 90; p. 84.
[25] Ibid.,p. 94; p. 88.
[26] Lacan seems to take his reference for this distinction from Freud's own comment that the 'admonitions of others' are 'conveyed to him by the medium of the voice' (ibid, pp. 94-96; pp. 88-90), thus again on a concept of language as the medium of intersubjective communication (cf. note 21 above):

> What is my desire? What is my position in the imaginary structuration? This position can only be conceived in so far as a guide is found beyond the imaginary, on the level of the symbolic plane, of the legal exchange which can only be embodied through verbal exchange between human beings. This guide who governs the subject is the ego ideal. (*Les écrits techniques de Freud,* p. 162.)

this being achieved by the introjection of someone who was once part of itself, the movement between them being the attempt to present-ify (make present or actual) their relation (what the subject is *(a))*. What Freud is describing is the impossible and continually re-asserted attempts of the subject to maintain the imaginary fiction of its own totality through which it was primordially constituted. The problem of a clash between an existential and formal ego ideal is raised, during the March 1954 seminar on this topic, by Serge Leclaire: 'either displacement of the libido takes place once more onto an image, an image of the ego, that is, onto a form of the ego, which we call ideal, since it is not like that of the ego as it is now, or as it once was — or else we call the ego ideal something which is beyond any one form of the ego, something which is strictly speaking an ideal, and which approximates more to the notion of idea or form'.[27]

The formal moment of the ideal ego is its structuration at the primary point of the mirror-phase, and the distinction between ideal ego and ego ideal resolves itself into the two moments of that phase, that of the corporeal image, prior and resistant to symbolisation, and that of the relation to the other, ultimately dependent on such symbolisation (the Other).

The experiment of the inverted vase is Lacan's illustration of these distictions. It falls into two stages, the first of which is a fairly well-known experiment of geometrical optics:

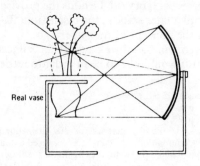

Real vase

FIG. 2

[27] Ibid., p.156.

By means of a spheric mirror, a real and inverse image can be produced of a vase which is upside down and concealed from sight. The image does not require an interposed screen for its observation but merely that the observing subject be situated in line with the point where the rays of light reflected off the mirror converge. This is the corporeal image of the subject and Lacan describes it as primary narcissism: 'This first narcissism is situated, if you like, on the level of the real image of my schema, in so far as that image makes it possible to organise the whole of reality within a certain number of pre-formed frames'.[28]

The corporeal image is identical for all mechanisms of the subject, and gives form to its *Umwelt*, in so far as it is a man or woman (and not, say, a horse). The unity of the subject depends on that image, and it becomes the basis for all future projection. The image of the upside down vase reversing itself into a position where it contains the diversity of the separate flowers (the original experiment is in fact the other way round) makes the experiment especially apt to demonstrate the slight access which the subject has to its own body.

In the second part of the experiment (Fig. 1), a virtual image is produced by means of a second mirror placed in front of the real image; the observer is now placed in such a position that she or he can see this virtual image without being able to see the real image of which it is the reflection; at each point it is the subject's necessary remove from the source of its own 'imagery' that is stressed. The virtual image is the place of secondary narcissism which enables the subject to situate its imaginary and libidinal relation to the world: 'to *see* in its place, and to structure as a function of that place and its world ... its *libidinal being*. The subject sees its being in a reflection in relation to the other, that is to say, in relation to the ego ideal'.[29]

---

[28] Ibid., p. 144.

[29] Ibid., pp. 144-145. The use of the other (small o) here is problematic given the earlier definition of the ego ideal in its relation to language; the author of the *Scilicet* article (cf. Part II) uses Other throughout; certainly there is a shift in Lacan's own usage from the small *a* as a reference to the imaginary other *(autre)* to its use as a reference to absence (the *objet petit a*). I take these shifts as indicative of the intrusion of the symbolic Other back over the imaginary relation. Cf. commentary by Jacques-Alain Miller, 'Table commentée des représentations graphiques', *Ecrits* (2nd edn), pp. 903-8:

the real image, henceforth designated as i(a), represents the specular image of the

The relationship posited here is given striking corroboration by Freud's own comment in a footnote to *Group Psychology and the Analysis of the Ego:* 'A path leads from identification by way of imitation to empathy, that is, to the comprehension of the mechanism by means of which we are enabled to take any attitude at all towards another mental life'[30] — especially when taken in conjunction with his separate observation on the 'narcissistic origin of compassion (which is confirmed by the word itself)' *(Mitleid).*[31]

How then does this place and structure inform the subject's future identifications? In *Group Psychology and the Analysis of the Ego,* Freud sets out to explain the relationship between this introjected ego ideal and the socialisation of the subject in a further group identification between egos. Taking the group phenomenon as the culmination of the deceptive function of identification, Lacan reformulates the question: 'how an object reduced to its most stupid reality, and yet assigned by a certain number of subjects the function of common denominator, thereby confirming what we will call its function as token, is capable of precipitating the identification of the ideal ego straight into that idiotic power of mis-chief that it basically reveals itself to be.'[32]

The power of the ego ideal to propel the subject into a position of dual submission to the master image introjected as ego ideal, and to those egos with which it posits itself as equivalent, becomes the starting-point for a second set of questions about the effective modes of identification, and their relationship to a demand which attempts to posit its own sufficiency, to retrieve or reconstitute a position of plenitude, and desire — the concept now introduced — which gradually undermines this certitude.

Freud posits three types of identification:

(a) identification as the original form of emotional tie with an object;

subject, whilst the real object *a* supports the function of the partial object, precipitating the formation of the body. We have here a phase prior to the mirror stage (according to an order of logical dependency) — *a phase which presupposes the presence of the real Other.* (pp. 904, my italics.)

[30] *Group Psychology,* p. 110n; p. 140n.

[31] Freud, *From the History of an Infantile Neurosis ('The Wolfman')* (1914) SE 17, p. 88; PF 9, p. 327.

[32] Lacan, 'Remarque sur le rapport de Daniel Lagache: "Psychanalyse et structure de la personnalité" ' (1960), *Ecrits,* p. 677.

(b) regressive identification as a substitute for a libidinal object-tie by means of introjection of the object on to the ego;

(c) identification which arises with a new perception of a (repressed) common quality shared with some other person who is not the object of the sexual instinct.[33]

I will start with the first form of identification to illustrate the problems which emerge from this new breakdown in relation to what has been presented so far, before going on to discuss them separately in terms of the Lacanian categories.

Freud first makes a distinction between identification and desire (object choice), giving the former precedence over the latter: 'In the first case one's father is what one would like to *be*, and in the second he is what one would like to *have*. The distinction, that is depends on whether the tie attaches to the subject or the object of the ego. The former kind of tie is therefore already possible before any sexual object choice has been made'.[34]

By making the small boy's pre-Oedipal identification with his father the model of primary identification, Freud clearly anticipates Lacan's stress on the alienating function of identification, and its close links with a potential rivalry which seeks to eliminate its object. Freud confirms the link by making this identification with the father, that is the primary socialisation of the subject, a derivative of the first, oral, phase of development: 'Identification, in fact, is ambivalent from the very first; it can turn into an expression of tenderness as easily as into a wish for

---

[33] The problem of sexual difference clearly informs the first two categories, since the second type of identification is obviously the prototype for the girl's identification with the lost primordial object (the mother), in fact one of the examples which Freud gives for category two is the male homosexual's identification with the mother. However, he also gives that of Dora's symptomatic identification with her father's cough *(Dora*, pp. 82-83; pp. 119-121), which shows that the second category is a pivotal point for identification based on sexual identity, and identification related to the repression of a secondary object of desire (the father). The third form of identification is illustrated by the 'smoked salmon' dream, in which the dreamer identifies with the woman she has unconsciously posited as her sexual rival. *(The Interpretation of Dreams,* pp.147-151; pp. 229-233) The relationship of this form of identification to a repressed object of desire, no longer an object of demand, is here clear (cf. Lacan's discussion of this dream in 'The direction of the treatment', pp. 256-263); this form of identification could also be taken as the model for the post-Oedipal identification of both girl and boy with the parent of the same sex.

[34] *Group Psychology*, p. 106; p. 135.

someone's removal. It behaves like a derivative of the first, *oral* phase of the organisation of the libido, in which the object which we long for and prize is assimilated by eating and is in that way annihilated as such'.[35]

Introjection of the ego ideal has its purely libidinal equivalent in the mechanism of incorporation, which acts here as a double reference to the cannibalistic relationship between mother and child (later to be stressed by Klein), and to the totem meal, where absorption of the father's body leads to the appropriation of his status and name. Only the first part of this dyad can strictly speaking be termed incorporation, since the second is its ritualised and social derivative, and is therefore related to the introjection of the ego ideal which had been defined as necessarily bound to language.

The totem meal now appears as a ritual symbolisation of the transcendence of those forms of rivalry (Oedipus as a secondary rivalisation) which only appear at the point where identification becomes contaminated with the question of desire. This question appears excluded from the unmitigated demand characteristic of the oral and anal phases of development which imply the possibility of the total incorporation or mastery of the object (the fiction of plenitude). Lacan reads the three types of identification posited by Freud in terms of the gradual intrusion of the axis of desire on to the axis of identification, an intrusion which can be measured against the shift from the drives of demand (oral, anal) to those of desire (scopic, invocatory) in which the physical distance of the object reveals the relation between subject and object to be necessarily disjunct. Note that it is precisely at the moment when those drives most relevant to the cinematic experience as such start to take precedence in the Lacanian topography that the notion of an imaginary plenitude, or of an identification with a demand sufficient to its object, begins to be undermined. The three forms of identification can tentatively be equated with three moments which correspond to the Lacanian division Real, Imaginary, Symbolic:

(a) privation (demand directed to a lost object);
(b) frustration (demand which cannot be given its object);
(c) castration (demand for which there is no object).

[35] Ibid, p. 105; pp. 134-135.

Each type of identification is thus taken as the model for a mode of relation (primary object-relation, regressive identification with libidinal object, identification between egos), a structure of insufficiency (privation, frustration, castration), and a tension between demand and desire with a corresponding set of alternative drives.

What is important here is that the demand of the subject is in each case directed outwards to an external object, and it is the relationship of this demand to the place of the object it claims that becomes the basis for identification. The earlier emphasis on ideal ego inevitably fades as both incorporation and introjection obscure the plane of a projected or objectifiable totality. The precedence of the Real in the Lacanian scheme, as the point of the subject's confrontation with an endlessly retreating reality, signals this definition of the subject in terms of an object which has been lost, rather than of a totality which it anticipates.

The reference for this can again be taken from Freud, in the path that leads from his early remarks on the loss of the object which characterises the infant's relation to the world (*The Project for a Scientific Psychology*) to the concept of repetition elaborated in the *Fort Da* game (*Beyond the Pleasure Principle*).[36] Thus in the first instance Freud indicates that the child's first utterance (the cry) is predicated on the missing object which it thereby represents, and in the second that the infant only finds or constitutes itself through the articulation and the repetition of the loss of the object in play: 'the alternation presence/absence only *makes sense* to the extent that the infant can identify itself with the reel of cotton as absent, which presupposes the logical foundation of its identification to a signifier which is missing'.[37] Taken together these instances point to what Lacan will call the constitution of the subject in the moment of its splitting (hence *Ichspaltung*), a moment which we can already discern in the fiction of self-representation — the subject sees itself as a whole only by being placed *elsewhere* — of the mirror-stage. It is the loss of the object and the relation of the subject to this loss — the knots which the subject gets into in its attempts to elide or re-place it — that Lacan terms the structure of desire.

[36] *Project for a Scientific Psychology*, pp. 366-367; *Beyond the Pleasure Principle*, pp. 14-17.
[37] 'Le clivage du sujet', p. 111.

II

At this point the two-dimensional optical schema is no longer adequate since the object is visible, or rather on the same dimension as the image which is its substitute. What is now needed is a means of representing the essential disjunction between the imaginary and the lost object as existing on a separate plane. The author of 'The Splitting of the Subject and Its Identification' takes the torus or solid ring to represent this disjunction, since operation or movement carried out on its surface circumscribes a central void which determines the limits of that movement while remaining essentially outside it. I will use these diagrams together with the first optical schema, as I think they most clearly illustrate the inadequacy of that schema and the need to reformulate the question of the subject in relation to the object of the scopic drive. The subject is now defined no longer in terms of reflection (the image) but in terms of differentiation (cuts, joining, disjunction).

The author of 'The Splitting of the Subject' quotes Freud to show how identification in itself depends on a repetition which can only be the mark of its own difference: 'The identification is a partial and extremely limited one and only borrows a single trait from the person who is its object'.[38] This single trait is the 'unique' trait since the whole series will depend on its pure repetition; the idea of unity is here rigorously dissociated from the idea of totality, at the basis of the earlier concept of *Gestalt*, and attached to the structural concept of a unit as a single element in an already functioning enumeration system. It is therefore called a unary rather than a unique trait, since it can only be articulated as that which is apparently identical. The example drawn on here is de Saussure's 8.45 Geneva-Paris express[39] which, although it can manifestly be a different train from that of the previous day, is yet identifiable as the same since it is different in function from the rest.

Thus Freud's remark, made in reference to the second form of identification, is extrapolated as the indication of a potentially structuralist concept of identity, where each element is distinct from its own origin, different at each new instance of its repetition, and identical only in its opposition to all the other elements in the

---

[38] *Group Psychology*, p. 107; p. 136.
[39] *Course in General Linguistics*, p. 107.

signifying chain. This concept was obviously implicit in Lacan's stress on the determinate role of the 'other' image in the mirror-phase; here it represents a new emphasis on *coupure* or splitting, of which the compulsive repetition of trauma will be the clinical counterpart: 'we see here a point that the subject can approach only by dividing itself into a certain number of agencies'.[40] The movement away from a stress on illusory totality and identity, to identity as a function of repeated difference can thus be seen as representing a shift in Lacan's emphasis from the Imaginary, to the structure of linguistic insistence as already underpinning moments prior to its intervening symbolisation.

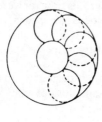   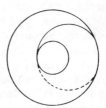

FIG. 3   FIG. 4

The first diagram (Fig. 3) shows the relationship of demand to privation, the circles repeating themselves in a helix around the ring representing demand in its repetitive function, while showing

(a) that demand cannot attain itself, but increases its distance from its point of departure at each turn, thereby testifying to its incapacity to seize the object which supports its own movement;

(b) that the point at which demand does meet up with itself is the point at which it has outlined the central void, but *without knowing it,* since it has no point of contact outside its own surface.

Here the subject identifies with the all-powerful signifier of demand from which it is indistinguishable; but already unable to signify the lost unit except by repeating it as different, it fades before that signifier.

In the second drawing (Fig. 4), the subject thinks it has gone the

---

[40] *The Four Fundamental Concepts,* p. 51.

round of its own space, but fails to distinguish between the space interior to its outer surface, and the central void which it has simultaneously circumscribed without realising it. The diagram illustrates the distinction between idealisation — a 'complete' rotation — and desire — a central void — of which there is no knowledge.

Turning next to Lacan's optical schema, the emphasis is now placed on the second mirror A, manipulated by the Other (*Autre*), so that whereas the first image depended on the fixity of the observing subject, the second virtual image is a function of the relationship between the rotation of mirror A and the field of space behind it. The distinction between projection and introjection, the image emitted and received, is now reinforced by the intervention of the Other as the locus of speech, which, investing the ego ideal with language, sets it up for subsequent identification with the Law. This role of the Other

(a) undermines the autonomy of the primary *Gestalt;*

(b) reveals its own position as exponent of desire, which means that it is seen to be determined by the same loss or void as that which underpins the demand of the subject itself.

The Imaginary can now be defined in terms of this intrusion of the Other, and the corresponding tension between the assumed plenitude of A and its gradual emergence as incomplete. Lacan criticises his first schema in these terms: 'we would be wrong to believe that the big Other of discourse can be absent from any distance taken up by the subject in its relation to the other, which is opposed to it as the small other, as belonging to the imaginary dyad.'[41]

This Other is now even referred back to the primary moment of the mirror-stage:

> For the Other, the place of discourse, always latent to the triangulation that consecrates that distance, is not yet so as long as it has not spread right into the specular relation in its purest moment: in the gesture with which the child in front of the mirror, turning to the one who is holding it, appeals with its look to the witness who decants, verifying it, the recognition of the image, of the jubilant assumption, where indeed *it already was.*[42]

[41] 'Remarque sur le rapport de Daniel Lagache', p. 678.
[42] Ibid.

The permeation of the Other over the specular relation therefore reveals the necessity of *appeal*, and hence the structural incompleteness of that relation, and then, through that, the irreducible place of desire within the original model:

> The problem is that our model throws no light on the position of the *objet a.* For as an image for a play of images, it cannot describe the function which that object receives from the symbolic... *a,* the object of desire, at the starting point at which our model situates it, is, as soon as it begins to function there ... the object of desire ... Which is why, reflected in the mirror, it does not only provide a' as the standard of exchange, the currency whereby the other's desire enters into the ideal ego's moments of transitivity. It is returned to the field of the Other as exponent of the desire in the Other.[43]

Thus the object is missing from the Other, while this still acts as the place wherein the subject alienates its own image and simultaneously grounds its desire.

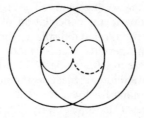

FIG. 5

In a next stage, the subject, having gone the round of its own impossibility, will simply displace on to the Other its conception of a full subjectivity or plenitude which it addresses to the Other as demand. Fig.5 is the model of frustration, as that moment when, basing its desire in this alienating image, the subject finds that its own demand as subject is identifiable with the desire of the Other; and the demand of the Other identifiable with its own desire. The outer circle of repetition can be seen to coincide with the central void of the secondary torus to which the first makes its appeal.

[43] Ibid., p. 682.

This can be taken as the new model for the imaginary structure, manifested most clearly in transference, when the neurotic directs its demand to the object of desire, the one object that cannot be demanded, and simultaneously submits its desire to the Other's demand; this latter expectation is recognisable as the basis for the impositions of the super ego. The author of 'The Splitting of the Subject' defines this relationship: 'It is this very moment that reveals what it is that binds the Other to the imaginary function, since it is through its identification to the specular image that the subject of privation now comes to differentiate, from those circles which can cancel each other out on the surface of the torus, those which are irreducible because they circumscribe a void'.[44]

In this way, the subject relies on the Other in the imaginary relation, not to constitute a full identity, but in order to circumscribe a void identified with the Other's demand; the object of desire at this point appears to be concealed within that demand, which acts as the metaphor for the unary trait. Specular identification replaces a previously undifferentiable series of repetitions with this new equivalence. The rigour of the subject's conformity is not due to the cancellation of a void, but to the simultaneous differentiation and displacement of that void which such identification permits. This mode of identification corresponds to the regressive mode of identification which is a substitute for the lost libidinal object tie; the subject identifies with the object of its demand for love.

In the final stage of the topography, the object of desire has been stamped as the effect of the impossibility for the Other to reply to demand. Henceforth 'the object is no longer an object of subsistence, but object of the ek-sistence of the subject: the subject there finds its place outside of itself, and it is to this function that the *obet a* of the first rivalry will ultimately be led'.[45] The moment of castration is that in which the Other reveals itself as exponent of desire or false witness, and it represents the final collapse of the Other as the guarantor of certitude. Desire is now the point of intersection between two demands, and is left over as that which simply cannot be signified. This form of identification could be defined as that which arises with a new perception of a common quality shared with someone who is not an object of sexual desire;

[44] 'Le clivage du sujet', p. 121.
[45] Ibid., p. 123.

it is identification now conditioned by its function as support of desire.

Having now demonstrated the distinction between the optical schema, as positing an autonomous Imaginary, and the torus as revealing the irreducible nature of the object of desire, the author of 'The Splitting of the Subject' points to the need for a diagram which could illustrate the possibility of grasping internally to the

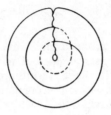

FIG. 6

model this irreducible void, which is now defined as the object of the analytic process (the subject's advent to desire). The model used is the cross-cap or projective plane. By means of a cut the model can be split into two separate parts, one of which will seize its central point and the other of which will appear as a Moebius strip. The latter now represents specular identification, the former the subject in its relation to desire. The model is difficult, but two basic factors should be retained:

(a) the cut which constitutes the subject in its dependent relation to the object of desire also allows the subject to *detach* itself from the specular illusion;

(b) the cut which detaches this fragment also determines the topological properties of the fragment which remains; hence the specular illusion as apparently separate, but always the *effect* of the basic structure of desire: 'the essential factor is that the *coupure* which detaches the object is that which simultaneously determines the topological properties of the fragment which remains and which does have an image in the mirror'.[46]

It is to the way in which this radical cut or *coupure* informs the

---

[46] Ibid., pp. 132-133.

structure of specularity itself, the subject's position in relation to the image rather than to the image it vehicles, that Lacan addresses himself in that part of his 1964 seminar entitled 'The Look as *objet petit a'*.[47] Projective geometry is now used to show the presence or insistence of desire inside those very forms which are designed to reproduce or guarantee the specular illusion itself (image, screen, spectator).

III

In the four seminars grouped under the heading 'The Look as *objet petit a'*, Lacan uses a series of models and anecdotes to challenge what he calls the idealising presumption whereby the subject assumes it 'can see itself seeing itself', persistently referring back to its own subjectivity a 'look' which manifestly pre-exists its intervention as subject. The Imaginary itself, through which the subject sets itself up as subject and the other as object, can be seen to contain a potential reversal — the subject is constituted as object by the Other — for which the structure of specularity is now taken as the model.

The dual screen relationship of the spectator in the cinema, described by Metz[48] — the screen on to which the film is projected and the internalised screen which introjects that imagery — is the exact counterpart of that process whereby the subject is endlessly 'pictured' or 'photographed' in the world:

> in the scopic field, the look is outside, I am looked at, that is to say, I am a picture.
>
> It is this function which lies at the heart of the subject's institution in the visible. What fundamentally determines me in the visible is the look which is outside. It is through the look that I enter into the light, and it is from the look that I receive its effect. From which it emerges that the look is the instrument through which the light is embodied, and through which — if you will allow me to use a word, as I often do, by breaking it up — I am *photo-graphed*.[49]

Thus the subject of representation is not only the subject of that

---

[47] *The Four Fundamental Concepts*, pp. 67-119.
[48] See Metz, 'The Imaginary Signifier'.
[49] *The Four Fundamental Concepts*, p. 106 (translations modified).

geometrical perspective whereby it reproduces objects as images:

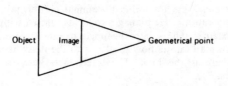

FIG. 7

it is also represent*ed* in that process, illuminated by the light emitted by the object of its own look, and thereby registered simultaneously as *object* of representation. Lacan relates the anecdote of the fisherman who pointed at a can of sardines floating on the water, and, turning to the young Lacan with a laugh, said: 'You see that can? Do you see it? Well, it doesn't see you'!.[50] Lacan attributes his discomfort at the 'joke' to his sudden realisation of the alien 'figure' he made within that community; but he goes on to use the anecdote to illustrate the *schize* between the eye and the look, since if the can couldn't *see* him, yet, as the converging point of the light which it emitted back to the observer, it was in a sense *looking* at him.

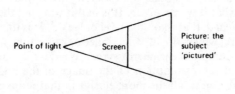

FIG. 8

The introduction of the screen demonstrates:

[50] Ibid., p. 95.

1. The subject's active intervention in the imaginary relationship, in which it is seized by the object of its look:

> Only the subject — the human subject, subject of desire which is man's essence — is not, unlike the animal, entirely taken in by this imaginary capture. He manages to locate himself within it. How? To the extent that he isolates the function of the screen and plays off it. Indeed man knows how to play with the mask as that beyond which there is the look. The screen acts here as the site of mediation.[51]

2. The role of desire within that relationship; an object veiled from sight by an over-intense light can be discerned only if a screen is interposed which partially obscures that light and/or the observing subject; the screen thus blocks the subject from the light in order to expose its object, and the 'look' of that object is seen to emerge only in this moment of partial elision:

> As soon as the subject attempts to accommodate itself to this look, it becomes that punctiform object, that vanishing point of being with which the subject confuses its own failing. Thus, of all the objects through which the subject can recognise its dependency in the register of desire, the look specifies itself as that which cannot be grasped.[52]

The screen therefore serves a dual function, as locus of the image off which the subject will play in an attempt to control its imaginary captation, and as a sign of the elusive relation between the object of desire — the look — and the observing subject: 'The subject presents itself as other than what it is, and what it is given to see is not what it wants to see. It is in this way that the eye can function as *objet a*, that is, on the level of lack'.[53] It is this look, as object of desire, which already functioned as a question mark over the asserted triumph of the mirror stage: 'What is manipulated in the triumph of the assumption of the image of the body in the mirror, is that object, all the more elusive in that it appears only marginally: the exchange of looks'.[54] The super-imposition of Lacan's two triangles:

[51] Ibid., p. 107.
[52] Ibid., p. 83.
[53] Ibid., p. 104.
[54] Lacan, 'De nos antécédents', *Ecrits,* p. 70.

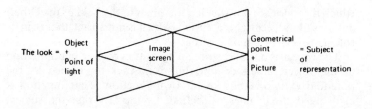

The look = Object + Point of light | Image screen | Geometrical point + Picture = Subject of representation

FIG. 9

illustrates the conjunction of screen and image which now reveals the elision both of the inaccessible object and of the subject as the guarantor of certitude: 'in so far as the picture enters into a relation with desire, the place of a central screen is always marked, which is precisely the means whereby, in front of the picture, I am elided as subject of the geometrical plane'.[55] Even the first triangle which demonstrated the laws of perspective contains a potential reversal, since the lines drawn from the object on to a surface to produce an image of that object, can be redirected onto a further plane to produce a gross deformation or anamorphosis. Conveniently for Lacan's demonstration, the most famous pictorial illustration of anamorphosis — Hans Holbein's *The Ambassadors*[56] not only challenges the subject's fixed relation to the picture, since it is only as the subject withdraws that the object can be discerned, but also demonstrates this challenge on the level of its content, since the object perceived as the subject moves aside is a human skull.

This whole section of the seminar appears as a repeated collapsing of the imaginary relation into desire, here related to death as the zero point of the subject. This central role of desire is read by Lacan into the passage in *Being and Nothingness* in which Sartre describes the observer at the keyhole, suddenly startled by the sound of approaching footsteps from his complacency as *voyeur*.[57] The subject is not just caught by a look which subjects it and cancels its position as 'pure' observation; it is caught by a look

[55] *The Four Fundamental Concepts*, p. 108.
[56] The picture forms the front cover of *The Four Fundamental Concepts*.
[57] *Jean-Paul Sartre, L'être et le néant*, 1943; tr. Hazel E. Barnes, *Being and Nothingness*, New York 1966, pp. 347-350.

which it cannot see but which it imagines in the field of the Other; and it is literally caught in the act, which is not an act, that is, in its role as *voyeur* or support of desire.

The *voyeur* is not, therefore, in a position of pure manipulation of an object, albeit distant, but is always threatened by the potential exteriorisation of his own function. That function is challenged three times over: first, by the fact that the subject cannot see what it wants to see (it is this which becomes the conditioning factor of voyeurism which deliberately distances its object); secondly, by the fact that it is not the only one looking; thirdly, that the reciprocity implied in this is immediately challenged, since the subject can never see its look from the point at which the other is looking at it. These three moments can be seen to correspond to the three moments of privation, frustration and castration: the subject is depossessed of its object, the subject posits a full equivalence between itself and another subject, the subject is led to realise that this apparent reciprocity is grounded on the impossibility of complete return.

IV

The gradual ascendancy of the question of desire over that of identification in Lacan's theory seems to raise several issues of potential importance for film theory. It is no coincidence that the late emergence of the concept of 'splitting' in Freud's own work (the 1927 paper of 'Fetishism' and the 1938 'The Splitting of the Ego in the Process of Defence') is echoed in Lacanian theory by the movement from a concept of *Gestalt* to one of identity as a function of repeated difference.[58] It does seem to me that certain propositions made by Christian Metz in his article 'The Imaginary Signifier' could be questioned in terms of that movement, and I will conclude by tentatively suggesting where this essay diverges from his position.

Metz's article sets itself the question 'What contribution can Freudian psychoanalysis make to the study of the cinematic signifier?' Its most important aspects for this discussion are the sections on the theoretician's relation to the film object (described in Kleinian/Lacanian terms as the imaginary restoration of the

[58] Freud, 'Fetishism' (1927), SE 21; PF 7; 'Splitting of the Ego'.

'good' object which the critical activity endlessly destroys and repairs), and the spectator's relation to the image on the screen (described more specifically in terms of Lacan's concept of the mirror-stage).

Metz distinguishes identification in the cinema from the primary identification of the subject with its body in the mirror, since the spectator's own body is not seen on the screen and, as a subject, it has already passed through this primary identification; it can therefore recognise objects in the world without needing to see itself as such. The spectator's identification with the image and/or characters on screen is therefore described as secondary, the subject's identification being primarily with the camera itself. This is the fantasy of the all-perceiving subject (subject and centre of the look) which is thus seen to be inscribed within the very apparatus of cinema itself. This same fantasy can be recognised in an idealist ontology of film which sees the development of cinema as an increasingly realistic appropriation of the world. Metz rightly challenges this 'delusion' or 'idealising presumption' (Lacan) of the centred subject, but he remains largely within the terms of the theory he is criticising. Thus for Metz, what deludes the subject is the sense of a perceptual mastery of the world, whereas what the spectator is in fact seeing are mere images demanding to be recognised as real (verisimilitude). The subject is, therefore, deluded by the nature of the perceptual phenomena, rather than by its very position as origin or centre of vision.

This stress on the absence of the object seen has as its corollary a notion of a full non-imaginary relation to the object, and the assigning of the invocatory and scopic drives to the realm of the imaginary *because of* the distance which underpins their relation to the object. As we have seen above, however, the scopic and invocatory drives, which could be said to specify the spectator's relation to the cinema, simply reveal the absence of the object which underpins the drive *per se,* rather than being characterised by an absence which can be equated with the physical absence of the object from the cinematic screen. What follows are a number of differences with Metz's arguments which lead on from these remarks:

1. Inasmuch as the Imaginary becomes conditioned by the object of desire exposed in the field of the Other, the Imaginary cannot simply be equated with Klein's 'good' and 'bad' objects,

even if the imaginary game she describes is at the basis of the first moments of that function.

2. The fact that the subject's own body is not on the screen does not necessarily distinguish its experience from that of the mirror stage; the subject never specularises its own body as such, and the phenomenon of transitivism demonstrates that the subject's mirror identification can be with another child.

3. The relationship of the mirror stage to the structure of the look is not a sequential one; the emergence of the latter in Lacan's theory throws into question the plenitude of the former in its very first moments, where the Other is not just the sign of an intervening symbolisation but also the exponent of desire; one cannot, therefore, refer to the mirror stage as primary identification, and to that of the look as secondary identification which is primary in the cinema; the question of secondary identification needs to be examined more closely in relation to Lacan's reading of the three modes of identification posited by Freud.

4. Since the structure of specularity undermines the Imaginary topic, certain aspects of that structure cannot be taken as marginal instances of the cinematic experience:

(a) The relationship of the scopic drive to the object of desire is not simply one of distance but of externalisation, which means that the observing subject can become object of the look, and hence elided as subject of its own representation (the *oeil derrière la tête*[59] could therefore be the means whereby the subject's position as spectator in the cinema is continually threatened); the illusion at the basis of the subject 'seeing itself seeing itself' does not only appear in the meta-activity of critical analysis, but is raised and challenged by the operations of the specular illusion *per se*.

(b) The intervention of the specular relation in the imaginary plane demonstrates that the structure of subjectivity, grounded on a decisive *coupure*, is in itself fetishistic: *(i)* fetishism has virtually no connection with Klein's 'good' object,[60] since the third term necessary to its formulation is completely excluded from her description of the child's paranoid-schizoid and then depressive

[59] This phrase of André Green's is quoted in Metz, 'The Imaginary Signifier', p. 49.

[60] 'The Imaginary Signifier', p. 75.

relationship to the mother; *(ii)* fetishism cannot be placed as a marginal instance of the cinematic experience, manifested by a passion for technique,[61] but must be re-centralised in relation to the subject's precarious control of that experience, precisely bcause that control is first affirmed by the subject's apparent centralisation in the cinema as subject of the geometrical plane; Metz's points about scopic perversion therefore need to be referred directly to those relating to the 'all-perceiving subject'; equally, the disavowal and affirmation which he ascribes to the reality status of the objects portrayed on the screen, and secondarily to the subject's critical posture in relation to the film, need also to be related to a query hanging persistently over the subject's position as centralised Ego.

5. All these points could perhaps be formulated in relation to the ambivalent function which Lacan ascribes to the screen itself, as the locus of a potentially ludic relationship between the subject and its imaginary captation, and the simultaneous sign of the barrier between the subject and the object of desire.

6. Finally, what Metz says of the 'presentified absence' of the object in the cinema, is, as he points out, equally applicable to any pictorial representation. Whether the density of the sensory register in the cinema makes this any more true of the cinema can perhaps best be queried by the story of Zeuxis and Parrhasios, used by Lacan to illustrate the distinction between lure or decoy and *trompe-l'oeil* or illusion; Zeuxis draws grapes on to a wall which act as a bait for unsuspecting birds, but Parrhasios goes one further by painting a veil on to a wall so effectively that Zeuxis turns to him and asks what lies behind it; in order to dupe a human subject: 'what one presents to her or him is a painting of a veil, that is to say, something beyond which she or he demands to see'.[62]

---

[61] Ibid., pp. 74-75.
[62] *The Four Fundamental Concepts*, p. 112.

The Cholmondeley Sisters, British School, Seventeenth Century, c. 1600-1610

8
The Cinematic Apparatus — Problems in Current Theory

A paradox seems to be emerging from recent developments in film theory.[1] On the one hand, within feminism, the debate about sexuality is being posed increasingly with reference to construction or representation (the dialogue with psychoanalysis). In this debate, the cinematic image is taken as both the model of and term for a process of representation through which sexual difference is constructed and maintained. This is in direct continuity with what has always been for women an attention to the 'image', the necessity recognised by feminism, and in a sense specific to it, of posing the political problem in terms of the constructed image: at its simplest, the question of 'how we *see* ourselves'; more especially for cinema, the question of woman as spectacle. What is crucial about these discussions is that they *start* from the question of sexual difference, this being the concept, or position, on which the analysis is based. On the other hand, as a corrective to earlier tendencies in semiotics (the problem of formalism)[2] and to the

---

[1] This article was written in response to feminist issues in relationship to film theory which had been raised at a conference on 'The Cinematic Apparatus' held at the Center for Twentieth Century Studies at the University of Wisconsin-Milwaukee in 1978. It was published in *The Cinematic Apparatus,* edited by Teresa de Lauretis and Stephen Heath, London 1980, pp. 172-186.

[2] The turn to psychoanalysis was undoubtedly part of the response to this problem of formalism, recognised in Metz's own work as the need for an account of the ceaseless working over by the particular film of the codes of cinema, the displacement of the cinematic in and through the filmic text. A similar shift can be

reductive ways of conceptualising the cinematic apparatus (simple notions of determination by the technological), an appeal is being made to psychoanalysis which seems systematically to ignore the question of sexual difference. This is all the more striking in that the appeal continually draws on concepts from psychoanalysis which were only produced in response to that question and hence can only be justified by it — or not, as the case may be (feminism's critique of psychoanalysis).

My concern here is not to enter into the debate within feminism about psychoanalysis but rather, taking up arguments made by Jean-Louis Comolli and Christian Metz, to look at something of this elision of sexual difference in their theorisation of the cinematic apparatus, to show how the concept of sexual difference functions as the 'vanishing point' of the theory and to suggest some of the possible repercussions for ways of thinking about film-making practice for women.[3]

I

Central to Comolli's account of cinema is the concept of analogy. The first question which needs to be asked is what is at stake in this concept. Initially it seems to work against two equally inadequate versions of cinematic history: cinematic perfectibility as the direct product of technological progress; cinema as a set of

seen in literary semiotics in the movement from a structural typology to textual analysis, from the structural analysis of narrative to the opening of the text in its disturbance in and of narrative codes. In both cases, attention is focused on the enunciation of the text (the place of the reader, spectator) as against the enounced (the organisation of the fiction): 'the psychoanalytic enquiry ... in comparison with the discourse of a more classical semiology shifts the point of focus from the statement [*énoncé*] to the enunciation [*énonciation*]' (Metz, 'The Imaginary Signifier', p. 3). It can then be asked why this shift has produced such radically different results in the two areas. On the one hand, in literary semiotics, the concept of sexual difference is posed as an inherent part of the redefinition (the placing and displacing of sexual difference taken as crucial to the process of writing itself), with an increasing stress on the avant-garde text, 'text' against 'the work' (cf. Barthes's 'From Work to Text', *Image, Music, Text*) and on the activity of the reader in the text. On the other hand, in cinema semiotics the problem of difference seems to have been elided with consequences that this article attempts to specify, and attention has been directed above all to the classic fiction film with the spectator defined in terms of an imaginary, essentially passive cohesion.

[3] Jean-Louis Comolli, 'Machines of the Visible', *The Cinematic Apparatus*.

heterogeneous social machines. Analogy serves to draw together the various instances of the cinematic apparatus — optics and the camera (realism and the ontology of the visible), the process of production (the perfect reproducibility of the photographic image, film as industrialised commodity), the process of projection (the spectator's identification with camera and/or fiction); referring in each case to a kind of technological programming of a desire for recognition.

In its original formulations, this was the basis of Metz's introduction of the concept of the imaginary into the metapsychology of film. It was then already clear that the main problem of that introduction was its definiton of the last of these three instances (the process of projection) in terms of the first (ontology of the visible), so that the imaginary fantasy of the spectator was her or his identification with a world mistaken as real (the cinema is always an image). By confining the concept of the imaginary within the debate about realism, Metz made the spectator's position in the cinema (the fantasy of the all-perceiving subject) a mirror-image of the error underpinning an idealist ontology of film (cinema as a ceaseless and gradually perfected appropriation of reality). More importantly, it made the delusion of the spectator the *effect* of that ontology, so that what was seen to be at work constantly correcting the delusion was an awareness that the cinematic image, despite its perceptual richness, was in fact not real, an awareness present alongside the delusion itself.

This was the first appearance of the concept of disavowal in the metapsychology of film; its adherence to a theory of perception and the problems thus produced were evident: 'Before this *unveiling of a lack* (we are already close to the cinema signifier), the child, in order to avoid too strong an anxiety, will have to double up its belief (another cinematic characteristic) and from then on for ever hold two contradictory opinions (proof that the real perception in spite of everything has not been without effect).[4]

On re-reading this now, the difficulties seem overwhelming. Firstly, since the effect of the cinematic apparatus is to conceal its distance from, or construction of, reality, how can it be compared with this instance of traumatic perception? Secondly, and crucially for feminism, the concept which Metz draws on is in itself problematic precisely *because of* the status it accords to the

[4] Metz, p. 70.

instance of perception (which is the basis of Metz's comparison). What the example refers to in Freud, and Metz completes the reference, is the discovery of female anatomy to the boy child, its 'revelation'. Apart from the difficulty of the exclusively male construction of the reference, the problem is its account of this moment exactly as a revelation, whereas in fact it is clear that the perception of an absence can have meaning only in relation to a presence or oppositional term, to a structure — that of sexual difference — within which the instance of perception *already finds its place*. This is the stress of those concepts developed by Freud — such as after-effect — which fight against the notion of immediate causality implicit in the passage quoted (and, it must be said, in certain aspects of Freud's own work) and which place the assumption of sexual difference within a structure of differences held elsewhere (the phallus as always already privileged) without which the moment of perception would strictly have no meaning. Thus it is that the aspect of the concept of disavowal which is most problematic within psychoanalytic theory itself and, not coincidentally, which has been most strongly objected to by feminism (the sight of castration, nothing to be seen as having nothing, Irigaray's *'rien à voir équivaut à n'avoir rien')*,[5] the concentration on the visual as *simply* perceptual, is the very aspect that Metz imports into the theory of the spectator's relation to the screen. The paradox is that the instance of disavowal only has meaning in relation to the question of sexual difference but is used within the theory only in relation to the act of perception itself. What this also means is that the illusion of imaginary identity is challenged solely by the unreality of the image (difference as the difference from the real object); that is, any challenge to the imaginary remains within the terms of the imaginary itself.

Note too for the moment that another effect of all this is the virtual disappearance of the concept of the unconscious: disavowal as a conscious 'I know, but...' — 'I know that it's not real, but I'll pretend while I'm here that it is.' This is important as it can easily produce discussion as to the intelligence or otherwise of the mass spectator-consumer of film (are they really duped or not?). It is also an essential distinction for feminism if disavowal is to be maintained in its relation to sexual difference without being open to justifiable feminist criticism (real inferiority as the

[5] Luce Irigaray, *Speculum of the Other Woman*, p. 48.

automatic deduction from a real perception).

To describe the cinematic apparatus as a 'machine of the visible' seems at first sight to be in direct line with this way of looking at cinema. In fact, Jean-Louis Comolli's description introduces a number of changes into the original argument from the basis of his work on technology, changes that are in a sense correctives to some of the problems just raised but in a way that again elides the central term of difference and that can this time be seen to have an immediate bearing on the idea of political cinema.

Analogy operates at a further level: as a reference to the industrialised series and to standardisation, with cinema as part of the mechanical manufacture of objects whose mass production at the end of the nineteenth century coincided with a social multiplication of images and a notion of the world as appropriable through its visibility. This suggests another form of disavowal, that of the process of production itself, all those aspects of the technological apparatus — photochemistry, grading, mixing — that are made subordinate to the visual image which the cinema perfects (or whose perfection the cinema reproduces) at a time when that image knows a real instability (photography as a potential disturbance or decentring of Renaissance vision — optical aberrations, refractions, retinal persistence, etc.). The photographic image is seen as the norm to which the cinema conforms. Thus, for example, the transposition of depth of field to shade, range and colour is taken as the response to developments in the photograph, as well as being part of a displacement of the codes of cinematic realism onto the more complex planes of narrative and fictional logic.

Now given the various elements of this argument, which would seem to demand a number of different ways of thinking about cinematic practice (the question of process and/or narrative), why do the concepts of analogy and disavowal reappear with such remarkable conformity to Metz's original definition? The problem is all the more striking in that there are specific questions which Comolli's work raises only to evade. First, what is the effect of the extension of the concept of analogy into the description of cinema as industrialised machine if not to reinforce the idea of cinema as simply the reproduction of imaginary identity? Cinema thus appears as a type of analogical machine for the programming of identity, a process written into the origins and history of the apparatus itself, something that would then have to be argued against specifically in making the case for the possibility of a political cinema. Secondly, what is the pertinence of stressing the invisible aspect of cinematic process if not to reintroduce, positively, the idea of film process and the material production of the image back into the film-making activity? And finally, given the emphasis on conformity to the photographic image ('it might be you', cinema as the possible recognition of oneself on screen) and the corresponding emphasis on forms of narrative logic, what types of identification and recognition are at stake? Metz himself distinguished cinematic identification from primordial mirror-identification on the grounds that the spectator did *not* actually see his or her own body on screen, and also placed narrative identification as secondary in the cinema to identification with the camera itself.[6] Comolli's use of analogy and self-recognition brings this 'secondary' identification — the history of specific forms of narrative organisation and of the images through which they have been produced and secured — back to the centre of the debate.

The answer to these questions is complex but the issues are not followed through in that complexity. Something of what happens can be grasped if one looks, precisely, at the way that Comolli uses the concept of disavowal. Here, it can be seen most clearly as a conscious 'I know, but...', relating to the fictional nature of cinematic representation (not quite identification with camera or character but rather with the world as seen). From this basis, it is translated into a privileging of the cinematic institution as the system of representation in which the threshold of mystification is at its lowest and whose radical potential is therefore highest. Disavowal is thus imperceptibly turned into a matter of intelligence or manipulation: 'there is no uncertainty, no mistake, no misunderstanding or manipulation'; and from there: 'it is necessary to suppose spectators to be total imbeciles, completely alienated social beings, in order to believe that they are throughly deceived and deluded by simulacra'; which leads to a specific justification and privileging of cinema: 'yet it is also, of course, this structuring disillusion which offers the offensive strength of cinematic representation and allows it to work against the completing, reassuring, mystifying re-presentations of ideology.'[7]

---

[6] Metz, pp. 48, 56.
[7] Comolli, pp. 140-141.

(This could almost be Brecht on the potential of cinema before he was brought up against censor, camera, subjective inserts ... .) The political potential of cinema is written into the process of disavowal itself (the 'I know' before the 'but...') and is simply a reversal of that process.

The point is not that there is anything wrong with constructing a positive theory of cinema on an incorrectly used concept of disavowal (an 'academic' objection); rather, it is that this has only been possible — as a kind of saving of cinema against industrial fetishism (in Marx's sense now) — by ignoring the real concept of difference which the use of disavowal constantly solicits and then at once loses 'sight' of, and which, if it were addressed, would demand a very different type of attention to the way that sexual difference and identification are construced across the cinematic space.

Take, for example, the model which Comolli uses for the cinema's self-designation as fiction, an analogical reproduction which is and is not a reproduction, and hence contains a potentially activated difference. It is surely no coincidence that that model is a painting of two women, 'a famous painting of the English school, *The Cholmondeley Sisters* (1600-10)'[8]; mothers and babies, alike and not alike, the reflection of each other but not quite. The model is illuminating in the very problems it raises. For what is the nature of a parallel between an image which is the effect of the suppression of the terms of its construction as in cinema and an image in which identity is split across two almost identical images? How can we refer to this image as if it simply represented that process of construction without addressing the socially recognisable forms through which identification is played out — reproduction/repetition posed twice over in the image of the sisters and their own reproduction again (the babies they hold)? And that the problem of representation be found across these two images of women unavoidably raises the question of woman *as* image, woman as guarantor and sanction of the image against the latent trouble *of* the image, the panic of the look produced ('panic and confusion of the look').[9]

This question of woman in the image as safeguard against the trouble of the image is surely what is at issue in any feminist

[8] Ibid., p. 138.
[9] Ibid.

discussion of cinema, and yet the model is taken and overlooked in this sense (ironically thereby confirming its function). What this produces is a definition of social relations, when they appear in the argument, purely in terms of submission and authority (the inverse corollary to a stress on manipulation of the visible world) — 'all that is filmable is the changing, historical, determined relationship of men and things [sic] to the visible...'[10] — and then within Comolli's own film, *La Cecilia,* (Italy/France, 1976), a use of woman in which her relationship to the cinema (the question of woman as image) is never posed. In this film, the story of a political commune, the woman appears as plenitude, as a totality of cinema, given as spectacle from the terms of her first appearance (a tracking shot which follows her as object of the men's look); or else as disturbance, as a figure who troubles community and image, when we see her lying diagonally on the grass, breaking across the frame in shots of her conversations with this or that member of the commune.

There seems, indeed, to be a direct sequence here: analogical repetition, disavowal, conscious knowledge, political cinema; with difference as either distance from reality or the social relations of men and things, and sexual difference as the missing term. It is, in fact, only because difference is set up in the argument through the notion of distance from reality that, in discussion, Comolli is able to justify the nature of the image of the woman, her use in this film, on the grounds that there was only this woman, that this *was* the reality (the actual history he is describing at the expense of, or forgetting, the history of his description, that is, of these familiar images of the woman as part of the history of cinema itself).

II

Something about the body, and hence potentially about the constitution of sexual difference, is nonetheless constantly present in these arguments. Thus Metz concluded his discussion of fetishism by reference to the cinema as a 'body', *physis*, literally material,[11] this being the precondition of its continuing effectivity;

[10] Ibid., p. 139.
[11] Metz, p. 75.

and through all the considerations of physical process (the repressed of cinema), the idea is finally there that what is lost is the very material or substance of cinema, a body to be recovered *for* cinema, and perhaps against the other bodies, the recognisable relations and identifications, played out on screen. Put like this, the idea has its attractions, the notion of a space that might be created against the dominant forms of cinematic representation. It is in this context that Comolli reintroduces depth into the image field as part of a theatricalisation of the shot, depth against cinema, and so against manipulative forms of fictional logic, 'bodies in space' ... women in depth? This is the danger, if the relationship between the problem of woman as image and the creation of an alternative narrative space is not formulated as such. For what happens here is that woman and space 'in depth' are identified as marginal, fetishised, one could say (what else can an insistence on depth outside its historically attested connotations really be?).

This question of process is one that comes up again and again. At its simplest, it goes as follows: once one starts to talk about a difference or break in the system of representation, to what extent does one remain, or have to remain, within the same psychoanalytic economy? Moments when the diegesis is broken in musical comedy or the internalisation of process into certain types of avant-garde film practice (and the two examples are often cited together), is this simply the difference beneath the disavowal? A difference which perhaps becomes even more difficult when the structure is recognised as that of sexual difference, because of the place and the image of woman then produced (the negative term). Or is it a more primordial difference, prior to or outside that construction, somehow retrievable through the very mobility which the photographic image sets itself to halt? The desire is to get outside the form of representation which demand and reproduce the socially coded objects of fetishism (at least recognised here as such). This is the question asked by Jean-François Lyotard: 'must the victim be on stage for *jouissance* to be intense?'[12] It is surely not by chance that the example he uses to raise that question again refers to a woman: the Swedish *posering*

---

[12] Jean-François Lyotard, 'L'àcinéma', *Cinéma: théorie, lectures,* special number of *Revue d'esthétique,* Paris 1973; tr. 'Acinema', *Wide Angle* 2:3, 1978, p. 59.

in which the erotic object is fixed an immobile, *posed*, woman as the object of the spectator's gaze who thus enjoys off bodies at a distance — in depth? ('Presently there exists in Sweden an institution called the *posering,* a name derived from the *pose* solicited by portrait photographers: young girls rent their services to these special houses, services which consist of assuming, clothed or unclothed, the poses desired by the client. It is against the rules of these houses — which are not houses of prostitution — for the clients to touch the models in any way ... it must be seen how the paradox is distributed in this case: the immobilisation seems to touch only the erotic object while the subject is found overtaken by the liveliest agitation.')[13]

Two separate points seem to be involved here, both of which need to be formulated in relation to feminism. On the one hand, there is the discussion as to types of object represented. This raises, for example, the whole question of the 'relative potency' of images as indicated by the films of the British avant-garde film maker Peter Gidal and his accounts of their practice: his concern to avoid the socially coded objects of fetishism, the refusal to produce and reproduce film images of women and hence the refusal to use images of women in his films — with the (symptomatic) duality that this then imposes: against anthropomorphic identification through the narrative relations of human figures (which means images of women or men), but also, as the inevitable stressed addition to the general rule, against images of women, specifically, and whether in or out of conventional narrative (the point Laura Mulvey will make in her essay 'Visual Pleasure and Narrative Cinema': that the image of the woman is the best way of stopping narrative flow without trouble, unpleasure).[14] At one level this position is clear, if pessimistic: the objects to be subjected to the film process should not be the culturally received objects of fetishism and censor. The fact that it is the image of the woman that here causes the split in the theory, forcing the film-making activity to think itself on two fronts, foregrounds this very problem of woman and representation. On another level, and on

[13] Ibid., p. 57.
[14] Laura Mulvey, 'Visual Pleasure and Narrative Cinema', *Screen,* 16: 3, Autumn 1975. Mulvey describes how the image of the woman can be a disturbance and rupture of narrative cohesion, but also how its transposition into spectacle (woman purely *as* image) serves to neutralise this disturbance, to hold it off.

the other hand, it can produce an effect which seems worrying and which relates to the general notions of space and economy that are introduced into certain discussions of avant-garde film. Thus Maureen Turim has argued that the general undecidability and fluctuation of spatial representation has as its analogy (no coincidence again) the model of the girl-child caught in and playing off a series of refracted mirrors: pre-mirror phase, unconstituted, fragmented, and at the same time defined and recognised as a girl, placed as somehow before representation and then projected onto the breakdown of cinematic space.[15] Once again the impetus is clear: the attempt to place woman somewhere *else*, outside the forms of representation through which she is endlessly constituted as image.

The problem is that this sets up notions of drive, rhythmic pulsing, eroticisation of energy pre-representation, a space of 'open viewing', which then makes film process itself socially — and sexually — innocent. Film process is then conceived as something archaic, a lost or repressed content ('continent'), terms to which the feminine can so easily be assimilated, as it has been in classical forms of discourse on the feminine as outside language, rationality, and so on; arguments which are now being revived as part of the discussion of psychoanalysis and feminism, the search for a feminine discourse, specific, outside.[16]

The dangers are obvious. That such arguments overlook the archaic connotations of these notions of energy and rhythm for women, at the same time that they render innocent the objects and processes of representation which they introject onto the screen, seems again to be not by chance.[17]

It may be possible to identify the problem more specifically by looking at the kind of theoretical discussion from which something of these arguments is drawn. Lyotard, in an article entitled 'The Unconscious as *Mise en Scène*', takes Freud's 1919 essay 'A Child is Being Beaten' and sets it against *The Interpretation of Dreams*, as sexuality against meaning. Freud is

---

[15] Maureen Turim, 'The Place of Visual Illusions', *The Cinematic Apparatus*.

[16] See especially Luce Irigaray, *This Sex Which Is Not One*.

[17] Turim raises this explicitly with reference to Lyotard's work: 'But the danger of a purely Lyotardian analysis is that in its concentration on the description of libidinal engagement it tends to ignore the representation that remains in the art object', Turim, pp. 146-147.

seen as moving away from language to drive, and the contradictions in the fantasy described in 'A Child is Being Beaten' are taken as the model for the breakdown of representation. In fact, Freud's essay illustrates at its clearest the relation of drive *to* representation (this latter not being a primary message even in *The Interpretation of Dreams* but fractured and problematised), to the problem of femininity no less. For what the fantasies of the female patients reveal is the difficulties and structuration of feminine sexuality across contradictions in subject/object positions and areas of the body — the desire of the woman is indeed 'not a clear message'[18] (whoever said it was?). Note also that Freud uses this very essay to attack Adler's theory of 'masculine protest' as the cause of all repression — why then, Freud asks, do boys suppress only the homosexual object and not the passive fantasy? The essay demonstrates that male and female cannot be assimilated to active and passive and that there is always a potential split between the sexual object and the sexual aim, between subject and object of desire. What it could be said to reveal is the splitting of subjectivity in the process of being held to a sexual representation (male *or* female), a representation without which it has no place (behind each fantasy lies another which simply commutes a restricted number of terms). All this needs to be spelt out because Lyotard uses Freud's essay for the idea of different, non-theatrical, representational space, a 'pictorial space of virtual bodies', another space again of 'open' viewing. We have to ask what, if the object itself is removed (the body or victim), is or could be such a space of open viewing (fetishisation of the look itself or of its panic and confusion)? And what does this do for feminism? Other than strictly nothing, dropping all images of women; or else an archaising of the feminine *as* panic and confusion, which is equally problematic, simply a re-introjection as feminine — the pre-mirror girl — of the visual disturbance against which the image of woman classically acts as guarantee.

The aim in all this for a model of desire which might be feminine, or at least outside the structuration of sexuality inherent in classic forms of representation is, however, important. For, returning to the concept of disavowal, to redefine that concept as the question of sexual difference is necessarily to recognise its

[18] Lyotard, 'The Unconscious as *Mise en Scène*', *Performance*, eds. Michel Benamou and Charles Caramello, Madison 1978, p. 94.

phallic reference: how woman is structured as image around this reference and how she thereby *comes to* represent the potential loss and difference which underpins the whole system (and it is the failure to engage with this that is the problem with Metz's and Comolli's work). What classical cinema performs or 'puts on stage' is this image of woman as other, dark continent, and from there what escapes or is lost to the system; at the same time as sexuality is frozen into her body as spectacle, the object of phallic desire and/or identification. There seems to be a genuine double bind here which reproduces itself on the level of the theory. For, if it is in relation to this phallic reference that woman is defined as different or outside and the organisation and cohesion of cinematic space is always also the securing of that reference, then the other side of this — the disturbance or trouble behind the cohesion itself — cannot be brought back into the cinematic space *for* women without thereby confirming the negative position to which she was originally assigned.

The problem appears in feminist discussion of what a feminine desire might be and can be posed interestingly with regard to Comolli's film — how exactly do we desire the woman in *La Cecilia*? On the one hand, there is the argument that it is some primordial desire that the image of the woman as full activates or potentiates (moment of fusion of, say, Lyotard and Klein[19] — a different space being a primordial archaic feminine sexuality, exactly woman in depth); and on the other, an argument which is less immediately attractive for feminism perhaps, that if she is desired at all, it can only be across a masculine identification, the only place within cinema for desiring a woman being a form of control through the look (the question of Sternberg's *Morocco* — what is really at stake in the famous shot when Dietrich kisses the

[19] *From* Freud, Melanie Klein concentrated on the pre-oedipal relationship between the mother and girl child; *against* Freud (the concept of the phallic phase), Klein argued for the girl's early (re-)cognition of specifically feminine bodily sensations. In fact, by tracing the Oedipus complex back to the earliest stages of child development, Klein could be said to have collapsed the concept of pre-oedipality altogether, while analysts drawing on her theories who have insisted on the girl's early awareness of feminine anatomy can be seen to return the girl child, and later the woman, to a natural bodily femininity against which everthing else is then described as a defensive or secondary 'aberration'. See Melanie Klein, 'Early Stages of the Oedipus Complex' (1928), *Contributions to Psychoanalysis,* London 1948, and Ernest Jones, 'The Phallic Phase'. For a fuller discussion of these issues, see Juliet Mitchell 'Introduction 1', *Feminine Sexuality.*

woman in the cafe?).

From this a further question can emerge, that of woman's own desire for her position as fetish (the splitting of subjectivity across masculine/feminine, the disjunction between anatomy and identification is perhaps at its clearest here since the woman is taken to desire herself but only through the term which precludes her). The question is posed by a very different film practice, that of Aimée Rankin and Steven Fagin's *Woman/Discourse/Flow* (USA, 1978), a film in which the problems of cinema as 'generalised strip-tease' ('cinema with its wandering framings, wandering like the look, like the caress,...a kind of permanent undressing, a generalised strip-tease'[20]) and of 'seeing oneself seeing oneself' (the risks inherent in recentring the spectator's look) are given specifically as the problem of the image of the woman in cinema. The film attempts to demonstrate the image of woman as the very difficulty of cinema: writing is used not just as a punctuating or literalisation of the image but equally of the woman's body as image (the body of the woman is written over and across with a whole theory of cinema and a whole romance of the woman, typed cards fixed to her body, phrases traced directly on her skin); we see the woman film maker Rankin filming her own body (the body is therefore inseparable from the gaze through which it is constituted); that body is gradually identified and framed, and then its loss precipitates the breakdown of the recognisable cinematic space as the camera begins a random pattern of movement which obliterates the field of vision, the depth of the image and its body. Which is not to say that there are not difficulties in the film: the relationship which seems to be posited between the woman's body and the grain of the film, body and grain as a kind of initial purity, the latter the natural process of the former (at the start of the first shot of the woman's body a focus pull takes us from the texture of film and skin into the argument of cinema and her image), the way in which the written discourse across the body of the woman can be seen as masquerade or the embodiment of a master discourse; and then, perhaps as a corrective to this, the moments when the engagement with the cinematic image seeks, through its voice over, to address another political space, more familiar notions, 'under his gaze', 'he doesn't care what I am inside', which appeal to a different and more

[20] Metz, p. 77.

familiar idea of women's oppression.

Finally we need to ask how to formulate in and through cinema, if one can at all, the relation between this constitution of the feminine and other forms of oppression and subjection for women, the attempt to hold the relation between the two. This was clearly the impetus behind Laura Mulvey and Peter Wollen's *Riddles of the Sphinx* (Britain, 1977). In one way, this is the other side of a query which is constantly raised for women: how to engage at all from a feminist position founded on notions of immediate or personal experience, the knowledge of one's own history, with forms or concepts of representation which depend for their analysis on the idea of the unconscious; how to move against the very nature of every day language, which leads to the question of *Riddles,* 'what would a politics of the unconscious be?'

There is no simple answer, but what is crucial to both these films is that they deal with the problem of cinema and the image of the woman simultaneously, the one as the problem of the other. They do so differently. Mulvey and Wollen's film attempts to create a series of positive images for women (the imaginary *for* women) which might also be seen as identifying women, through the very difficulty of this attempt, with what is archaic, outside, or even regressive (the movement of the film's narrative, the story of the central character, Louise, is a movement back from the impossible political struggle to her personal and finally prehistoric past).

Posing the question in these terms — the problem of woman and cinema, the problem of cinema as that constitution of the feminine described here — is the logical outcome of putting the concept of sexual difference back into discussion of the cinematic apparatus. To say that it has been overlooked is simply to confirm the very problem that I have tried to outline.

9
Woman as Symptom

There is a way of talking about film today which assumes a natural
transformation of the cinema, something simply taking place in
terms of its increased accessibility — as if a technological
revolution was occurring in which the apparatus of cinema would
be automatically transformed by its increased access to a greater
number of people.[1] In this argument certain concepts are used and
certain issues are privileged, like, for example, whether or not we
are actually losing our audience, or the idea of information as the
dominant function of cinema, as opposed to, say, fiction and
fictionality — that is, the question of what type of fictions the
apparatus of cinema actually constructs. A kind of collapsing
occurs in which problems of fiction and identification are
dissolved into those of technology and communication. Here I
want to talk about the other side of this emphasis, the processes of
identification — of 'imaginary' identification as Jacques Lacan
calls it — which are specifically involved in the very apparatus, or
dispositif, of cinema itself.[2] I want to suggest that the idea of an
unproblematic transformation of cinema through a change of
technology, or of access, is at least open to question, especially

[1] First given as a conference presentation at the Venice Biennale Film Festival
Conference *Cinema in the Eighties* which was held in Venice in 1979; published in
Cinema in the Eighties: Proceedings of the Meeting (Venice: Edizione 'La Biennale di
Venezia', 1980), pp. 23-25.
[2] See Jean-Louis Baudry, 'Le dispositif', *Communications* 23, 1975 (tr. 'The
Apparatus', *Camera Obscura* 1, 1976).

when we hear about someting as fascinating (in every sense of the term) as Shirley Clarke's *Love Tapes,* which she described as video images of women watching themselves talk about love and which seem to enact such a blown-up recurrence of the question of self-image, a veritable scenario of love and self-love, of self-recognition and identification.[3]

What I want to do therefore is take certain concepts like those of the imaginary and identification which have been used in the last five or six years in the analysis of cinema, concepts which were part of the movement away from the idea of a semiological science, indicate some of their difficulties and show how these relate to some of the problems of the cinema as we are presently trying to understand it.[4]

For semiology, the movement was away from questions of the strictly formal organisation of the cinematic product into questions of enunciation and specularity, and the key concept in that shift was that of the 'imaginary' brought into the analysis of film by Christian Metz in his crucial article on 'The Imaginary Signifier': 'In the field of film as in other fields, the psychoanalytic itinerary is *from the outset a semiological one,* even (above all) if in comparison with the discourse of a more classical semiology it shifts from attention to the *énoncé* to concern for the *énonciation* ... It has very often, and rightly been said that the cinema is a technique of the imaginary'.[5]

For Metz, this concept belonged to something he called the death of cinema in so far as the focus now was on textual systems as opposed to cinematic codes and on the way in which each film reworks and displaces the codes of previous films — a kind of putting to death of the cinema that has gone before it. It was in this context that Metz first turned his attention to those aspects of cinema which exceed the film product itself and which demand an investigation of how cinema is implicated in a whole structure which goes beyond the fact of the film and the place of the

---

[3] Shirley Clarke was one of the leading avant-garde documentary film makers working in America in the 1950s. She described her *Love Tapes* during an intervention at the conference.

[4] For a fuller discussion of these issues in relation to the film theories of Christian Metz and Jean-Louis Comolli, and a more detailed exposition of the concept of the 'Imaginary' see 'The Cinematic Apparatus: Problems in Current Theory' and 'The Imaginary' in this collection.

[5] Metz, 'The Imaginary Signifier', p. 3.

spectator in that process. The concept of the 'imaginary' was used here to refer to the way in which in narrative cinema the spectator identifies with the camera itself and is seduced into a regime of specularity, caught by the very apparatus itself and then identifying, necessarily, with the positions of desire and sexuality which each individual film puts into play.

Immediately, however, a paradox emerged or something which I would call a slippage in the theory, which has a number of crucial effects for some of the terms which are being used today in the analysis of cinema. For the question which Metz asked in relation to the imaginary, the question through which he brought the concept into the analysis of film, was 'What contribution can Freudian psychoanalysis make to the study of the cinematic signifier?'[6] But in so far as the project of semiology was a move away from the concept of the cinematic code, there is a slight paradox already that the role of psychoanalysis is to emphasize the specifically cinematic. What this leads to is an omission of certain concepts from psychoanalysis which are crucial to an understanding of the whole apparatus of cinema — notably that of sexual difference.

According to Metz, cinema is the most *imaginary* of representational apparatuses because its perceptual presence is more acute and tangible than any other system of representation, at the same time as that representation is in fact more enigmatic, more absent, missing in the strict sense of the term (the idea of an encounter which necessarily took place before the spectator's experience of the film). Thus the concept of the imaginary became confined to the question of perception, the reality of what was seen on the screen, with the corresponding insistence that, while the spectator is more duped in the cinema than in any other art form, she or he is nonetheless aware of that process and is therefore strictly in a position which psychoanalysis would call one of disavowal: 'I know (that what I am seeing is not real) but (I will pretend whilst I am here that it is)'. The problem starts here, however, in that for psychoanalysis the actual reference for the notion of disavowal is to the concept of sexual difference, to that moment when the boy child for the first time perceives the difference between his body and that of the girl, an image which is absolutely unentertainable for the boy — whereupon he disavows

[6] Ibid., p. 42.

what he sees.[7]

It is this description which has been at the heart of the feminist polemic with Freud, but there are two ways of reading it. One is simply to refer it to that instance of perception and to make of it nothing *other* than a moment of perception which is immediately effective in its results, which means that the sight itself (with the associated connotation of inferiority) has an immediate psychological effect on the child. The other way of reading this moment is to see that it has absolutely no meaning outside a structure of sexual difference (the point at which boys and girls must define themselves *as* different) within which socially and historically the male term is already privileged. More crucially, it is only in terms of this fundamental question of how sexual difference comes to be read by the child that the concepts of perception and disavowal brought into the metapsychology of film can be understood. Yet the concept is used purely with reference to the act of perception and not to the structure of sexual difference in terms of which alone it has any logic.

The same thing happens with the concept of the imaginary, for once again it only has meaning with reference to a system of fiction through which the viewing subject entertains a false image of herself or himself as a totality, thereby closing off or repressing the problem of difference which undermines any fictional cohesion or identity of self. For we need to remember that the imaginary, of which the cinema may well be the most privileged and efficient machine, is precisely a *machine*, an apparatus in which what is at stake is a repression of refusal of the difficulty of sexuality itself. The imaginary falls under the structure of disavowal insofar as the refusal of sexual difference is already figured by the subject in the earliest attempts to constitute an illusory mastery of self. Sexuality, and specifically sexual difference, are therefore the terms which need to be centred in the analysis and consideration of cinema if those concepts from psychoanalysis are to have any meaning (we need to ask why this detaching of the concepts has in fact taken place), and if that movement away from a classical semiology is to have its proper effects.

At the same time, something is going on which seems to involve a kind of coincidence, if not exactly a complicity, between

---

[7] Freud, 'The Dissolution of the Oedipus Complex' and 'Some Psychical Consequences of the Anatomical Distinction Between the Sexes'.

developments within psychoanalytic theory, within the semio-logical analysis of cinema and even within the industry of cinema itself. Thus in the analysis of film as a textual system (notably in the work of Raymond Bellour and the journals *Camera Obscura* and *Screen* on Hollywood narrative films), it is a particular logic of desire that is identified as produced and reproduced by the cinematic machine. A logic through which cinema as an apparatus tries to close itself off as a system of representation, but constantly comes up against a vanishing-point of the system where it fails to integrate itself and then has to refuse that moment of difference or trouble by trying to run away from it or by binding it back into the logic and perfection of the film system itself.[8]

And in Lacanian psychoanalysis there has been a similar and related emphasis, through the concept of the *'pas tout'*, that is, the 'not all' of any system of representation, the idea that there is no such system, however elaborated or elevated it may be, in which there is not some point of impossibility, its other face which it endlessly seeks to refuse — what could be called the vanishing-point of its attempt to construct itself as a system. And in so far as the system closes over that moment of difference or impossibility, what gets set up in its place is essentially an image of the woman. We can recognise in this account the scenario of sexual fantasy. It is again the crucial point within the theory: the system is constituted as system or whole only as a function of what it is attempting to evade and it is within this process that the woman finds herself symbolically placed. Set up as the guarantee of the system she comes to represent two things — what the man is not, that is, difference, and what he has to give up, that is, excess:

> On the one hand the women becomes, or is produced, precisely as what he is not, that is, sexual difference, and on the other as what he has to renounce, that is, *jouissance*.[9]

The psychoanalytic approach to these question therefore

[8] See in particular Raymond Bellour, 'L'évidence et le code', *L'analyse du film*, Paris 1979 (tr. 'The Obvious and the Code', *Screen* 15:4, Winter 1974-75) and 'Enoncer', in ibid. (tr. 'Hitchcock, The Enunciator' *Camera Obscura* 2, 1977); Kari Hanet, 'Bellour on *North by Northwest'*, *Psychoanalysis and the Cinema: Edinburgh '76 Magazine*, London 1977; Stephen Heath, 'Film and System: Terms of Analysis', *Screen* 16: 1, Spring 1975 and 16: 2, Summer 1975.

[9] Lacan, *D'un discours qui ne sera pas semblant*, 6, pp. 9-10.

parallels or echoes those analyses of cinema which have addressed themselves to the way in which the woman gets set up, not simply as a certain *image,* something which can be criticised historically or sociologically, but as a *guarantee* against the difficulties of the cinematic system itself.

Three films can convey a sense of the way in which the difficulty of the system as a problem of cinema comes to be inscribed across the body of the woman: *Carrie* (Brian de Palma, 1978); *Coma* (Michael Crichton, 1978); and *Fedora* (Wilder, 1978). Each of them illustrates a kind of panic of this process, that is, a panic at the centre of cinematic enunciation itself. Each film produces a self-consciousness of cinema, a kind of commentary on the very apparatus of the film, but then this very self-consciousness is reduced to the question of the body of the woman, of what is at stake in constituting her as the object (and subject) of the look.

In *Carrie,* the story of a woman with parapsychological powers, there is a form of reference to or playing off (a teasing) of cinema which runs right through the film. It starts with the opening shot where the camera moves up and down the body of the girl in the shower and then lights on her menstruation — the end point and trauma of the sequence for camera, Carrie herself and spectator alike. It then moves to the very end of the film when the screen splits to show the effects of Carrie's crazed vision (one half of the image) on the rest of the town (the other half). In both of these instances, which are key moments in the film, what is important is not just the classic and obviously disturbing image of the woman which makes her destructiveness so literally an effect of her body (the unavoidable link which the film produces between that first and last shot). More important is the fact that the movement and play of cinema, the risks that it takes with itself — for these are both moments when the film draws attention away from narrative to its own technique — are drawn back into the problem of the woman and become in this case almost an effect of her look. Rather as if the way that this film works over its own traces and foregrounds its operations and codes is covered and even cancelled out by the relentless focus on her gaze (Carrie as the evil eye).

What links these films for me — and recognising of course that this is an arbitrary selection — is the way that they take something about classical Hollywood cinema and either twist it, perfect it, inflate it or break it, and then draw that moment back into a question about the very form of the image of woman in film. Thus in *Coma* there is a kind of perfecting of the hermeneutic code, the basic code of detection and suspense, but also its inversion because it is a woman who occupies the place normally given to the male protagonist, for example in Hitchcock's films. The central woman character tries to uncover why her woman friend, and then others before her, have gone into coma and then disappear in the hospital where she works. But what this releases is a kind of paranoia across the whole space of her investigation as she starts to believe that everyone is against her. As if there was an excess or danger in the very idea of the woman as detective (the idea that she might actually *look*) which produces its paranoid reversal although there is in fact only one villain in the film. The film then has to forget this spiral of paranoia which goes way beyond anything that the narrative can finally resolve. The film tidies up the narrative (the classical Hollywood ending where the heroine is saved by her man) but the anxiety which it has unleashed around the woman remains in excess.[10] This apart from the more obvious fact that the film is, at a much cruder level, about investigating, looking into, rendering unconscious — quite literally — the body of the woman.

In *Fedora*, the process is almost too obvious — the reference to surgery, the cosmetic, the very image of the woman as the image of a dying cinema. It is the story of a film star ravaged by plastic surgery who demands of her daughter that she takes up, identifies with, and masquerades in her place, a demand that can only be refused finally by the suicide of the daughter. Staged like the death of Anna Karenina, this death is the opening shot of the film. But there is one thing which is important in this context about *Fedora*, something for which it was criticised by a number of critics. There is a moment in the film, before we are told the truth about Fedora and her daughter, before the point when the ugliness of what the cinema machine has done to this woman is revealed as the consequence of the interaction between the mother and child, when the daughter is seen to be mad and when that madness can only be seen as an effect of the apparatus and history of cinema itself, since none of us yet know, neither the audience nor the chief male protagonist, what lies behind that madness, that is, the fact

[10] For an extensive analysis of this film, to which these brief remarks are indebted, see Elizabeth Cowie, 'The Popular Film as Progressive Text — a discussion of *Coma*', *m/f* 3, 1979 and 4, 1980.

that it has a cause — the story which the film goes on to describe. That moment then has to be forgotten or refused, it has to be turned into a psychological drama about the relation between the mother and daughter; it cannot simply be held as a troubling or accusation of cinema itself. *Fedora* has been criticised precisely because of the length of that moment before everything is explained, before we are, as it were, told the truth of the story at the cost of that other more troubling truth which resides in the machinery of cinema itself. The comparison has been made with Hitchcock's *Vertigo* in which there is also a long period of narrative time in which neither the protagonist nor the audience know what is going on (that the woman who has appeared in the narrative is in fact the same as the woman we thought to be dead). What seems to be unacceptable, therefore, is that we should not *know*, that there should be a disturbance which cannot be resolved into the terms of an explanation, and which might persist, as the problem of cinema's relation to itself. What this film does, therefore, is to set up the image of woman *as* cinema (the film star) in such a way as to simultaneously refer to and disavow the problem *of* cinema, which is explicitly in *Fedora* its *death* (the film is a nostalgic rework by Wilder of his own *Sunset Boulevard* with William Holden as the star once again).

I want to end by telling a story which represents for me a model for the whole apparatus of cinema, a short story by Anais Nin from her collection *Delta of Venus,* the pornographic stories she wrote in the 1940s with Henry Miller for one hundred dollars a day (the person commissioning the stories thought they would send her on a life of debauchery, but according to Nin they sent her to sainthood instead). The story is called 'The Veiled Woman' and it is very simple — I will only give here the rudiments of the story.[11]

There is a man in a bar and he sees a veiled woman and this woman is with a man. The woman leaves the bar and the man comes up to the first man and tells him that he is completely dominated by the caprices of a woman who will only make love to a man if she has never seen him before and will never see him again. He then offers to pay the first man (George) to satisfy the desires of this woman. So George goes to make love to this woman and is given fifty dollars and there is a long description of the taxi

[11] Anais Nin, 'The Veiled Woman', *Delta of Venus* (1969), London 1978, pp. 84-91 and Preface, p. 11.

drive, how he is blindfolded and then arrives at a house where the mirrors are so bright that he can't see anything and how he then makes love to the woman. The whole episode is presented through the point of view of the man, what he sees and what he is thinking and feeling throughout. He then leaves, is haunted by the experience for months which he cannot repeat with any other woman, and then one evening a man comes up to him in a bar and tells him of an extraordinary experience: a man who approached him and offered, for a fee of a hundred dollars, to let him see a magnificent love scene. And when the first man (George) asks him to describe the scene, he recognises it as the very scene in which he had participated. A detailed analysis of this story would be out of place here especially in that I want it to serve merely as an emblem in which one detail in particular is crucial. For although the writer does not tell you as such, it is clear that the money that the first man received for making love to the woman is the money that the second man paid to see the scene (fifty to a hundred dollars so there is a doubling of the primary investment at stake). Thus behind this staging, or '*mise en scène*', of desire with the woman at the centre (knowable and unknowable, blinding and veiled and yet the ultimate object of the gaze), there is a whole circulation of money, fantasy, and exhibition which can only be represented on the outskirts of the scene itself. If cinema is a commodity caught in a system of exchange, what price the image of the woman in that process?

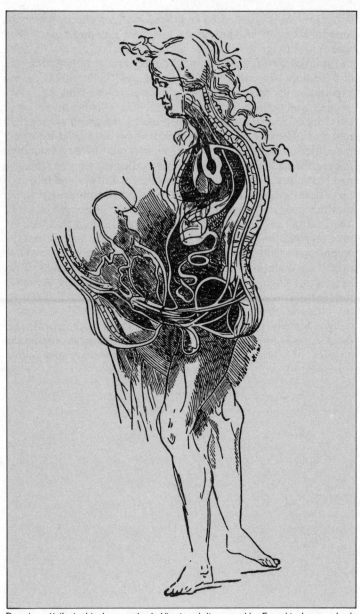

Drawing attributed to Leonardo da Vinci and discussed by Freud in *Leonardo da Vinci, A Memory of His Childhood*

10
Sexuality in the Field of Vision

In an untypical moment Freud accuses Leonardo of being unable to draw[1]. A drawing done in anatomical section of the sexual act is inaccurate. What is more it is lacking in pleasure: the man's expression is one of disgust, the position is uncomfortable, the woman's breast is unbeautiful (she does not have a head). The depiction is inaccurate, uncomfortable, undesirable and without desire. It is also inverted: the man's head looks like that of a woman, and the feet are the wrong way around according to the plane of the picture — the man's foot pointing outwards where the woman's foot should be, and her foot in his place. In fact, most of Freud's monograph on Leonardo is addressed to the artist's *failure*, that is, to the restrictions and limitations which Leonardo himself apparently experienced in relation to his potential achievement. Freud takes failure very seriously, even when it

[1] Sigmund Freud, 'Leonardo da Vinci and a Memory of his Childhood', p. 70n; p. 159n. This essay was written for the catalogue of the exhibition *Difference: On Representation and Sexuality*, held at the New Museum of Contemporary Art, New York, December-February 1984-85 and at the Institute of Contemporary Arts, London, September-October 1985, pp. 31-33. The exhibition, curated by Kate Linker, included works by Ray Barrie, Victor Burgin, Hans Haacke, Mary Kelly, Silvia Kolbowski, Barbara Kruger, Sherry Levine, Yve Lomax, Jeff Wall and Marie Yates. There was also a film and video exhibition in conjunction with the art exhibition in New York, curated by Jane Weinstock. Only part of the drawing discussed here is now attributed to Leonardo, see 'Leonardo da Vinci', PF 11, p. 161n.

refs to someone who, to the gaze of the outside world, represents the supreme form of artistic success. But in this footnote on the sexual drawing, Freud goes beyond the brief of the largely psychobiographical forms of interpretation that he brings to Leonardo's case. He relates — quite explicitly — a failure to depict the sexual act to bisexuality and to a problem of representational space. The uncertain sexual identity muddles the plane of the image so that the spectator does not know where she or he stands in relationship to the picture. A confusion at the level of sexuality brings with it a disturbance of the visual field.

An artistic practice which sets itself the dual task of disrupting visual form and questioning the sexual certainties and stereotypes of our culture can fairly return to this historical moment (historical analytically as well as artistically, since the reference to Leonardo is now overlaid with the reference to the beginnings of psychoanalysis itself). Not for authority (authority is one of the things being questioned here), but for its suggestiveness in pointing up a possible relation between sexuality and the image. We know that Freud's writing runs parallel to the emergence of 'modern' art; he himself used such art as a comparison for the blurred fields of the unconscious psychic processes which were the object of his analytic work.[2] But in this footnote on Leonardo's failure in the visual act, we can already see traced out a specific movement or logic: that there can be no work on the image, no challenge to its powers of illusion and address, which does not simultaneously challenge the fact of sexual difference, whose self-evidence Leonardo's drawing had momentarily allowed to crumble.[3]

The rest of Freud's writing shows that sexual difference is indeed such a hesitant and imperfect construction. Men and women take up positions of symbolic and polarised opposition against the grain of a multifarious and bisexual disposition, which Freud first identified in the symptom (and genius...) before recognising its continuing and barely concealed presence across the range of normal adult sexual life. The lines of that division are

[2] Freud, 'The Dissection of the Psychical Personality', p. 79; p. 112 (passage retranslated by Samuel Weber in *The Legend of Freud,* p. 1).

[3] Peter Wollen makes a similar point on the relationship between perceptual and sexual contradiction in Manet's Olympia in 'Manet — Modernism and Avant-Garde', *Screen* 21: 2, Summer 1980, p. 21.

fragile in exact proportion to the rigid insistence with which our culture lays them down; they constantly converge and threaten to coalesce. Psychoanalysis itself can therefore explain the absence of that clear and accomplished form of sexuality that Freud himself had unsuccessfully searched for in the picture.

Freud often related the question of sexuality to that of visual representation. Describing the child's difficult journey into adult sexual life, he would take as his model little scenarios, or the staging of events, which demonstrated the complexity of an essentially visual space, moments in which perception *founders* (the boy child refuses to believe the anatomical difference that he sees)[4] or in which pleasure in looking tips over into the register of *excess* (witness to a sexual act in which he reads his own destiny, the child tries to interrupt by calling attention to his presence).[5] Each time the stress falls on a problem of seeing. The sexuality lies less in the content of what is seen than in the subjectivity of the viewer, in the relationship between what is looked at and the developing sexual knowledge of the child. The relationship between viewer and scene is always one of fracture, partial identification, pleasure and distrust. As if Freud found the aptest analogy for the problem of our identity as human subjects in failures of vision or in the violence which can be done to an image as it offers itself to view. For Freud, with an emphasis that has been picked up and placed at the centre of the work of Jacques Lacan, our sexual identities as male or female, our confidence in language as true or false, and our security in the image we judge as perfect or flawed, are fantasies.[6] And these archaic moments of disturbed visual representation, these troubled scenes, which expressed and unsettled our groping knowledge in the past, can now be used as theoretical prototypes to unsettle our certainties once again. Hence one of the chief drives of an art which today addresses the presence of the sexual in representation — to expose the fixed nature of sexual identity as a fantasy and, in the same gesture, to trouble, break up, or rupture

[4] Freud, 'Some Psychical Consequences of the Anatomical Distinction between the Sexes', p. 252, pp. 335-336.
[5] Freud, *From the History of an Infantile Neurosis*, pp. 29-47; pp. 80-81.
[6] On the centrality of the visual image in Lacan's topography of psychic life, and on enunciation and the lying subject see 'The Imaginary' and 'Dora — Fragment of an Analysis', note 24, in this collection.

the visual field before our eyes.

The encounter between psychoanalysis and artistic practice is therefore *staged,* but only in so far as that staging has *already taken place.* It is an encounter which draws its strength from that repetition, working like a memory trace of something we have been through before. It gives back to repetition its proper meaning and status: not lack of originality or something merely derived (the commonest reproach to the work of art), nor the more recent practice of appropriating artistic and photographic images in order to undermine their previous status; but repetition as insistence, that is, as the constant pressure of something hidden but not forgotten — something that can only come into focus now by blurring the field of representation where our normal forms of self-recognition take place.

The affinity between representation and sexuality is not confined to the visual image. In fact, in relation to other areas of theoretical analysis and activity, recognition of this affinity in the domain of the artistic image could be said to manifest something of a lag.[7] In one of his most important self-criticisms,[8] Barthes underlined the importance of psychoanalysis in pushing his earlier exposé of ideological meanings into a critique of the possibility of meaning itself. In his case studies Freud had increasingly demonstrated that the history of the patient did not consist of some truth to be deciphered behind the chain of associations which emerged in the analytic setting; it resided within that chain and in the process of emergence which the analysis brought into effect. Lacan immediately read in this the chain of language which slides from unit to unit, producing meaning out of the relationship between terms; its truth belongs to that movement and not to some prior reference existing outside its domain. The divisions of language are in themselves arbitrary and shifting: language rests on a continuum which gets locked into discrete units of which sexual difference is only the most strongly marked. The fixing of language and the fixing of sexual identity go hand in hand; they rely on each other and share the same forms of instability and risk. Lacan read Freud through language, but he also brought out, by

---

[7] For discussion of these issues in relation to film, see Laura Mulvey's crucial article, 'Visual Pleasure and Narrative Cinema', and also Jane Weinstock's article in *Difference: On Representation and Sexuality.*

[8] Roland Barthes, 'Change the Object Itself'.

implication, the sexuality at work in all practices of the sign. Modernist literary writing could certainly demonstrate, alongside the syntactic and narrative shifts for which it is best known, oscillations in the domain of sexuality, a type of murking of the sexual proprieties on which the politer world of nineteenth-century realist fiction had been based. Although the opposition between the two forms of writing has often been overstated, it is no coincidence that, in order to illustrate this tension between 'readerly' and 'writerly' fiction, Barthes chose a story in which the narrative enigma turns on a castrato (Balzac's *Sarrasine*).[9] The indecipherable sexuality of the character makes for the trouble and the joy of the text.

It is worth pausing over the implications of this for a modernist and postmodernist artistic practice which is increasingly understood in terms of a problematic of reading and a theory of the sign. Again, the historical links are important. Freud takes modern painting as the image of the unconscious. But the modernist suspension of the referent, with its stress on the purity of the visual signifier, belongs equally with Saussure who, at the same time, was criticising the conception of language as reference and underlining the arbitrary nature of the sign (primacy to the signifier instead of language as a nomenclature of the world). Lacan's move then simply completes the circuit by linking Saussure back to Freud. The unconscious reveals that the normal divisions of language and sexuality obey the dictates of an arbitrary law undermining the very possibility of reference for the subject since the 'I' can no longer be seen to correspond to some pre-given and permanent identity of psycho-sexual life. The problem of psychic identity is therefore immanent to the problem of the sign.

The same link (of language and the unconscious) can be made to that transition to postmodernism which has been read as a return of the referent, but the referent as a problem, not as a given.[10]

---

[9] Barthes, *S/Z*.

[10] Leo Steinberg defined postmodernism as the transition from nature to culture; this is reinterpreted by Craig Owens, 'The Allegorical Impulse — Towards a Theory of Postmodernism', *October* 12-13, Spring and Summer 1980, esp. pp. 79-80, and also Douglas Crimp, 'On the Museum's Ruins', *October* 13, Summer 1980. Craig Owens has recently used Freud's account of the creative impulse in a critical appraisal of the Expressionist revival, 'Honor, Power and the Love of Women', *Art and Artists,* January 1983.

Piles of cultural artefacts bring back something we recognise but in a form which refuses any logic of the same. The objects before the spectator's eyes cannot be ordered: in their disjunctive relation, they produce an acuter problem of vision than the one which had resulted when reference was simply dropped from the frame. Above all — to return to the analogy with the analytic scene — these images require a reading which neither coheres them into a unity, nor struggles to get behind them into a realm of truth. The only possible reading is one which repeats their fragmentation of a cultural world they both echo and refuse.

At each point of these transitions — artistic and theoretical — something is called into question at the most fundamental level of the way we recognise and respond to our own subjectivity and to a world with we are assumed to be familiar, a world we both do and do not know. Yet in each of these instances, it is precisely the psychoanalytic concepts of the unconscious and sexuality, specifically in their relationship to language, which seem to be lost.

Thus the modernist stress on the purity of the visual signifier easily dissolves into an almost mystic contemplation. Language can be used to rupture the smoothness of the visual image but it is language as pure mark uninformed by the psychoanalytic apprehension of the sign. Cultural artefacts are presented as images within images to rob them of the values they seem naturally to embody, but the fundamental sexual polarity of that culture is not called into account. Finally, meaning is seen to reside in these images as supplement, allegory or fragment, but with no sexual residue or trace — the concept of textuality is lifted out of psychoanalytic and literary theory but without the sexual definition that was its chief impetus and support.

Across a range of instances, language, sexuality and the unconscious *in their mutual relation* appear as a present-absence which all these moments seem to brush against, or elicit, before falling away. The elisions can be summarised schematically:

— purity of the visual signifier and the unconscious as mystique (no language);

— language as rupture of the iconicity of the visual sign (no unconscious);

— cultural artefacts as indictment of the stereotype (no sexual difference);

— reading as supplement, process or fragment (no sexual

determinacy of the signifier or of visual space).

Artists engaged in sexual representation (representation *as* sexual) come in at precisely this point, calling up the sexual component of the image, drawing out an emphasis that exists *in potentia* in the various instances they inherit and of which they form a part.[11] Their move is not therefore one of (moral) corrective. They draw on the tendencies they also seek to displace, and clearly belong, for example, within the context of that postmodernism which demands that reference, in its problematised form, re-enter the frame. But the emphasis on sexuality produces specific effects. First, it adds to the concept of cultural artefact or stereotype the political imperative of feminism which holds the image accountable for the reproduction of norms. Secondly, to this feminist demand for scrutiny of the image, it adds the idea of a sexuality which goes beyond the issue of content to take in the parameters of visual form (not just what we see but how we see — visual space as more than the domain of simple recognition). The image therefore submits to the sexual reference, but only in so far as reference itself is questioned by the work of the image. And the aesthetics of pure from are implicated in the less pure pleasures of looking, but these in turn are part of an aesthetically extraneous political space. The arena is simultaneously that of aesthetics and sexuality, and art and sexual politics. The link between sexuality and the image produces a particular dialogue which cannot be covered adequately by the familiar opposition between the formal operations of the image and a politics exerted from outside.

The engagement with the image therefore belongs to a political intention. It is an intention which has also inflected the psychoanalytic and literary theories on which such artist draw. The model is not one of applying psychoanalysis to the work of art (what application could there finally be which does not reduce one field to the other or inhibit by interpretation the potential meaning of both?). Psychoanalysis offers a specific account of sexual difference but its value (and also its difficulty) for feminism, lies in the place assigned to the woman in that differentiation. In his essay on Leonardo, Freud himself says that once the boy child sees what it is to be a woman, he will 'tremble for his masculinity'

---

[11] For a discussion of some of these issues in relation to feminist art, see Mary Kelly, 'Re-viewing Modernist Criticism', *Screen* 22: 3, Autumn 1981.

henceforth.[12] If meaning oscillates when a castrato comes onto the scene, our sense must be that it is in the normal image of the man that our certainties are invested and, by implication, in that of the woman that they constantly threaten collapse.

A feminism concerned with the question of looking can therefore turn this theory around and stress the particular and limiting opposition of male and female which any image seen to be flawless is serving to hold in place. More simply, we know that women are meant to *look* perfect, presenting a seamless image to the world so that the man, in that confrontation with difference, can avoid any apprehension of lack. The position of woman as fantasy therefore depends on a particular economy of vision (the importance of 'images of women' might take on its fullest meaning from this).[13] Perhaps this is also why only a project which comes via feminism can demand so unequivocally of the image that it renounce all pretensions to a narcissistic perfection of form.

At the extreme edge of this investigation, we might argue that the fantasy of absolute sexual difference, in its present guise, could be upheld only from the point when painting restricted the human body to the eye.[14] That would be to give the history of the image in Western culture a particularly heavy weight to bear. For, even if the visual image has indeed been one of the chief vehicles through which such a restriction has been enforced, it could only operate like a law which always produces the terms of its own violation. It is often forgotten that psychoanalysis describes the psychic law to which we are subject, but only in terms of its *failing*. This is important for a feminist (or any radical) practice which has often felt it necessary to claim for itself a wholly other psychic and representational domain. Therefore, if the visual image in its aesthetically acclaimed form serves to maintain a particular and oppressive mode of sexual recognition, it does so only partially and at a cost. Our previous history is not the petrified block of a

[12] 'Leonardo da Vinci and a Memory of his Childhood', p. 95; pp. 186-187.

[13] The status of the woman as fantasy in relation to the desire of the man was a central concern of Lacan's later writing; see *Encore*, especially 'God and the Jouissance of The Woman' and 'A Love Letter' in *Feminine Sexuality*, and the commentary, 'Feminine Sexuality — Jacques Lacan and the *école freudienne*', in this collection.

[14] Norman Bryson describes post-Albertian perspective in terms of such a restriction in *Vision and Painting: The Logic of the Gaze*, London 1983.

singular visual space since, looked at obliquely, it can always be seen to contain its moments of unease.[15] We can surely relinquish the monolithic view of that history, if doing so allows us a form of resistance which can be articulated *on this side of* (rather than beyond) the world against which it protests.

Among Leonardo's early sketches, Freud discovers the heads of laughing women, images of exuberance which then fall out of the great canon of his art. Like Leonardo's picture of the sexual act, these images appear to unsettle Freud as if their pleasure somehow correlated with the discomfort of the sexual drawing (the sexual drawing through its failure, the heads of laughing women for their excess). These images, not well known in Leonardo's canon, now have the status of fragments, but they indicate a truth about the tradition which excludes them, revealing the presence of something strangely insistent to which these artists return. *'Teste di femmine, che ridono'*[16] — laughter is not the emphasis here, but the urgent engagement with the question of sexuality persists now, as it did then. It can no more be seen as the beginning, than it should be the end, of the matter.

[15] See Lacan on death in Holbein's 'The Ambassadors', *The Four Fundamental Concepts*, pp. 85-90.

[16] 'Leonardo da Vinci and a Memory of his Childhood', p. 111; p. 203. An exhibition entitled *The Revolutionary Power of Women's Laughter*, including works by Barbara Kruger and Mary Kelly was held at Protetch McNeil, New York, January 1983.

Bibliography

Acton, William. *A Practical Treatise on Diseases of the Urinary and Generative Organs.* London: Churchill, 1851.

— *Prostitution, considered in its moral, social and sanitary aspects, in London and other large cities, with proposals for the mitigation and prevention of its attendant evils.* London: Churchill, 1857.

— *The Contagious Diseases Act, Shall the Contagious Diseases Act be applied to the civilian population.* London: Churchill, 1870.

Adams, Parveen. 'Representation and Sexuality', *m/f* 1, 1978.

Althusser, Louis. 'Freud and Lacan', *La Nouvelle Critique,* 1964; tr. Ben Brewster, *New Left Review* 55, March-April 1969.

Anderson, Perry. 'Origins of the Present Crisis', *New Left Review* 23, January-February 1964.

— 'Components of the National Culture', *New Left Review* 50, July-August 1968.

— *In the Tracks of Historical Materialism.* London: New Left Books/Verso, 1983.

Ashbee, Henry S. *Index librorum prohibitorum.* London: privately printed, 1877.

Barrett, Michèle. *Women's Oppression Today.* London: New Left Books/Verso, 1980.

Barrett, Michèle and McIntosh, Mary. 'Narcissism and the Family: A Critique of Lasch', *New Left Review* 135, September-October 1982.

Barthes, Roland. 'La mythologie aujourd'hui', *Esprit* 1971; tr. Stephen Heath, 'Change the Object Itself', *Image, Music, Text.* London: Fontana, 1977.

— 'De l'oeuvre au texte', *Revue d'esthétique* 3, 1971; tr. 'From Work to Text', *Image, Music, Text.*

236

— *S/Z*. Paris: Seuil, 1970; tr. Richard Miller, *S/Z*. New York: Hill and Wang, 1974.

Baudry, Jean-Louis. 'Le dispositif', *Communications* 23, 1975; tr. 'The Apparatus', *Camera Obscura* 1, 1976.

Beer, Gillian. *Darwin's Plots: Evolutionary Narrative in Darwin, George Eliot and Nineteenth Century Fiction*. London: RKP, 1983.

Bellour, Raymond. 'The Obvious and the Code', *Screen* 15: 4, Winter 1974-75.

— 'Hitchcock, the Enunciator', *Camera Obscura* 2, 1977.

— *L'analyse du film*. Paris: Albatros, 1979.

Benveniste, Emile. 'La nature des pronoms', *Problèmes de linguistique générale*. Paris: Gallimard, 1966; tr. 'The Nature of Pronouns', *Problems in General Linguistics*. Florida: University of Miami Press, 1971.

— De la subjectivité dans le langage', *Problèmes de linguistique générale;'* tr. 'Subjectivity in Language', *Problems in General Linguistics*.

Bernheimer, Charles and Kahane, Claire. *In Dora's Case: Freud, Hysteria, Feminism*. New York: Columbia; London: Virago, 1985.

Bourneville, P. Regnard. *Iconographie photographique de la Salpêtrière*. Paris 1876-78.

Bryson, Norman. *Vision and Painting: The Logic of the Gaze*. London: Macmillan, 1983.

Burchill, Louise. 'The Last Word of this Adventure: Interview with Julia Kristeva', *On the Beach* 1984.

Chase, Cynthia. 'The Decomposition of the Elephants: Double-Reading *Daniel Deronda'*, *PMLA* 93: 2, March 1978.

Chodorow, Nancy. *The Reproduction of Mothering: Psychoanalysis and the Sociology of Gender*. Berkeley: University of California Press, 1978.

Cixous, Hélène. *Portrait de Dora*. Paris: des femmes, 1976.

Comolli, Jean Louis. 'Machines of the Visible', *The Cinematic Apparatus*, ed. Teresa de Lauretis and Stephen Heath. London: Macmillan, 1980.

Cooper, David. 'Freud Revisited', *New Left Review* 20, May-June 1963.

— 'Two Types of Rationality', *New Left Review* 29, January-February 1965.

Coward, Rosalind. *Patriarchal Precedents*. London: RKP, 1982.

Cowie, Elizabeth. 'Woman as Sign', *m/f* 1, 1978.

— 'The Popular Film as Progressive Text — a discussion of *Coma'*, *m/f* 3, 1979; 4, 1980.

Crimp, Douglas. 'On the Museum's Ruins', *October* 13, Summer 1980.

Davidson, A. 'Assault on Freud', *London Review of Books,* 5 July 1984.

De Man, Paul. *Allegories of Reading*. New Haven and London: Yale University Press, 1979.

Derrida, Jacques. 'Freud et la scène de l'écriture', *L'écriture et la*

différence. Paris: Seuil, 1967; tr. Alan Bass, 'Freud and the Scene of Writing', *Writing and Difference*. Chicago: Chicago University Press, 1978.

— 'La double séance', *La dissémination*. Paris: Seuil, 1972; tr. Barbara Johnson, 'The Double Session', *Dissemination*. Chicago: Chicago University Press, 1981.

— 'La facteur de la vérité, *Poetique* 21, 1975; tr. Willis Domingo, James Hulbert, Moshe Ron and M. -R. L., 'The Purveyor of Truth', *Yale French Studies* 52, 1976.

— 'Fors', preface to Nicolas Abraham and Maria Torok, *Cryptomanie, le verbier de l'homme aux loups*. Paris: Aubier-Flammarion, 1976; tr. 'Fors — the Anglish Words of Nicolas Abraham and Maria Torok', *The Georgia Review* 31: 1, 1977.

— *La carte postale*. Paris: Flammarion, 1980.

— 'Géopsychanalyse "and the rest of the world" ', *'Géopsychanalyse, les souterrains de l'inconscient,* ed. René Major. Paris: Confrontations, 1981.

Deutsch, Helene. 'The Significance of Masochism in the Mental Life of Women', *International Journal of Psychoanalysis* 11, 1930.

Dews, Peter. 'The *Nouvelle Philosophie* and Foucault', *Economy and Society* 8: 2, 1979.

Didi-Huberman, Georges. *Invention de l'hystérie, Charcot et l'iconographie photographique de la Salpêtrière*. Paris: Macula, 1982.

Dyhouse, Carol. *Girls Growing Up in Late Victorian and Edwardian England.* London: RKP, 1981.

Eagleton, Terry. *Literary Theory, An Introduction*. Oxford: Blackwell, 1983.

Eliot, George. *Middlemarch* (1871-72). Harmondsworth: Penguin, 1965.

— *Daniel Deronda* (1876). Harmondsworth: Penguin, 1967.

— *The Lifted Veil* (1878). London: Virago, 1985.

Eliot, T. S. *'Hamlet'* (1919), *Selected Prose of T. S. Eliot,* ed. Frank Kermode. London: Faber, 1975.

— 'Tradition and the Individual Talent' (1919), *Selected Prose of T. S. Eliot.*

— 'The Use of Poetry and the Use of Criticism' (1933), *Selected Prose of T. S. Eliot.*

Felman, Shoshana. *La folie et la chose littéraire*. Paris: Seuil, 1978; trs. N. M. Evans and Shoshana Felman, *Writing and Madness.* Ithaca: Cornell University Press, 1986.

— ed. *Literature and Psychoanalysis, The Question of Reading: Otherwise, Yale French Studies* 55/56, 1977. New Haven: Yale University Press, 1982.

Fenichel, Otto. 'The Drive to Amass Wealth' (1934), *Collected Papers,* second series. London: RKP, 1955.

— A Critique of the Death Instinct' (1935), *Collected Papers,* first series,

1954.
— 'The Symbolic Equation: Girl = Phallus', *Psychoanalytic Quarterly* 18: 3, 1949.
Firestone, Shulamith. *The Dialectic of Sex* (1970). London: The Women's Press, 1979.
Florio, John. tr. *The Essays of Michael, Lord of Montaigne* (1603). London and New York: Routledge and Sons, 1885.
French, Marilyn. *Shakespeare's Division of Experience.* London: Jonathan Cape, 1982.
Freud, Sigmund. 'Observations of a Severe Case of Hemi--Anaesthesia in a Hysterical Male' (1886), *The Standard Edition of the Complete Psychological Works* (SE). London: Hogarth, 1955-74, SE 1.
— 'Preface and Footnotes to Charcot's Tuesday Lectures' (1892-94) SE 1.
— *Project for a Scientific Psychology* (1895 (1887)), SE1.
— *The Origins of Psychoanalysis,* letters to Wilhelm Fliess, Drafts and Notes, 1887-1902, ed. Marie Bonaparte, Anna Freud, Ernst Kris, London: Imago, 1954.
— with Josef Breuer, *Studies on Hysteria* (1893-95), SE 2, *Pelican Freud Library.* Harmondsworth: Penguin, 1976-85, PF 3.
— *The Interpretation of Dreams* (1900), SE 4-5, PF 4.
— 'Fragment of an Analysis of a Case of Hysteria' ('Dora') (1905 (1901)), SE 7, PF 8.
— *Three Essays on the Theory of Sexuality* (1905), SE 7, PF 7.
— 'Psychopathic Characters on the Stage' (1942 (1905 or 1906)), SE 7.
— 'Leonardo da Vinci and a Memory of his Childhood' (1910), SE 11, PF 14.
— 'Formulations on the Two Principles of Mental Functioning' (1911), SE 12, PF 11.
— 'On the Universal Tendency to Debasement in the Sphere of Love' (1912), *Contributions to the Psychology of Love,* 2, SE 11, PF 7.
— 'The Dynamics of Transference' (1912), *Papers on Technique* (1911-1915), SE 12.
— 'Observations on Transference Love' (1915 (1914)), *Papers on Technique,* SE 12.
— *Totem and Taboo* (1913), SE 13, PF 13.
— 'On Narcissism: An Introduction' (1914), SE 14, PF 11.
— 'The Unconscious' (1914), *Papers on Metapsychology,* SE 14, PF 11.
— 'Mourning and Melancholia' (1915), SE 14, PF 11,
— 'From the History of an Infantile Neurosis' ('The Wolfman') (1918 (1914)), SE 17, PF 9.
— 'The Psychogenesis of a Case of Homosexuality in a Woman' (1920), SE 18, PF 9.
— *Beyond the Pleasure Principle* (1920), SE 18, PF 11.
— *Group Psychology and the Analysis of the Ego* (1921), SE 18, PF 12.

— 'Negation' (1925), SE 19, PF 11.
— 'Fetishism' (1927), SE 21, PF 7.
— 'Female Sexuality' (1931), SE 21, PF 7.
— 'The Dissection of the Psychical Personality' (1932), *New Introductory Lectures,* SE 22, PF 2.
— 'Femininity' (1933), *New Introductory Lectures,* SE 22, PF 2.
— *Moses and Monotheism* (1939 (1937-39)), SE 23, PF 13.
Gidal, Peter. 'On Julia Kristeva', *Undercut* 12, 1984.
Gilbert, Sandra and Gubar, Susan. *The Madwoman in the Attic.* New Haven: Yale University Press, 1979.
Green, André. *Un oeil en trop.* Paris: Minuit, 1969; tr. Alan Sheridan, *The Tragic Effect, Oedipus Complex and Tragedy.* Cambridge: Cambridge University Press, 1979.
— *Le discours vivant, le concept psychanalytique de l'affect.* Paris: Presses Universitaires de France, 1973.
— *Hamlet et HAMLET.* Paris: Balland, 1982.
H. D. *Tribute to Freud* (1944). Boston: Godine, 1974.
Habermas, Jürgen. *Knowledge and Human Interests.* London: Heinemann, 1972.
Hamon, Marie-Christine. 'Le langage-femme existe-t-il?', *Ornicar* 11, 1977.
— 'Les feministes sont misogynes!', *Des femmes analystes parlent, Libération,* 19-20 January 1980.
Heath, Stephen. 'Film and System: Terms of Analysis', *Screen* 16: 1, Spring 1975, 16: 2, Summer 1975.
Horney, Karen. 'On the Genesis of the Castration Complex' (1924), *Feminine Psychology.* London: RKP, 1967.
— 'The Flight from Womanhood' (1926), *Feminine Psychology.*
Ingleby, David. 'The Ambivalence of Psychoanalysis', *Free Associations, Radical Science* 15, 1984.
Irigaray, Luce. *Speculum de l'autre femme.* Paris: Minuit, 1974: tr. Gillian Gill, *Speculum of the Other Woman.* Ithaca: Cornell University Press, 1985.
— *Ce sexe qui n'en est pas un.* Paris: Minuit, 1977; tr. Catherine Porter, *This Sex Which Is Not One.* Ithaca: Cornell University Press, 1985.
Jacobus, Mary. 'A Question of Language: Men of Maxims and *The Mill on the Floss',* in Elizabeth Abel ed., *Writing and Sexual Difference.* Chicago: University of Chicago Press; Brighton: Harvester, 1982.
Jacoby, Russell. *The Repression of Psychoanalysis, Otto Fenichel and the Political Freudians.* New York: Basic Books, 1983.
Jakobson, Roman. 'Why Mama and Papa?' (1959), *Studies on Child Language and Aphasia.* The Hague: Mouton, 1971.
Jameson, Fredric. *The Political Unconscious: Narrative as a Socially Symbolic Act.* London: Methuen, 1981.
Johnson, Barbara. 'The Frame of Reference: Poe, Lacan, Derrida', *Yale*

French Studies 55/56, 1977; reprinted in Robert Young ed., *Untying the Text*. London: RKP, 1981.

Jones, Ann Rosalind. 'Julia Kristeva on Femininity: The Limits of a Semiotic Politics', *Feminist Review* 18, November 1984.

Jones, Ernest. 'The Theory of Symbolism', *British Journal of Psychoanalysis* 11: 2, 1916.

— 'The Early Development of Female Sexuality', *IJPA* 8, 1927.

— 'The Phallic Phase', *IJPA* 14: 1, 1933.

Kelly, Mary. 'Re-viewing Modernist Criticism', *Screen* 22: 3, Autumn 1981.

Klein, Melanie. 'The Early Stages of the Oedipus Conflict' (1928), *Contributions to Psychoanalysis*. London: Hogarth, 1948.

— 'The Importance of Symbol Formation in the Development of the Ego', *IJPA* 11, 1930.

Kristeva, Julia. *Semeiotikè, Recherches pour une sémanalyse*. Paris: Seuil, 1969.

— *La révolution du langage poétique*. Paris: Seuil, 1974; excerpts from Part 1 tr. *The Kristeva Reader*, ed. Toril Moi. Oxford: Blackwell, 1986.

— *Des Chinoises*. Paris: des femmes, 1974; tr. Anita Barrows, *About Chinese Women*. London: Marion Boyars, 1977.

— 'Polylogue', *Tel Quel* 57, Spring 1974; tr. Thomas Gora, Alice Jardine, Leon S. Roudiez, 'Polylogue', *Desire in Language*, ed. Leon S. Roudiez. Oxford: Blackwell; New York: Columbia, 1980.

— 'Sujet dans le langage et pratique politique', *Tel Quel* 58, Summer 1974.

— 'La femme, ce n'est jamais ça', *Tel Quel* 59, Autumn 1974; tr. Marilyn August, 'Woman can never be defined', *New French Feminisms*, ed. Elaine Marks and Isabelle Courtivron. Brighton: Harvester, 1981.

— 'Ellipse sur la frayeur et la séduction spéculaire', *Communicatons* 23, 1975; tr. Dolores Burdick, 'Ellipsis on Dread and the Specular Seduction', *Wide Angle* 3: 2, 1979.

— 'D'une identité l'autre', *Tel Quel* 62, Summer 1975; tr. 'From One Identity to Another', *Desire in Language*.

— 'Pourqoi les Etats Unis?', with Marcelin Pleynet and Phillippe Sollers, *Tel Quel* 71-73, Autumn 1977; tr. 'The US Now: A Conversation' *October* 6, Fall 1978, also in *The Kristeva Reader*.

— 'Un nouveau type d'intellectuel: le dissident', *Tel Quel* 74, Winter 1977; tr. *The Kristeva Reader*.

— 'La littérature dissidente comme réfutation du discours de gauche', *Tel Quel* 76, Summer 1978.

 — 'Le temps des femmes', *34/44: Cahiers de recherche de science de textes et documents* 5, Winter 1979; tr. Alice Jardine and Harry Blake, 'Women's Time', *Feminist Theory: A Critique of Ideology*, ed. Nannerl O. Keohane, Michelle Z. Rosaldo, Barbara C. Gelpi. Chicago: Chicago University Press; Brighton: Harvester, 1982.

— 'Il n'y a pas de mâitre à langage', *Nouvelle Revue de Psychanalyse, Regards sur la Psychanalyse en France,* 20, Autumn 1979.

— *Pouvoirs de l'horreur, essai sur l'abjection.* Paris: Seuil, 1980; tr. Leon S. Roudiez, *Powers of Horror.* New York: Columbia University Press, 1982.

— *Histoires d'amour.* Paris: Denoel, 1983.

— 'Mémoires', *Infini* 1, 1983.

— *'Histoires d'amour* — Love Stories', *Desire,* ed. Lisa Appignanesi. London: Institute of Contemporary Arts, 1983.

Lacan, Jacques. 'Le stade du miroir comme formateur de la fonction du Je' (1936), *Ecrits.* Paris: Seuil, 1966; tr. Alan Sheridan, 'The mirror stage as formative of the function of the I', *Ecrits: A Selection.* London: Tavistock, 1977; also tr. Jan Meil, 'The Mirror Phase', *New Left Review* 51, September-October 1968.

— 'Cure psychanalytique à l'aide de la poupée fleur', *Revue française de la psychanalyse* 4, 1949.

— 'Intervention sur le transfert' (1951), *Ecrits;* tr. Jacqueline Rose, 'Intervention on transference', *Feminine Sexuality, Jacques Lacan and the école freudienne,* eds. Juliet Mitchell and Jacqueline Rose. London: Macmillan, 1982; New York: Norton, 1983.

— 'Fonction et champ de la parole et du langage en psychanalyse' (1953), *Ecrits;* tr. 'The function and field of speech and language in psychoanalysis', *Ecrits: A Selection.*

— *Le séminaire I: Les écrits techniques de Freud* (1953-54). Paris: Seuil, 1975; tr. John Forrester, *Freud's Writings on Technique.* Cambridge: Cambridge University Press, 1987.

— *Le séminaire II: Le moi dans la théorie de Freud et dans la technique de la psychanalyse* (1954-55). Paris: Seuil, 1978; tr. Sylvana Tomaselli, *The Ego in Freud's Theory and in the Technique of Psychoanalysis.* Cambridge: Cambridge University Press, 1987.

— 'D'une question préliminaire à tout traitement possible de la psychose' (1955-56), *Ecrits;* tr. 'On a question preliminary to any possible treatment of psychosis', *Ecrits: A Selection.*

— 'L'instance de la lettre dans l'inconscient ou la raison depuis Freud' (1957), *Ecrits;* tr. 'The agency of the letter in the unconscious or reason since Freud', *Ecrits: A Selection.*

— 'Les formations de l'inconscient', *Bulletin de Psychologie* 2, 1957-58.

— 'Propos directifs pour un congrès sur la sexualité féminine (1958), *Ecrits;* tr. 'Guiding remarks for a Congress on Feminine Sexuality', *Feminine Sexuality.*

— 'La signification du phallus' (1958), *Ecrits;* tr. 'The meaning of the phallus', *Feminine Sexuality.*

— 'La direction de la cure et les principes de son pouvoir' (1958), *Ecrits;* tr. 'The direction of the treatment and the principles of its power', *Ecrits: A Selection.*

— 'A la mémoire d'Ernest Jones: sur sa théorie de symbolisme' (1959), *Ecrits.*

— 'Desire and the interpretation of desire in *Hamlet', Yale French Studies* 55/56, 1977.

— 'Remarque sur le rapport de Daniel Lagache: "Psychanalyse et structure de la personnalité" ' (1960), *Ecrits.*

— *Le séminaire XI: Les quatre concepts fondamentaux de la psychanalyse* (1964). Paris: Seuil, 1973; tr. Alan Sheridan, *The Four Fundamental Concepts of Psychoanalysis,* London: Hogarth, 1977.

— 'De nos antécédents...', *Ecrits.*

— *Le séminaire XVII: L'envers de la psychanalyse* (1969-70), unpublished typescript.

— *Le séminaire XVIII: D'un discours qui ne sera pas semblant* (1970-71), unpublished typescript.

— 'Une lettre d'âmour', 'Dieu et la jouissance de La femme', *Le séminaire XX: Encore* (1972-73). Paris: Seuil, 1975; tr. 'A love letter', 'God and the Jouissance of The Woman', *Feminine Sexuality.*

— *Le séminaire XXI: Les non-dupes errent* (1973-74), unpublished typescript.

— 'Séminaire du 21 janvier 1975', *Ornicar?* 3, May 1975.

Laing, R. D. 'Series and Nexus in the Family', *New Left Review* 15, May-June 1962.

— 'What is Schizophrenia?', *New Left Review* 28, November-December 1964.

Leavis, F. R. *The Great Tradition.* London: Chatto and Windus, 1948.

Lemoine-Luccioni, Eugénie. *Partage des femmes.* Paris: Seuil, 1976.

Lerner, Laurence ed. *Shakespeare's Tragedies, An Anthology of Modern Criticism.* Harmondsworth: Penguin, 1963.

Leverenz, David. 'The Woman in Hamlet', *Representing Shakespeare: New Psychoanalytic Essays,* eds., Coppélia Kahn and Murray Schwartz. Baltimore and London: Johns Hopkins, 1980.

Lyotard, Jean-François. 'L'àcinéma', *Cinema: théorie, lectures.* Paris, Klincksieck, 1973; tr. 'Acinema', *Wide Angle* 2: 3, 1978.

— 'The Unconscious as *Mise en Scène', Performance,* Michel Benamou and Charles Caramello eds.. Madison: Coda Press, 1978.

Masson, Jeffrey. *Freud: The Assault on Truth — Freud's Suppression of the Seduction Theory.* Boston and London: Faber, 1984.

MacCabe, Colin. *The Talking Cure: Essays in Psychoanalysis and Language.* London: Macmillan, 1981.

MacLaren, Angus. *Birth Control in Nineteenth Century England.* London: Croom Helm, 1978.

MacRobbie, Angela. 'Strategies of Vigilance, an Interview with Gayatri Chakravorty Spivak', *Block* 10, 1985.

Mannoni, Maud. *L'enfant, sa 'maladie' et les autres.* Paris: Seuil, 1967; tr. *The Child, his 'Illness' and the Others.* London: Tavistock, 1970.

Metz, Christian. 'Le signifiant imaginaire', *Communications* 23, 1975; tr. Celia Britton, Anwyl Williams, Ben Brewster, Alfred Guzzetti, *Psychoanalysis and Cinema: The Imaginary Signifier.* London: Macmillan, 1983.

Miller, Nancy. 'A Conversation between Adrienne Rich and Roland Barthes', *Feminism/Theory/Politics,* forthcoming 1986.

Millett, Kate. *Sexual Politics* (1969). London: Virago, 1977.

— 'Beyond Politics? Children and Sexuality', *Pleasure and Danger,* ed. Carole S. Vance. Boston and London: RKP, 1984.

Mitchell, Juliet. 'Why Freud?', *Shrew,* November-December 1970.

— *Psychoanalysis and Feminism.* London: Allen Lane, 1974.

— *Women: The Longest Revolution.* London: Virago, 1984.

Montrelay, Michèle. 'Recherches sur le féminité, *Critique* 26, 1970, revised in *L'ombre et le nom.* Paris: Minuit, 1977; tr. Parveen Adams, 'Inquiry into Femininity', *m/f* 1, 1978.

— 'La passion de la perte', *Des femmes analystes parlent, Libération,* 19-10 January 1980.

Mulvey, Laura. 'Visual Pleasure and Narrative Cinema', *Screen* 16: 3, Autumn 1975.

Nin, Anais. 'The Veiled Woman', *Delta of Venus* (1969). London: W. H. Allen, 1978.

Owens, Craig. 'The Allegorical Impulse — Towards a Theory of Postmodernism', *October* 12, Spring 1980, 13, Summer 1980.

— 'Honor, Power and the Love of Women', *Art and Artists,* January 1983.

Plaza, Monique. 'Pouvoir "phallomorphique" et psychologie de "la Femme" ', *Questions feministes* 1, 1977; tr. ' "Phallomorphic" Power and the Psychology of "Women" ', *Ideology and Consciousness* 4, 1978.

Reich, Wilhelm. *Reich Speaks of Freud, Conversations with Kurt Eissler,* ed. Mary Higgins and C. M. Raphael. New York: Farrar, Straus and Giroux, 1967.

Rivière, Joan. 'Womanliness as Masquerade', *IJPA* 10, 1982; reprinted in *Formations of Fantasy,* London: RKP, 1986.

Roudinesco, Elisabeth. 'Histoire de la psychanalyse en France', *Infini* 1, 1983.

Roustang, François. *Un destin si funeste.* Paris: Minuit, 1976; tr. Ned Lukacher, *Dire Mastery.* Baltimore and London: Johns Hopkins, 1982.

Rowbotham, Sheila, Segal, Lynne, Wainwright, Hilary. *Beyond the Women.* New York: Monthly Review Press, 1975.

Rubin, Gayle. 'The Traffic in Women', *Towards an Anthropology of Women,*ed. Rayna Reiter. New York: Monthly Review Press, 1975.

— 'Thinking Sex: Notes for a Radical Theory of the Politics of Sexuality', *Pleasure and Danger.*

Rustin, Michael. 'A Socialist Consideration of Kleinian Psychoanalysis', *New Left Review* 131, January-February 1982.

Saada, Jeanne Favret. 'Excusez-moi, je ne faisais que passer', *Les Temps Modernes* 371, June 1977.

Safouan, Moustafa. 'L'oedipe, est-il universel?', *Etudes sur l'oedipe.* Paris: Seuil, 1974; tr. Ben Brewster, 'Is the Oedipus Complex Universal?', *m/f* 5/6, 1981.

— 'La sexualité féminine dans la doctrine psychanalytique', *Scilicet* 5, 1975, reprinted in *La sexualité féminine dans la doctrine freudienne.* Paris: Seuil, 1976; tr. 'Feminine sexuality in psychoanalytic doctrine', *Feminine Sexuality.*

— *L'échec du principe du plaisir.* Paris: Seuil, 1979; tr. Ben Brewster, *Pleasure and Being — Towards a Psychoanalytic Theory of Hedonism.* London: Macmillan, 1983.

Saint Theresa. *The Complete Works,* ed. Silverio de Santa Teresa P.. English edition: Peers: London, Sheed and Ward 1946.

Sartre, Jean-Paul. *L'être et le néant.* Paris: Gallimard, 1943; tr. Hazel E. Barnes, *Being and Nothingness.* New York: Methuen, 1966.

Saussure, Ferdinand de. *Cours de linguistique générale* (1915), ed. Tullio de Mauro. Paris: Payot, 1972; tr. Roy Harris, *Course in General Linguistics.* London: Duckworth, 1983.

Sayers, Janet. 'Psychoanalysis and Personal Politics: A Response to Elizabeth Wilson', *Feminist Review* 10, 1982.

Scilicet. 'La phase phallique et la portée subjective du complexe de castration', *Scilicet* 1, 1968; tr. 'The phallic phase and the subjective import of the castration complex', *Feminine Sexuality.*

— 'Le clivage du sujet et son identification', *Scilicet* 2-3, 1970.

Segal, Hannah. 'Notes on Symbol Formation', *IJPA* 38, 1957.

Shakespeare, William. *Hamlet*, Variorum ed. H. H. Furness, 15th ed. Philadelphia: Lippincott, 1877.

— *Hamlet*, ed. H. Jenkins. London: Methuen, 1982.

Showalter, Elaine. 'Feminist Criticism in the Wilderness', *Writing and Sexual Difference,* ed. Elizabeth Abel. Chicago: Chicago University Press, 1980.

— 'Shooting the Rapids: Feminist Criticism in the Mainstream', *Oxford Literary Review* 8: 1-2, 1986.

Spivak, Gayatri Chakravorty. 'Love me, love my ombre, elle', *Diacritics,* Winter 1984.

Stoller, Robert. 'A Contribution to the Study of Gender Identity',

IJPA 45, 1965.

Stone, Jennifer. 'The Horrors of Power: A Critique of Kristeva', *The Politics of Theory,* ed. Francis Barker. Colchester: Essex University, 1983.

Thomson, E. P. 'The Peculiarities of the English', *Socialist Register 1965.* London: Merlin Press, 1965.

Turim, Maureen. 'The Place of Visual Illusions', *The Cinematic Apparatus,* ed. Teresa de Lauretis and Stephen Heath. London: Macmillan, 1980.

Veith, Ilza. *Hysteria, the History of a Disease* (1965). London: University of Chicago Press, 1975.

Walkowitz, Judith. *Prostitution and Victorian Society: Women, Class and the State.* Cambridge: Cambridge University Press, 1980.

Weber, Samuel. *The Legend of Freud.* Minneapolis: University of Minnesota Press, 1982.

Weinstock, Jane. 'Sexual Difference and the Moving Image', *Difference: On Representation and Sexuality.* New York: New Museum, 1984; London: Institute of Contemporary Arts, 1985.

Weir, Angie and Wilson, Elizabeth. 'The British Women's Movement', *New Left Review* 148, November-December 1984.

Wilson, Elizabeth. 'Psychoanalysis: Psychic Law and Order', *Feminist Review* 8, 1981.

Winnicott, D. W. 'Split-Off Male and Female Elements found clinically in Men and Women: Theoretical Inferences' (1966), *Psychoanalytic Forum* 4, ed. J. Linden. New York 1972.

— 'Mirror-Role of Mother and Family in Child Development' (1967), *Playing and Reality.* London: Tavistock, 1971.

— 'Creativity and its Origins', *Playing and Reality.*

Wollen, Peter. 'Manet-Modernism and Avant-Garde', *Screen* 21:2, Summer 1980.

Young, Robert. ed. *Untying the Text: A Post-Structuralist Reader.* London: RKP, 1981.

— 'Psychoanalytic Criticism: Has It Got Beyond a Joke?', *Paragraph* 4, October 1984.

Index